CONTEMPORARY APPROACHES TO GEOGRAPHY VOLUME 3: ENVIRONMENTAL GEOGRAPHY

Series editor: Charles Rawding

Chris Kington Publishing

© Charles Rawding, Vanessa Holden and Ann Worsley 2010

All rights reserved. No part of this publication may be reproduced, stored in retrieval system, copied or transmitted without written permission from the publisher except that the materials may be photocopied for use within the purchasing institution only.
A catalogue record for this book is available from the British Library.

Written by:
Charles Rawding, Vanessa Holden and Ann Worsley

Edited by:
Giles Flitney

Design by:
Character Design
& Tom Kington

Printed in China by:
1010 Printing International Ltd

The right of Charles Rawding, Vanessa Holden and Ann Worsley to be identified as authors of this Work has been asserted by them in accordance with sections 77 and 78 of the Copyright, Designs and Patents Act 1988.

Published by Chris Kington Publishing, an imprint of Optimus Education: a division of Optimus Professional Publishing Limited
Registered office: 33-41 Dallington Street, London EC1V 0BB
Registered number: 05791519
Tel: 0845 450 6407 Fax: 0845 450 6410

www.optimus-education.com

ISBN 978-1-899857-98-2

Foreword

Contemporary Approaches to Geography is a series of texts for geography teachers designed to introduce the latest ideas from geography in higher education to the secondary geography teacher, while at the same time demonstrating how these ideas can be used in the delivery of examination specifications for 14 to 18 year olds. In recent years there have been significant innovations in teaching the subject at Key Stage 3 as a freeing up of the National Curriculum has enabled teachers to introduce newer ideas into the subject. However, in many cases the introduction of new ideas has not continued into the examination years, largely as a result of constraints, real or imagined, relating to examination specifications. At a time when new examination specifications are being introduced across both GCSE and A Level, it seems timely to offer new approaches that can be effectively incorporated into the classroom ensuring the relevance and topicality of geography and cementing its place as a central component of the curriculum.

The structure of the books has been guided by the headings of the range of examination specifications available across England, Wales and Northern Ireland, and there is cross-reference to these specifications provided in an appendix (see p209). However, these texts have not been designed with a specific specification in mind. Indeed, the authors would argue that the growing tendency for senior examiners to write textbooks designed to 'deliver' their specification is a trend that could result in school geographies being artificially constrained within particular fixed frames of reference. This should be considered of particular concern given the rate at which the subject is changing. These texts argue that what is required is an ability to think geographically, which will enable students to understand and interpret changing geographies as they are encountered.

Within the texts, you will find significant elements of the personal geographies of the authors. In this text, for instance, one author has made use of local case studies such as Clough Bottom Farm, Lancashire, while another has incorporated her own research in Papua New Guinea. Such an approach has been taken deliberately as it reinforces the importance of developing the personal geographies of students to enable them to think geographically. In similar vein, the extensive use of photographs within the texts reflects the beliefs of the authors that students must 'see' the real world in terms of its geographies in order to understand the relevance of the subject.

A central theme of the texts is that geographies (a deliberate plural) can only be understood in the context of modern society and by investigating the linkages between themes. Indeed, it might be argued that it is time to reconsider the prevailing thematic approach within school geography if we are to achieve effective synthesis and explanation. Each chapter attempts to make these linkages explicit by clearly signposting where connections with other chapters can be made; these cross-references have been made across all three books and it is intended that the three books be regarded as an integrated collection.

Embedded within the narrative, there is a range of suggested teaching activities, some of which have been further developed and have been provided in electronic format on the accompanying CD-Rom. Additional teaching resources, including a more extensive collection of photographs, have been provided on the CD-Rom and are signposted in the text. The 'Points for consideration' contained within the text are designed to trigger discussion and thought and to encourage the reader to continue to innovate. At the end of each chapter there are suggestions for possible website usage and a short selection of possible further reading. A full bibliography is provided at the end of the book.

Contents

Acknowledgements	x
The authors	xi
Introduction	1
Thinking geographically	1
What are environmental geographies	3
The social construction of environmental geographies	3
1. Ecosystems – Charles Rawding and Ann Worsley	5
Introduction	5
Populations, communities and ecosystems	6
Biomes and biogeographical regions	7
The Mediterranean biome	9
The tropical biome	9
The coastal sand dune ecosystem: the psammosere	11
Habitats and niches	12
Understanding ecosystems	14
Ecosystem services	15
Biodiversity	15
Valuing ecosystems	17
Ecosystems under pressure	18
Forest ecosystems and change	22
Afforestation in the Lake District	23
The National Forest	24
The impact of energy usage on biodiversity	24
The effects of ecosystem change on human health	26
Ecosystem thresholds	29
Summary	30
Endnotes	31
Useful website	31
2. Climate and weather – Vanessa Holden and Charles Rawding	33
Introduction	33
The role of the Sun	33
The dynamics between land masses and oceans	34
The importance of topographical features	37

Contents

Atmospheric pressure and winds	38
Mid-latitude depressions	41
The measurement of wind	42
Atmospheric moisture and the hydrological cycle	44
Clouds	45
Biomes	47
Extreme global weather	48
Hurricanes	48
Hurricane Katrina and New Orleans	49
Tornadoes	52
Thunderstorms	54
Local climatic variations	55
The British Isles	56
Air masses	57
Weather fronts	59
Forecasting weather	60
Synoptic charts	60
Summary	63
Endnotes	63
Useful websites	63

3. Climate change – Vanessa Holden   65

Introduction	65
How climate works	66
Evidence of short-term changes: direct evidence	67
Weather stations	67
Satellite measurements	68
Sea levels	68
Melting of global snow and ice stores	70
Evidence of long-term changes: proxy evidence	71
Lake sediments	71
Peat bogs	73
What's wrong with climate change?	74
Biodiversity and ecosystems	74
Agriculture and food supply	74
Rising sea levels	76
Marine ecosystems	78
Human health	78
Water availability	79
How can human-induced changes be stabilised?	79
Internationally	79
United Kingdom	80
Summary	82
Endnotes	82
Useful websites	82

4. Energy – Charles Rawding — 85

Introduction	85
Historical geographies of energy	85
The current situation	86
Energy production from fossil fuels	86
Coal	86
Oil production	88
Peak oil?	91
Energy from wood and deforestation	92
Carbon capture and storage (CCS) and decarbonisation	92
Carbon-neutral energy production	93
Carbon footprints	93
Nuclear power	94
Renewable energy	95
Hydroelectric power	95
Wind power	97
Solar power	99
Biofuels	99
Tidal and wave power	102
Geothermal	102
The localisation of energy	103
Energy and development	107
Energy futures	107
Summary	107
Useful websites	108
Further reading	108

5. Food supply – Charles Rawding — 109

Introduction	109
The involvement of government	110
Food supply and diet	111
Population and food supply	112
Globalisation and food	114
Food miles	116
The example of Kenya	119
Alternative food networks (AFNs)	120
Fairtrade	120
Organic farming	121
Clough Bottom Farm, Lancashire	122
The ethics of food supply	123
Food supply and carbon footprints	124
Local cropping practices in less economically developed countries	126
Forestry	127
Food security and food shortages	128

Summary	**132**
Endnotes	132
Useful websites	133

6. Sustainability – Vanessa Holden — 135

Introduction – what is 'sustainability'?	135
Social development and sustainability	**137**
Social development in LEDCs	138
Social development in MEDCs	140
Economic growth and sustainability	**141**
Economic growth in LEDCs	141
Economic growth in MEDCs	144
Transport and sustainability	**146**
Natural ecosystems and sustainability	**148**
Sustainability and biodiversity	**150**
Human use of natural resources	**152**
Energy and sustainability	**153**
Sustainability and political processes: the role of Agenda 21	**153**
Summary	**155**
Useful websites	155

7. Environmental management – Charles Rawding — 157

Introduction	**157**
Issues in environmental management	**158**
Land degradation	158
Agricultural practices	**159**
Soil erosion	159
Soil erosion: the Dust Bowl of the United States	159
Chemical contamination	160
Water scarcity	**161**
Salinity	**163**
Nutrient cycles	**163**
Desertification	**164**
Tackling desertification in China	166
Forest environments	**166**
Coastal, marine and freshwater environments	**169**
Marine and freshwater environments: examples from the United States	171
Fisheries	**171**
Restoring biodiversity	**173**
Biodiversity on the Lincolnshire Wolds	173
Metals, oil and the environment	**175**
The restoration of damaged environments	**176**
Environmental disasters	**178**
Bhopal 1984	178

Waste management	179
Summary	181
Endnotes	181
Useful websites	181

8. Globalisation – Charles Rawding — 183

Introduction	183
Global environmental trends	183
Economic development and environmental issues	185
Global intergovernmental actions	186
Trade, industry and the environment	187
Climate change: the ultimate globalisation?	189
Initiatives focusing on global interdependence	190
Global governance?	191
Transnational environmental movements	193
Pollution and transnational activism: an example from South Africa	194
Shipbreaking: a green industry?	195
The globalisation of fauna and flora	196
The globalisation of food	198
Regional perspectives on global issues	201
Linking the local to the global	203
Summary	203
Endnotes	205
Useful websites	205

References — 207

Examination specification references — 209

Index — 213

Acknowledgements

The authors are grateful to a large number of former Edge Hill University Geography PGCE trainees who have provided a range of inputs, particularly in terms of teaching ideas provided. We would especially like to thank Lucy Rushton, Briley Habib and Amy Laurence for the materials and advice that they have provided. We would also like to thank Ann Chapman for her work on a large number of the figures in the text. In addition, a number of colleagues have provided much valued support: Graham Lymbery and Michelle Newton from Sefton Metropolitan Borough Council's coastal defence team, Dr Barbara Lang, Dr Alan Bedford, Gerry Lucas and Steve Suggitt from Edge Hill University.

Individual teaching ideas or resources have been acknowledged where appropriate within the text.

Photography

All photographs are by Charles Rawding unless otherwise indicated.

The authors

Dr Vanessa Holden is a Research Fellow in Geography and member of the Environmental Change Group at Edge Hill University. The focus of much of her research is on coastal geomorphology and sedimentology, particularly with regard to the impacts of sea-level rise on the natural environment. She gained extensive practical experience as a consultant in private industry in the area of economic development and environmental matters. With a healthy fascination for coastal issues, she maintains a holistic approach to geography, believing it to be essential to truly understanding contemporary topics such as climate change and adaptation by people and ecosystems.

Dr Charles Rawding is Geography PGCE Course Leader at Edge Hill University. His main research interests lie in curriculum innovation in school geography and the links between school and academic geography. He has published extensively on geography education. His most recent books have been: *Reading our Landscapes: Understanding changing geographies* (Chris Kington Publishing, 2007) and *Understanding Place as a Process* (Geographical Association, 2007).

Professor Annie Worsley is a Chartered Geographer and Programme Leader for the BSc Hons Environmental Science at Edge Hill University. She is Chair of the Environmental Change Group and Vice-Chair of the Sefton Coast Partnership. Following her work on environmental change in the Highlands of Papua New Guinea, her work centres on the role of humans in environmental change and includes investigating coastal changes over the Holocene, how communities adapt to climate change and the impacts of air quality on health. All these diverse, yet geography-centred themes are supported by collaborative partnerships with practitioners and stakeholders including the National Health Service, Health Protection Agency, borough councils, Department for Environment, Food and Rural Affairs and the European Union.

Introduction

Thinking geographically

This book is one in a series of three, designed to cover the principal aspects of geography as defined by examination specifications in England, Wales and Northern Ireland. The series has been divided according to recent practice into human, environmental and physical geographies (note: environmental geography is a relatively recent addition to what was previously a dualism within the subject). However, a key theme running through the books is that it is essential that students are assisted in making links between the different areas of geography. Quite simply, if they are to become good geographers, they must be able to synthesise information and draw conclusions across a range of topics – something which has not been aided by the modularisation of the education system. To assist the reader in identifying these links, margin notes under the heading 'Making the links' [☞] have been included, in order to suggest where there are links between chapters in the three books.

Stressing the need for effective synthesis raises the question: what exactly does 'thinking geographically' entail? A section on 'thinking geographically' from Doreen Massey (figure 1) demonstrates what to think geographically might entail. It is an extremely good starting point for any discussion of what geography is, who geographers are and what purposes they serve in modern society.

> There is an argument – about climate change – that goes like this.
>
> '…the UK's contribution to global emissions of greenhouse gas is only a small percentage.'
>
> '…there's not much point in taking responsibility for our own place when India and China are growing as they are.'
>
> Now I might have found that a comforting argument. But it seems it is a totally inadequate geography.
>
> What that 'small percentage' counts is the greenhouse gas emissions from the United Kingdom directly. In that sense, it treats the UK as an isolated entity.
>
> But it is not.
>
> That calculation, it seems, misses out the effect of all the things we import from elsewhere (many of them, indeed, from China [☞]). We demand those goods, but we do not count as our own the pollution of producing them.
>
> Nor does that 'small percentage' take into account the role of UK companies in production around the world. It has been estimated, for instance, that something like 15% of global carbon emissions derives from companies listed on the London Stock Exchange. Our economy is said to benefit from those companies. So what responsibilities do we, as UK citizens, have towards them?

Figure 1: Thinking geographically

See accompanying CD-Rom

Thinking geographically.doc

See Volume 1: Human Geography, ch 6, Industrial geographies (p128).

> I could go on. The point is this. That 'small percentage' is meaningless in an interconnected world. We cannot pretend that because all that greenhouse gas emission doesn't happen here it doesn't happen because of us …that we are in no way implicated.
>
> But surely, might come the reply, we are improving? The UK is on course to meet its Kyoto target.
>
> Indeed it is. But why? Well, largely because:
> - we have allowed our manufacturing to collapse
> - we closed the mines and dashed for gas
> - we opted for an economy based on services and, especially, on finance.
>
> It is not so much that we are behaving better, as that:
> - we have exported our pollution
> - and we have reshaped the UK's role in the global economy.
>
> And that reshaping has also reshaped the geography of the UK itself, as:
> - manufacturing regions have declined
> - the north-south divide has widened
> - our economy revolves more and more around London's financial sector.
>
> Forget that comforting geography of small percentages. These are some of the other geographies that lie behind responsibilities for climate change.

Source: Professor Doreen Massey, *GA Magazine*, Spring 2008, p5.

Teaching idea 1

Present students with a copy of the extract in figure 1 and firstly ask them to highlight those sections they consider to be human/environmental/physical geography. Then ask them to produce a mind map showing the connections between the elements in the passage. How can this exercise help them to think geographically?

See Volume 1: Human Geography, ch 6, Industrial geographies (p128-132).

See ch 1, Ecosystems (p20).

The series of books attempts to demonstrate these links. For instance, chapter 6 of *Volume 1: Human Geography* looks in detail at the development of industry in China; at one level this can be seen as a classic example of industrial development based initially on low-cost labour, government policies, foreign investment and so on. However, it can also be seen as an example of the interdependence of nations, since the UK has come to rely heavily on Chinese imports [🔗], while at the same time China has been seen as a major culprit in terms of the emission of greenhouse gases and pollution more generally. However, it is demand from countries such as the UK that has resulted in the growth of Chinese industry, with smoke from Chinese factories and power stations entering the atmosphere, our atmosphere, everyone's atmosphere. The concept of an 'ecological footprint' [🔗] can be usefully deployed here to illustrate the global interrelations of environmental impacts and to reconnect the apparent dislocation between production and consumption.

What are environmental geographies?

Lambert and Morgan (2010: 4) argue that, 'a productive way of thinking about the work of geography teachers in schools is to see the subject as a way of helping young people understand and make sense of the modern adventure. This is because its content is concerned with the social processes that make up the modern project'. It could be argued that the development of environmental geography as a third strand of the academic subject of geography is partly a reflection of the changing perceptions of modern world, and what Lechner (2009: 260) refers to as 'the greening of world society'. The extent to which world society has become green is, of course, a highly contentious issue, but its very discussion indicates the significant changes that have occurred in terms of environmental perception and awareness in the last half century. The growth of the environmental movement has occurred during a period where we have increasingly seen the Earth as an integrated planet. The images of Earth sent back by the Apollo space missions (1961-1975) provided the context and a powerful visual stimulus for such an approach.

Several of the key concepts being investigated in this book go to the heart of this alleged 'greening' and also highlight the apparent contradictions between concepts such as 'development', 'sustainability' and 'environmentalism'. With all these notions, it is also important to recognise that an understanding of the environment may well be very personal and place and time-specific. Indeed, it may be more useful to consider multiple environmental understandings and the social context within which they arise.

The social construction of environmental geographies

If geographical explanation is to have wide-ranging relevance it must incorporate a multiplicity of views and perspectives. Leaving open the possibility of many stories and perspectives provides insights into society which could not otherwise be achieved (Massey et al, 1999). In this construction of society, the modern idea of 'difference' casts social and spatial categories and divisions between peoples and environments as a natural and therefore unproblematic fact of life. Such an approach ensures the relevance of the subject in the classroom by enabling students to take seriously their own living or everyday geographies.

> **Teaching idea 2**
>
> Ask students to investigate a contentious environmental issue in their local area – what different perspectives on the issue can they identify from the various positions taken over the disputed example?

A theme running through significant elements of this book relates to the differing perceptions of wealthier countries and less economically developed countries (LEDCs) with regards to environmental issues [☞]. Put simply, many of the LEDCs question why they should be forced to submit to the demands of the wealthiest nations in the name of the common good, when those now-wealthy nations were free to exploit their own natural environments in the relatively recent past as they pursued their own industrialisation policies. Clearly, one's perception of the importance of tropical rainforests is very different depending on who you are. Equally, the view of a well-

See ch 8, Globalisation (p187).

Introduction

See ch 7, Environmental management (p176-177).

See Volume 1: Human Geography, ch 5, Rural geographies (p104-106).

paid miner [🔗] in a British coal mine about the nature of his surroundings is likely to be quite different from that of local residents with no economic attachments to mining. On the other hand, increasing concerns about rural pollution due to farming activities in the UK [🔗] did not emerge until the wealthier middle classes began to move into rural communities in the 1980s, and started to object to long-standing, but environmentally undesirable, agricultural practices.

The book has been structured to provide a range of interlinked insights into environmental geographies. Chapter 1 investigates notions of ecosystems and their importance to the function of the planet. Chapters 2 and 3 look more specifically at the importance of weather and climate, with chapter 3 focusing on, arguably, the most pressing environmental issue facing the planet today, the implications of climate change. Chapter 4, in many ways, links to chapter 3 with its consideration of geographies of energy. If there is one area where the dynamic nature of geography is highlighted, it is the changing nature of approaches to geographies of energy over the last 50 years. Chapter 5 looks at the relationship between food supply and the environment. Chapters 6 and 7 both look at issues relating to the possibilities for effective environmental management. Chapter 6 tackles the politically and socially desirable, but highly problematic, notion of sustainability, while chapter 7 looks more closely at environmental management practices around the globe. Finally, chapter 8 highlights the globalised nature of so many aspects of environmental geography.

One of the principal purposes of this book is to demonstrate how the latest thinking in higher education can, where appropriate, be incorporated into the geography classroom in the secondary school. This text does not deliver chunks of knowledge to be imparted to the class, indeed it argues strongly against such an approach. As geographers, we need to move away from notions of fixed content and skills towards concepts and strategies for addressing complexity, difference and uncertainty and the permanence of shifting positions. This also involves challenging structured and ordered views of the world and moving towards more complex and multifaceted perspectives (Mitchell, 2009: 54). This book is an attempt to help people, both teachers and students, to think geographically in order to apply that thinking to whatever situation they need to understand.

Ecosystems

Charles Rawding and Ann Worsley

Introduction

The term 'ecosystem' has been a part of ecology and biogeography for more than 100 years.[1] In this time, its use has varied, but it has greatly influenced geographical thinking and has, in the past 50 years, come to be used and incorporated within broader themes such as sustainability and development. It was pioneering work, undertaken by a young American, Frederic Clements (Colinvaux, 1990), that saw the introduction of the notion of the organismic community, ie the ecosystem. Travelling across the American Midwest in the late 19th century, Clements' observations on the impact of wagon trains, migrating buffalo and hunting parties led him to describe how vegetation communities respond to natural, physical factors and to factors such as grazing intensity and human impact. He coined the term 'ecosystem' and wrote about how the communities of plants and animals he observed were closely related within distinctive units of area [☞]. In the early 20th century, a British ecologist, Tansley (1939), further developed the idea of ecosystems so that they became part of mainstream ecology and biogeography.

In the latter half of the 20th century, the use of the term ecosystem became mainstream, but, at the same time, new ideas and terminology developed as ecologists and biogeographers discovered and wrote about planetary scale systems. The term 'biosphere' is used to denote the zone in which all life occurs, and is thus planetary in scale. It includes the totality of life, but can refer simply to the sum total of organisms on Earth. Importantly, biosphere overlaps other planetary components, namely lithosphere, atmosphere and hydrosphere, and indeed, life can be found in all three. Thus the planetary systems can be represented by a series of overlapping areas (figure 1.1) which demonstrate the important role life plays in each. The work by James Lovelock has gone much further. In his seminal book, *The Ages of Gaia*, Lovelock (1989, 2009) cleverly explains how life on Earth exerts control over atmosphere, lithosphere and hydrosphere, seeing Earth as a self-stabilising mechanism, regulating atmospheric chemistry, and thus rendering the planet inhabitable. This view of the Earth's biosphere as a planetary ecosystem is very important – in particular, because it strongly conveys the impression of living flora and fauna interacting with and regulating their physical environments.

See Volume 1: Human Geography, ch 9, Geographies of health and environment (p178).

Figure 1.1: Biosphere, hydrosphere, atmosphere and lithosphere as overlapping and interacting components of planet Earth

See Biosphere.ppt

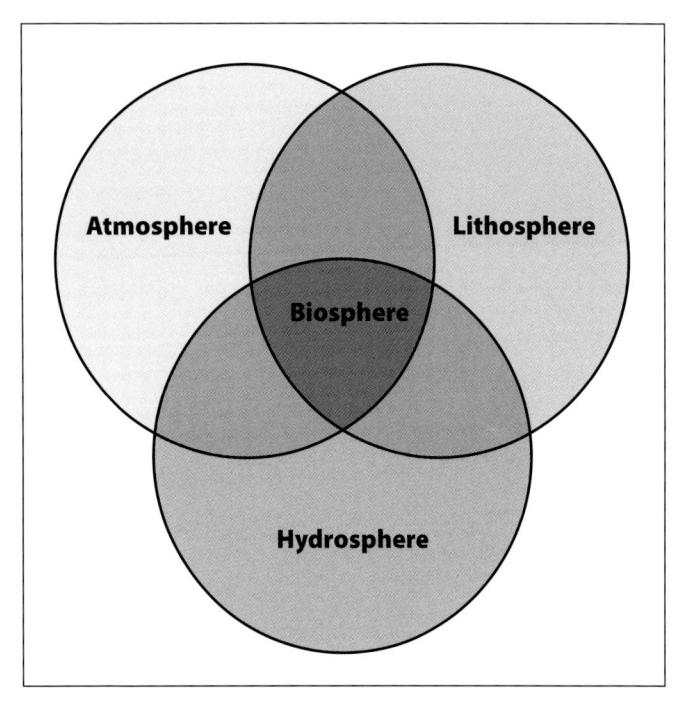

Figure 1.2:
Scales (ranks) of organisation in ecology and geographical enquiry

See accompanying CD-Rom

Ecosystems.doc

Organisation in ecology	Vegetation system in geography	Students
Biosphere	Biosphere	Planet Earth
Ecosystem	Biome	Country
Community	Regional/local ecosystem	County
Population	Habitat	Town
Organism	Niche	Street name House name or number

Within biogeography and ecology, the scale at which enquiry and investigation varies is considerable so, in this context, the terminology employed becomes critical. Figure 1.2 shows the scale of organisation and therefore geographical enquiry in vegetation studies. To help your students, it might be useful to consider the hierarchy in terms of an address.

Populations, communities and ecosystems

A population is a group of organisms of the same species living within a unit of area. This could include a population of pine trees in an upland forest, the human population of a country or the population of termites in an African termite mound. Critical factors include the population size or abundance, age structure, changes in size over time, and factors which affect numbers, eg migration. Understanding what factors affect population size is a key area of research in ecology and biogeography and has enormous implications for conservation, resource management and the understanding of human impacts on ecosystems.

Populations, of course, do not occur in isolation, but they coexist with others to form ecological communities. The term 'community' is rather more abstract, since communities do not exist as physically discrete entities with distinct boundaries. Nevertheless, it is an important concept to consider. Boundaries, such as they are, can be drawn subjectively, even though in many cases they exist due to physical features, such as mountain ranges, pond size and so on. In addition, human activity can devise boundaries, because we tend to try to compartmentalise the landscape into units of area, such as fields. But even where we can describe a community qualitatively or quantitatively, organisms may migrate in or out of that landscape, and thus the definition of community is subject to change. However, the community as a concept, and as a grouping of populations, is still valid and is widely used in ecology. Indeed, the organisation of communities is a major research theme in ecology and biogeography.

A community of organisms and the physical environment with which it interacts is known as an ecosystem. The term 'ecosystem' is often used in a variety of ways, and in place of other terms such as 'landscape' and 'environment'. It is used to describe a specific land system or unit of area made of interrelated components such as landforms, rock type, soils, climate and organisms. This ecosystem concept, described by Tansley in the 1930s, thus has great value because it focuses upon the living organisms and their physical environment. Ecosystem has come to mean the geographical unit of air, earth and water that includes and incorporates all living organisms. The ecosystem approach has great value in geography, since it conceptualises and studies environment in a holistic and integrated way. Since the concept of community includes only living organisms and ignores physical and chemical environmental factors, it is more appropriate to use the term 'ecosystem' because this represents the interactive system – ie the living organisms, their physical surroundings and features and the processes that link them all together.

Biomes and biogeographical regions

At a global level, it is possible to divide the planet into biogeographical zones or realms, which in turn are divided into biogeographical regions or biomes (figure 1.3). These biomes [☞] may be described as major terrestrial vegetation communities, which are often defined by the similarity of the dominant plants. Each biome is distinguished by its own combination of climate and major life forms, in particular, the major plant species that are dominant, showing a considerable degree of homogeneity. Each biome covers an extensive geographical area, and is also distinguished by its major soil types. Although the demarcation of biomes is often rather arbitrary, the global patterns and interrelationships between climate, vegetation and soils cannot be underestimated. One key factor which is also distinguished by its connection to vegetation, climate and soils is plant productivity – ie the amount of organic dry matter that accumulates in a single growing season, measured in g carbon m^{-2} yr^{-1}.[2]

See ch 2, Climate and weather (p47).

Figure 1.3: Biogeographical realms and biomes

See accompanying CD-Rom

World biomes.ppt

It is also possible to view the Earth in terms of the productivity of the vegetation, as seen in the NASA image shown in figure 1.4 on p8. The global snapshot shows where

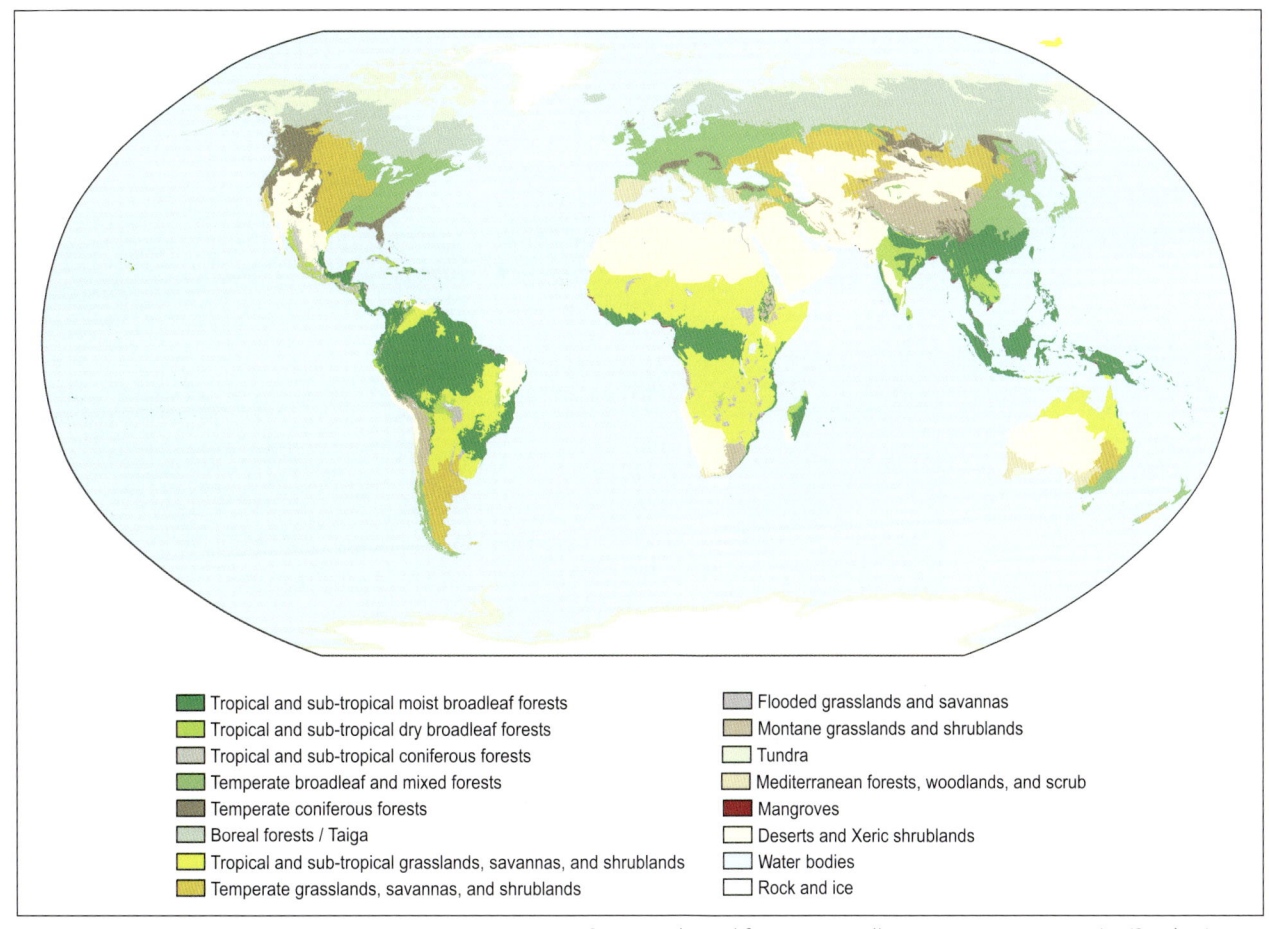

- Tropical and sub-tropical moist broadleaf forests
- Tropical and sub-tropical dry broadleaf forests
- Tropical and sub-tropical coniferous forests
- Temperate broadleaf and mixed forests
- Temperate coniferous forests
- Boreal forests / Taiga
- Tropical and sub-tropical grasslands, savannas, and shrublands
- Temperate grasslands, savannas, and shrublands
- Flooded grasslands and savannas
- Montane grasslands and shrublands
- Tundra
- Mediterranean forests, woodlands, and scrub
- Mangroves
- Deserts and Xeric shrublands
- Water bodies
- Rock and ice

Source: adapted from www.millenniumassessment.org/en/Synthesis.aspx using data from WWF: http://worldwildlife.org/science/data/item1875.html

Chapter 1: Ecosystems

Teaching idea 1.1

Making connections: using global maps of biomes, climate regions, soil zones and plant productivity (see figure 1.3 on p7), ask students to investigate the link between each. Why do tropical zones have high productivity? What is the relationship between this productivity and climate? What factors in climate regions contribute to plant productivity and soil formation? What do the similarities and differences between the maps tell us about the relationships between climate soils and vegetation?

**Figure 1.4:
Global vegetation**

See accompanying CD-Rom

Global vegetation.ppt

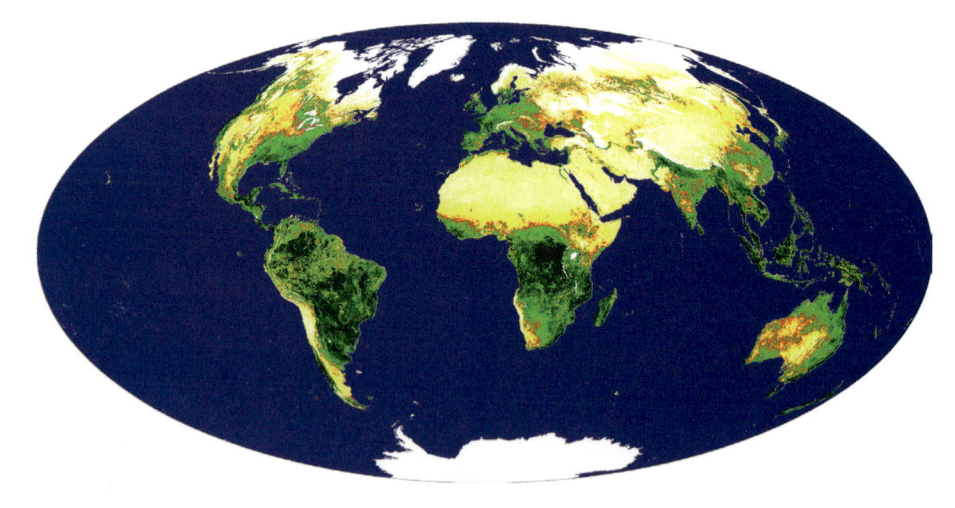

Source: MODIS Land Science Team, NASA. *http://visibleearth.nasa.gov/view_rec.php?id=274*

**Figure 1.5:
The Mediterranean biome**

See accompanying CD-Rom

Mediterranean vegetation.ppt

PHOTOS: (TOP AND BOTTOM RIGHT) ANN WORSLEY

Contemporary Approaches to Geography Volume 3: Environmental Geography   Chris Kington Publishing

green foliage is being produced by land plants (green and dark green show greater productivity; yellow shows little or no production, while red is a boundary zone). The image has been produced on the basis of the terrestrial biosphere breathing in carbon dioxide for photosynthesis.

The Mediterranean biome

Named after the Mediterranean region, this biome occurs in several areas around the world. It is characterised by hot, dry summers and wet, mild winters. This means that very little of the annual precipitation falls in the months of June, July and August (in the northern hemisphere), and peak rainfall tends to occur in the autumn. Wherever this biome does occur globally, we say that the natural vegetation is Mediterranean in character, because it has the same features in terms of plant communities and soils types, as well as climatic regime. The classic community is one dominated by a mixture of woodland and dense shrub-type vegetation which is principally sclerophyllous (ie adapted to lengthy seasonal drought by producing leathery or waxy leaves which help to reduce water loss by transpiration). The climatic climax community is evergreen oak, but much of this kind of woodland has disappeared from the Mediterranean region. The woodland communities are characterised by trees such as pine or evergreen oak and, in the Mediterranean basin itself, by the olive.

The contemporary vegetation community is often given the name 'mattoral'. The structure of the mattoral, its constituent flora and character, suggest that it has long been influenced by human activity, both through the grazing of animals and land clearance by burning. Indeed, many of the plant species show distinctive and remarkable adaptations to surviving fire and grazing. The mattoral can be subdivided into:

- maquis (dense shrub vegetation of more than 75% total cover, 1 to 5 metres in height but with little in the way of ground flora, dominated by species such as tree heath, juniper, myrtle and buckthorn)
- garrigue (scattered low, mostly evergreen shrubs up to 1 metre in height, ground cover 25 to 50%, dominated by species such as rosemary, thyme, lavender, sage, broom and rock rose)
- pseudo-steppe (made up of grasses, annuals such as clover and thistle, and bulbs such as asphodels, with ground cover of less than 25%).

In many places, the Mediterranean biome is characterised by soils that have suffered erosion or considerable degradation, following thousands of years of agricultural activity. Soils such as rendzina, terra rossa and terra fusca are also distinguished by their deep red and brown colours and give rise, along with the vegetation, to many typical images of the Mediterranean.

The tropical biome

This is the most complex and diverse biome on the planet, and it occurs where temperature and rainfall are at their highest all year round. Unlike in the UK, or in the Mediterranean biome, where seasonality of precipitation and temperature plays an enormous part in plant productivity, there is a distinct lack of change over the year;

temperature fluctuations are relatively small and water availability is always high. This makes for optimum growth. What curbs growth is the amount of sunlight available for plants, and so they must compete to obtain light for photosynthesis. They do this by utilising an enormous range of strategies to either reach the light, or adapt to low light intensity on the forest floor. Other plants have large leaves which help to intercept light, and many have drip tip leaves which enable the drainage of excess rainfall while promoting transpiration. Some trees have leaf stalks that follow the passage of the Sun across the sky so they can always absorb the maximum amount of light. Often leaves in the upper layer of the forest (the canopy layer) are small and leathery (or waxy) to reduce the loss of water, but this will also enable more light to reach the lower branches and leaves. To compete for light, other species have developed different growth strategies: some have long stems (or trunks) such as lianas (vines); others grow on the main trunks or branches of the main trees (eg ferns, orchids), and some are heterotrophs – ie they grow on the forest floor and obtain their nutrients by tapping into the trunks of trees or from decaying vegetation. The tree species themselves have distinctive growth forms to support biomass in the competition for light: many species have broad woody buttresses at the base of the trunk to channel stem flow and dissolved nutrients to the roots.

Figure 1.6: Tropical forest

See accompanying CD-Rom

Tropical forest.ppt

Tropical rainforests cover less than 6% of the Earth's surface; however, more than half of all the world's plant and animal species may be found here. It is estimated that the tropical forests contribute more than 40% to the Earth's oxygen derived from vegetation. Unlike temperate soils, which can be deep and rich, the soils under tropical rainforests are often thin, infertile and deeply weathered or leached. High temperature and moisture availability mean very rapid decomposition by bacteria with subsequent rapid take-up by the vegetation. Consequently, biomass is almost entirely held within the living vegetation community. However, like the Mediterranean, soils (known generally as oxisols) are often very red. This is because of the rapid transformation and movement up and down the soil profile of iron and aluminium with water.

The coastal sand dune ecosystem: the psammosere

Coastal sand dune systems have long been considered as ecosystems because they contain common environmental features and habitats which can be differentiated on the basis of ecology and geomorphology. Typically, a transect from the high water mark inland displays change with distance from the sea. Figure 1.7 clearly shows that several biotic and abiotic factors control the composition of vegetation, soil development and the morphology of the dunes. The most important factors are wind speed (which affects sand accretion rates and dune stability), temperature, water retention, salinity and the amount of salt spray, the accumulation of organic matter and calcium carbonate and pH. Typical coastal sand dunes are made up of a sequence of classic features [☞] including embryo, mobile and fixed dunes, dune slacks and blow-outs. Each type has distinctive morphologies and plant communities. The abiotic and biotic factors acting as controls to plant growth also act as indirect controls on morphology and give rise to the classic plant succession or sere. Where additional factors, such as human activity or climate forcing factors affecting wind, waves and ultimately sediment budgets, vary, the 'classic' sequence of vegetation succession may be interrupted or changed.

See Volume 2: Physical Geography, ch 3, Coasts (p74).

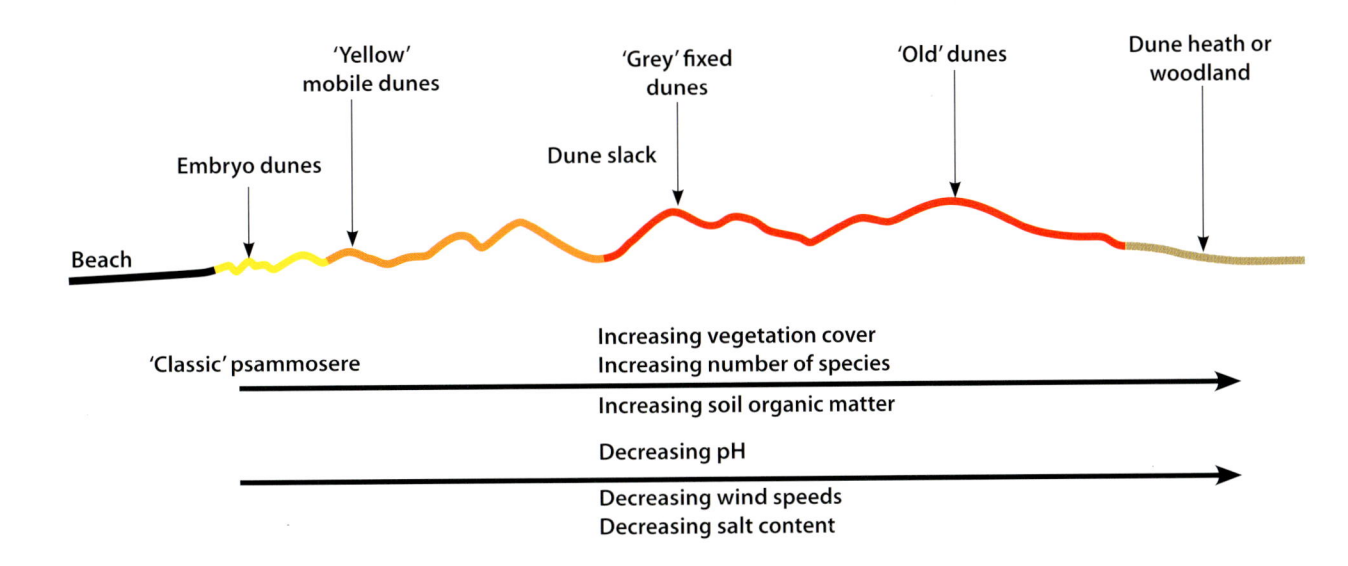

Figure 1.7: Cross-section of a typical psammosere

Psammosere.ppt

**Figure 1.8:
Coastal ecosystems – the Sefton Coast**

See accompanying CD-Rom

Coastal ecosystems.ppt

Habitats and niches

The success of an organism depends upon its ability to derive the energy to grow and ensure the survival of its species. The limits to that success depend on a large number of variables which may be abiotic (non-living, eg soil pH) or biotic (living, eg disease). Habitat refers to the physical space or place occupied by organisms at any one time during their lifetime (life cycle). Habitats are characterised by distinguishable environmental factors to which the organism is adapted and which it can tolerate. More specifically, the niche refers to the specific factors that limit survival, growth and reproduction. A fundamental niche is the maximum area in which a species can tolerate any given set of environment-limiting factors without competition from other species. The realised niche is that area in which the benefits from the environmental factors are further limited by competition from other organisms.

Teaching idea 1.2

A look at biomes

Ask students to select a biome and provide a series of photographs illustrating key aspects/features about it, eg key plant species, key animal species, a soil description, climatic characteristics [💿]. What features demonstrate how the plants and/or animals have adapted to their environment? What are the critical abiotic and biotic factors that exert control over plant populations here? What impacts have people had on the vegetation communities here?

See accompanying CD-Rom

See Mediterranean vegetation.ppt as an example

Chapter 1: Ecosystems

**Figure 1.9:
Wetland ecosystems**

See accompanying CD-Rom

Wetland ecosystems.ppt

a. Speke Hall Lake, Liverpool, Merseyside
Wetland ecosystems are unique, biologically diverse and provide many varied habitats for flora and fauna. This small lake, surrounded by fields and woodland provides food and shelter for many species.

b. Roudsea, Cumbria
Wetlands are among some of the most diverse ecosystems on the planet. They are rich in nutrients and thus provide unique habitats for a large range of flora and fauna in the muds, waters and at their edges.

Among the UK's most important types of wetland ecosystem are bogs, which develop from lakes in a process known as hydroseral succession.

This picture shows the edge of a wetland system that is undergoing succession. The specialist plants (here reeds called phragmites) each have their own unique habitat requirements. Some prefer and can cope with more waterlogging than others. At the same time, they trap inorganic debris and organic detritus which gradually build up the level of sediment. Then other plants, again with their own unique set of needs, take over. In this way, the wetlands gradually infill, first becoming a bog and then eventually becoming fully terrestrialised as a dryland system, usually as woodland.

c. Roudsea, Cumbria
Over time the wetland, which is dominated by water plants such as lilies and along the edge of the body of water by reeds (in reed swamps), becomes colonised by grasses and sedges together with trees and shrubs (such as alder, birch and hazel), and the very muds become stabilised by roots and the accumulation of organic and inorganic matter.

d. Deepdale, near Arnside, Lancashire
Gradually infilling, the wetland ecosystem is transformed into a landscape which looks very different. In this photo the reeds have disappeared and, although there is still some standing water, it is surrounded by trees which are encroaching upon the peat which accumulates as plants die off.

e. Roudsea, Cumbria
As sediments accumulate, gradually tree and shrub species that can cope with waterlogging begin to invade. In this case the tree in the foreground is birch.

f. Blea Tarn, Langdale, Cumbria
Larger lakes and wetlands undergo the same transformations as over time inorganic and organic debris accumulates, infilling the lake to produce distinctive and varied habitats for flora and fauna.

g. Fishouse Moss, near Roudsea, Cumbria
Eventually, hydroseral succession is completed and all standing water disappears, leaving a landscape transformed.

h. Roudsea, Cumbria
Larger trees such as oaks finally colonise the wetland when the muds have been transformed into soils over time.

See Wetland ecosystems.ppt as an example

> **Teaching idea 1.3**
>
> **Investigating ecosystems**
>
> Ask students to select an ecosystem, eg psammosere, woodland or wetland ecosystem [👁]. Again, provide students with a series of images of key plant and animal species. What abiotic and biotic factors are important in the selected ecosystem? Why are these factors important? How do these factors influence the development and structure of the chosen ecosystem? What are the main human impacts in this ecosystem?

Understanding ecosystems

Ecology is the study of the relationships of plants and animals to each other and to their environment, while an ecosystem may be defined as the community of plants and animals (biotic factors) together with the physical environment that sustains them (abiotic factors). The concept of an ecosystem is a deliberate attempt to focus on the characteristics of, and interrelationships between, the elements of the environment and its living inhabitants. These inhabitants may be permanent or temporary, and an understanding of the wide range of flows within such a system is essential to interpreting the dynamics of the ecosystem. Most ecosystems are considered to be open systems with inputs such as sunlight and rainfall, and outputs in the form of various types of detritus (waste). Ecosystems vary greatly in size and composition, from a small community of microbes in a drop of water, to the entire Amazon rainforest. Selecting an appropriate boundary is dependent on the issue under discussion.

The complexity of many ecosystems makes them robust under a range of conditions, such as the random removal of species; however, they may prove to be highly vulnerable if what are termed 'keystone species' are removed. The removal of keystone species may result in the extinction of other dependent species, or alternatively result in significant imbalances occurring within ecosystems as a result of the loss of function of keystone species. This would appear to be currently the case with a range of marine ecosystems where the top predators have been overfished resulting in dramatic growth of now predator-free species such as jellyfish and algal blooms.

Ecosystems also operate within a range of tolerances where survival is possible. These can relate to temperature, soil moisture content, precipitation or alternatively anthropogenic influences such as pollution or resource exploitation. The tolerance range of ecosystems is greater than that of individual species within the ecosystem, a factor which reinforces the desirability of sustained biodiversity within ecosystems (see *Sustainability and biodiversity* on p150).

The very existence of the human race, and that of the millions of species with which the planet is shared, is dependent on the health of our ecosystems. However, people are putting increasing strain on the world's ecosystems. They are being modified by human kind at an unprecedented rate, with only a partial understanding of the implications this will have in terms of the future sustainability of livelihoods and environments (see *Human use of natural resources* on p152).

Ecosystem services

Ecosystem services are the functions that are provided by ecosystems that are of major importance to human wellbeing. The Millennium Ecosystem Assessment (*www.millenniumassessment.org*) describes four categories of ecosystem services:

- supporting, eg nutrient cycling, soil formation and primary production
- provisioning, eg the production of food, fresh water, materials or fuel
- regulating, eg climate and flood regulation, water purification, pollination and pest control
- cultural, eg aesthetic, spiritual, educational and recreational services.

Biodiversity

Biodiversity [☞] is simply a contraction of the term 'biological diversity' and relates to the variations of life on Earth. As such, there are two principal strands to biodiversity: species diversity, which refers to the range of different species within a region, and habitat diversity, which refers to the range of habitat types within a region. Biodiversity includes diversity at the genetic level, as between individuals in a population, or between plant varieties, the diversity of species, and the diversity of ecosystems and habitats. Biodiversity encompasses more than just variation in appearance and composition. It also includes diversity in abundance (such as the number of genes, individuals, populations or habitats in a particular location), distribution (across locations and through time) and behaviour, including interactions among the components of biodiversity, such as between pollinator species and plants, or between predators and prey. Biodiversity also incorporates the relations between human societies and the environments within which they function. Although five major extinction events have been recorded over the history of the planet, the large number and variety of genes, species and ecosystems in existence today are the ones with which human societies have developed, and on which people depend.

See ch 7, Environmental management (p173).

Concerns over the loss of biodiversity across the globe resulted in the Convention on Biological Diversity (*www.cbd.int*) being signed at the UN Conference on Environment and Development (Rio de Janeiro, 1992) [☞] and coming into force in 1993. The aim of the convention is to conserve biological diversity and to promote the sustainable use of species and ecosystems, while at the same time endeavouring to ensure an equitable sharing of the economic benefits of genetic resources.

See ch 8, Globalisation (p186).

Biodiversity provides the basis for ecosystems and the services they provide, and as such it is essential for human survival. People rely on biodiversity in their daily lives, often without realising it. At one level, biodiversity provides essential products, such as food and fibres, whose values are widely recognised. However, biodiversity also underpins a much wider range of services, many of which are less valued, and in some cases their importance is poorly understood by wider society. For instance, bacteria and microbes that transform waste into usable products, insects that pollinate crops and flowers, coral reefs and mangroves that protect coastlines, and the biologically-rich landscapes and seascapes that provide enjoyment are only a few of the services provided. Although much more remains to be understood about the relationships between biodiversity and ecosystem services, it is well established that if the products

See ch 7, Environmental management (p158).

and services that are provided by biodiversity are not managed [🔗] effectively, future options will become ever more restricted. Poor people tend to be the most directly affected by the deterioration or loss of ecosystem services, as they are the most dependent on local ecosystems, and often live in places most vulnerable to ecosystem change. This is particularly the case for the rural poor. At a more general level, effectively functioning ecosystems are extremely important, as buffers against extreme climate events, as carbon sinks to ameliorate the impacts of global warming, and as filters for waterborne and airborne pollutants.

Current losses of biodiversity are having a range of impacts which are restricting future development options. Ecosystems are being transformed, and, in some cases, irreversibly degraded. A large number of species have become extinct in recent history or are threatened with extinction, while reductions in animal and plant populations are widespread, and genetic diversity is widely considered to be in decline. Current changes to biodiversity on land, and in the world's fresh and marine waters, are more rapid than at any time in human history, and have led to degradation in many of the world's ecosystem services.

See ch 4, Energy (p85).

The increasing use of energy [🔗] by modern society is having a significant impact on biodiversity. Growing requirements for energy are resulting in changes in species and ecosystems. This can be seen at a range of levels. In poorer areas of the less developed world, the traditional use of biomass fuels, such as locally collected timber, is under threat as populations grow. At a global level, where climate change is being driven by fossil-fuel use, species ranges and behaviour are altering in consequence. Such changes are likely to have very significant knock-on effects for society, with probable outcomes including changing geographical patterns of infectious diseases, and an increased awareness of the arrival of 'alien' and potentially damaging species in areas where they had previously been absent.

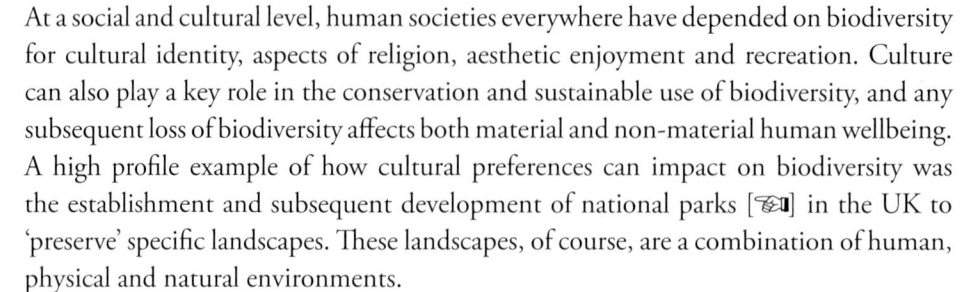

See Volume 1: Human Geography, ch 2, Geographies of tourism (p36).

At a social and cultural level, human societies everywhere have depended on biodiversity for cultural identity, aspects of religion, aesthetic enjoyment and recreation. Culture can also play a key role in the conservation and sustainable use of biodiversity, and any subsequent loss of biodiversity affects both material and non-material human wellbeing. A high profile example of how cultural preferences can impact on biodiversity was the establishment and subsequent development of national parks [🔗] in the UK to 'preserve' specific landscapes. These landscapes, of course, are a combination of human, physical and natural environments.

See ch 7, Environmental management (p172).

Although many losses of biodiversity, including the degradation of ecosystems, are slow or gradual, they can lead to sudden and dramatic declines in the capacity of biodiversity to contribute to human wellbeing. The collapse of the Canadian cod fishery [🔗] during the 1990s illustrates this well. The effectiveness of ecosystem services depends on biodiversity. It is this biodiversity that enables an ecosystem to function effectively and to supply benefits to people (see figure 1.10 on p17).

Teaching idea 1.4

Ask students to identify aspects of biodiversity that can be related to human culture, for instance harvest festivals in church, or landscape appreciation and tourism. What impact might a loss of biodiversity have on such cultural practices?

Provisioning	food, fuel or fibre as the end product
Regulating	pollination
Cultural	spiritual or aesthetic benefits, or cultural identity
Supporting	micro-organisms cycling nutrients and soil formation

Source: adapted from UNEP, 2007.

Figure 1.10:
The roles of biodiversity in the supply of ecosystem services in agriculture

See accompanying CD-Rom

Ecosystems.doc

Valuing ecosystems

The contribution of biodiversity-dependent ecosystem services to national economies is substantial. Although attempting to place an economic value on ecosystem services is new, it is likely that policy decisions using such approaches will benefit significantly in terms of trade-offs between economic development and ecosystem management [☞].

See ch 7, Environmental management (p166).

Values

Ecosystem	Value (US$)	Category
Annual world fish catch	58 billion	Provisioning
Anti-cancer agents from marine organisms	Up to 1 billion	Provisioning
Global herbal medicine market	Approx 43 billion (2001)	Provisioning
Honeybees as pollinators for agriculture crops	2–8 billion	Regulating
Coral reefs for fisheries and tourism	30 billion	Cultural (tourism)/regulating (coastal protection)

Costs

Ecosystem	Cost (US$)	Category
Mangrove degradation in Pakistan	20 million in fishing losses 500,000 in timber losses 1.5 million in feed and pasture losses	Provisioning Regulating
Newfoundland cod fishery collapse	2 billion + tens of thousands of jobs	Provisioning

Source: adapted from UNEP, 2007.

Of those ecosystem services that have been assessed, it is estimated that about 60% are currently degraded or being used unsustainably. Such unsustainable use is impacting on areas such as fisheries, waste treatment and detoxification, water purification, natural hazard protection, the regulation of air quality, the regulation of regional and local climate, and erosion control. Decline in a critical species at a local scale will have an adverse impact on ecosystem services, even if that species is not threatened globally. Most of this degradation can be attributed to an increase in demand for specific elements, such as fisheries, wild meat, water, timber, fibre and fuel. At a global scale, population growth and increasing levels of consumption, which have led to increased demand for ecosystem services and energy, are the principal factors impacting upon biodiversity.

Figure 1.11:
Valuing ecosystems?

See accompanying CD-Rom

Ecosystems.doc

Agriculture throughout the world is dependent on biodiversity. Yet agriculture is also the largest driver of genetic erosion, species loss and conversion of natural habitats. Changes in agricultural production techniques and loss of diversity may well have an adverse effect on the sustainability of agriculture. For example, the diversity and numbers of pollinators are affected by habitat change. Although some crops, such as rice and maize, do not require animal pollination, the decline of pollinators has long-term consequences for major food crops such as fruit trees and vegetables in many parts of the world. Genetic erosion, the loss of local populations of species, and the loss of cultural traditions associated with agricultural practices are often closely interlinked. The transition from traditional to commercially developed varieties of food crops is often associated with rates of genetic erosion in crop and livestock production systems throughout the less developed world. Such genetic erosion reduces the options of small farmers in terms of mitigating the impacts of environmental change and reducing vulnerability, particularly in marginal farming areas such as the arid and semi-arid lands of Africa and India.

It should be stressed here that similar genetic erosion occurred in the developed countries as their farming practices were transformed during the 19th and 20th centuries. However, wealthier societies are better able to cope with the economic consequences of environmental degradation.

Ecosystems under pressure

Over the recent past, humans have changed ecosystems more rapidly and extensively than during any comparable period of time. This has resulted in a substantial and largely irreversible loss in the diversity of life on Earth. Perhaps perversely, many of the changes that have been made to ecosystems have contributed to substantial net gains in human wellbeing and economic development. However, these gains have been achieved at growing costs in the form of the degradation of many ecosystem services and the exacerbation of poverty for some groups of people. Unless these issues are addressed, future generations will not be able to benefit to anywhere near the same extent from the Earth's ecosystems.

See Volume 1: Human Geography, ch 7, Development geographies (p144).

The Millennium Ecosystem Assessment highlights major issues that revolve around the fact that ecosystem degradation is reaching dangerous new levels. For instance, environmental degradation is a serious barrier to achieving the UN Millennium Development Goals [🖘] (*www.un.org/millenniumgoals*). The *intention* to eradicate famine and disease worldwide cannot be accomplished in the face of ongoing environmental damage. A disproportionate amount of this damage is being inflicted on the underdeveloped countries and the poorest people in the world (see figure 1.12 on p19). On a more positive note, the assessment does demonstrate that, with appropriate policies and actions, it may be possible to reverse the degradation of many ecosystem services over the next 50 years. However, the changes in policy and practice required are substantial and have yet to be effectively implemented.

The pressures of world population growth and economic development have had a massive impact on the world's biomes. Some 60% of world ecosystem services have been degraded. In more than half of the world's 14 biomes, 20 to 50% of their surface areas have already been converted to croplands. For the developed regions of the world, much of this conversion took place during periods of rapid industrialisation and population growth, from the late 18th century through to the

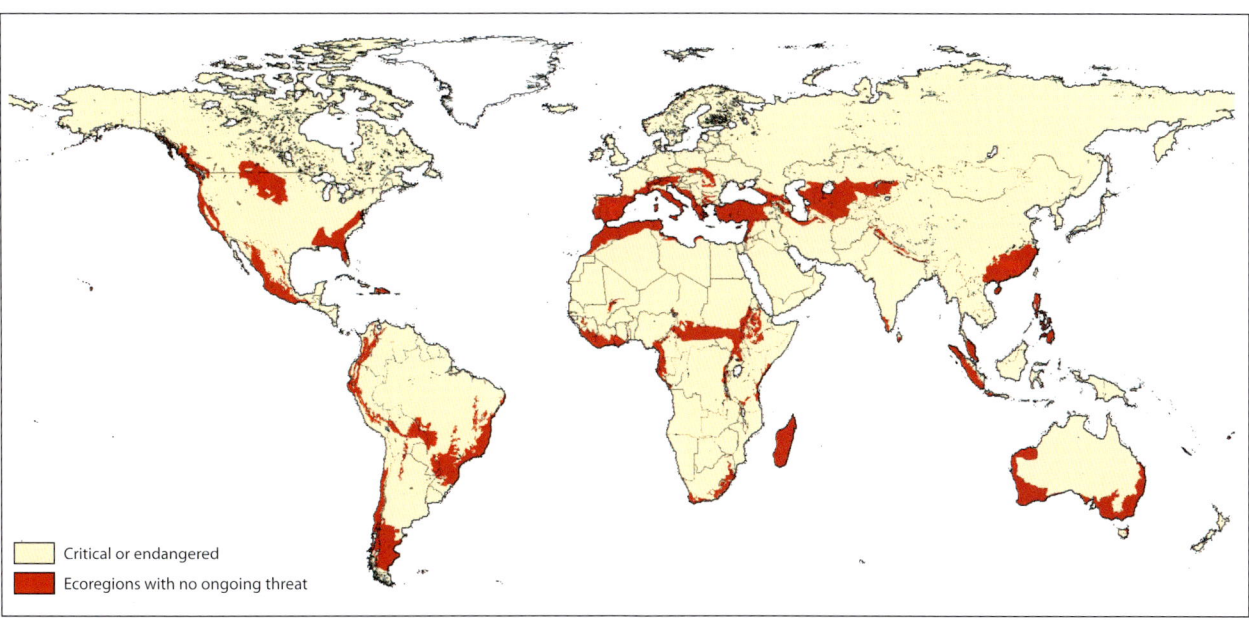

Chapter 1: Ecosystems

Critical or endangered
Ecoregions with no ongoing threat

Source: adapted from UNEP, 2007: 163.

**Figure 1.12:
Critical or endangered terrestrial ecosystems**

See accompanying CD-Rom

Endangered ecosystems.ppt

Teaching idea 1.5

Ask students to look at figure 1.12 and investigate in more detail one of the 'critical or endangered' terrestrial ecosystems. What forms of environmental damage are currently occurring? Why is this happening? What can be done to rectify the situation?

early 20th century. In the less developed areas of the world, change has occurred more recently. For instance, tropical dry broadleaf forests have undergone the most rapid conversion since 1950, followed by temperate grasslands, flooded grasslands and savannahs.

Developments in technology have also impacted on ecosystem conversion, with approximately 50% of inland water habitats being transformed for human use during the 20th century, as technologies for water management have been developed. Some 60% of the world's major rivers have been interrupted by dams and diversions, reducing biodiversity as a result of the flooding of habitats, the disruption of flow patterns, the isolation of animal populations and the blocking of migration routes. River systems are also being significantly affected by water withdrawals, leaving some major rivers nearly or completely dry. Such trends have become increasingly obvious in the wealthier countries of the world, as populations have grown in areas that are considered to have a desirable (ie dry and sunny) climate, such as the south-western USA and the Mediterranean coasts of Europe. In the Earth's oceans, coral reefs are seen to be particularly under threat.

One attempt to provide data on this topic has been the World Wide Fund for Nature's Living Planet Index (LPI) (*www.panda.org*), which tracks the global populations of more than 1,000 vertebrates. These vertebrates are divided into terrestrial, marine and freshwater categories. All three categories have shown worrying declines over the past 30 years, with an overall decline of about 30% since 1970 (see figure 1.13 on p20).

Figure 1.13:
Left: Living Planet Index,1970-2005.
Right: Humanity's ecological footprint, 1960-2005

See accompanying CD-Rom

Living planet .ppt

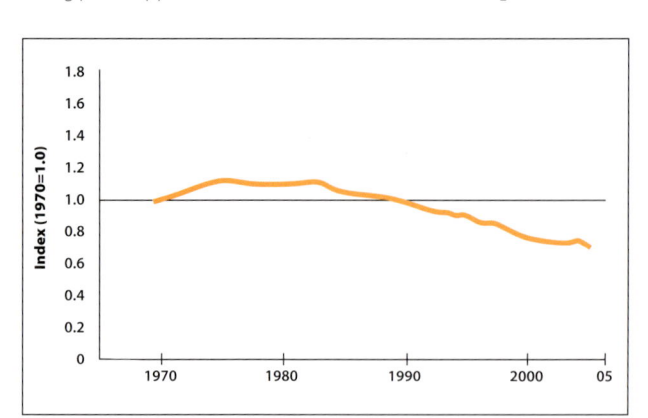

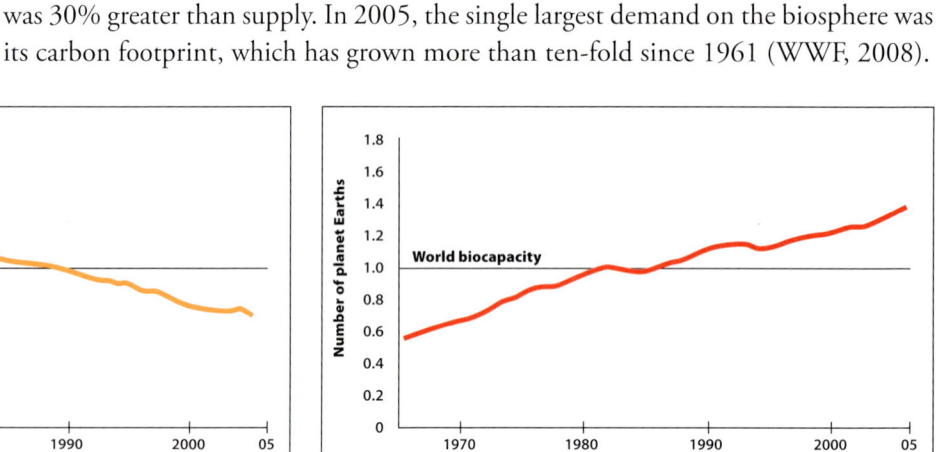

At the same time, humanity's ecological footprint has more than doubled over the period 1961 to 2005. The ecological footprint is the measure of humanity's demand on the biosphere in terms of the area of biologically productive land and sea required, both to provide the resources we use and to absorb our waste. In 2005, the global ecological footprint was 17.5 billion global hectares (a global hectare (gha) is a hectare with world-average ability to produce resources and absorb wastes). On the supply side, the total productive area, or biocapacity, was 13.6 billion gha. A country's footprint is the sum of all the cropland, grazing land, forest and fishing grounds required to produce the food, fibre and timber it consumes, to absorb the wastes emitted when it uses energy, and to provide space for its infrastructure. Since people consume resources and ecological services from all over the world, their footprint totals these areas, regardless of where they are located on the planet. Humanity's footprint first exceeded the Earth's total biocapacity in the 1980s; by 2005, demand was 30% greater than supply. In 2005, the single largest demand on the biosphere was its carbon footprint, which has grown more than ten-fold since 1961 (WWF, 2008).

Source: adapted from WWF, 2008: 2.

See ch 4, Energy (p99).
See ch 8, Globalisation (p191).

At the present time, tropical forest ecosystems are most likely to be affected by human activity (see below). This is largely as a result of forest clearance for agricultural expansion (including the growth of biofuel [💿] plantations). The fragmentation of large areas of forest is already resulting in the degradation of the largest remaining areas of species-rich forest blocks in the Amazon and Congo basins. Forest clearance also poses problems for species such as mountain gorillas, which survive in only four remaining areas of forest in central Africa, in national parks in Burundi, Uganda and Rwanda. These parks are now isolated elements in an area of recently cleared and managed farmland. Needless to say, gorillas and farms do not mix, and the gorilla populations are coming under serious threat in areas where the implementation of government policies may be less than effective [💿] (Adams, 2009: 261).

The expansion of cultivated areas for ranching, and the production of grain and biofuels, are also having a major impact on woodland-savanna areas such as the Cerrado region in north-eastern Brazil. This area has a pronounced dry season, and supports a unique array of drought- and fire-adapted plant species and endemic bird species. Large mammals such as the giant anteater, giant armadillo, jaguar and maned wolf also still survive here (*www.biodiversityhotspots.org*).

The intensification of shifting cultivation cycles, as population pressures increase, is also having an impact on biodiversity. For instance, studies in north-east India have shown that, where shifting cultivation has shortened to a five to ten-year cycle, there are significant implications for birds and plant species richness: a fallow period of 25 years for birds and 50 to 75 years for plants is necessary to maintain the composition of the ecosystem (Adams, 2009: 261-2).

Alongside forest ecosystems, marine and coastal ecosystems are also expected to continue to be degraded, as a result of continued and intensified fishing, eutrophication triggered by land-based activities, and coastal conversion for aquaculture. Impacts are most likely to be felt among the large species, including top predators. It is expected that there will be considerable declines, and some extinctions are likely to occur.

Figure 1.14: Impacts on biodiversity as a result of development pressures

See accompanying CD-Rom

Impacts on biodiversity.doc

Pressures	Impacts	Implications for ecosystem services and human wellbeing	Examples
Habitat conversion	• Decline in natural habitat • Fewer species • Fragmentation of landscapes • Soil degradation	• Increased agricultural production • Loss of water regulation potential • Reliance on fewer species • Decreased fisheries • Decreased coastal protection • Loss of traditional knowledge	Between 1990 and 1997, about 6 million hectares of tropical forest were lost annually, with the highest rates in South-east Asia, followed by Africa and Latin America.
Invasive alien species	• Competition with, and predation of, native species • Extinction • Genetic contamination	• Loss of traditionally available resources • Loss of potentially useful species • Losses in food production • Increased costs for agriculture, forestry, fisheries, water management and human health	The comb jelly, *mnemiopsis leidyi*, accidentally introduced in 1982 by ships from the US Atlantic coast, dominated the entire marine ecosystem in the Black Sea, competing with native fish for food and resulting in the destruction of 26 commercial fisheries.
Over-exploitation	• Extinct and decreased populations • Alien species introduced • Fewer species	• Decreased availability of resources • Decreased incomes • Increased environmental risk • Spread of diseases from animals to humans	An estimated 1 to 3.4 million tonnes of wild meat (bushmeat) are harvested annually from the Congo Basin. This is believed to be six times the sustainable rate. It is estimated that the value of the trade in Côte d'Ivoire was US$150 million/year, representing 1.4% of the GNP.
Climate change	• Extinctions • Expansion or contraction of species ranges • Changes in species compositions and interactions	• Changes in resource availability • Spread of diseases to new ranges • Changes in the characteristics of protected areas • Changes in resilience of ecosystems	Polar marine ecosystems are very sensitive to climate change, because a small increase in temperature changes the thickness and amount of sea ice on which many species depend. The livelihoods of indigenous populations living in sub-arctic environments subsisting on marine mammals are threatened, since the exploitation of the marine resources is directly linked to the seasonality of sea ice.
Pollution	• Higher mortality rates • Acidification	• Decrease in productivity • Loss of coastal protection, with the degradation of reefs and mangroves • Eutrophication, leading to loss of fisheries	Over 90% of land in the European Union is affected by nitrogen pollution. This results in eutrophication, and increases in algal blooms with impacts on biodiversity, fisheries and aquaculture.

Source: adapted from UNEP, 2007: 168.

Ecosystems are also being placed under pressure as a result of invasive alien species being introduced, accidentally or otherwise, into environments from which they were previously absent. Concerns about such issues in the UK have led to newspaper headlines such as 'The 15 plants killing our countryside' (*The Observer*, 17 May 2009). In this instance, the article relates to government proposals to prevent garden centres from selling popular plants which have 'escaped' into the wild. Examples of such plants include varieties of pond weed that are used as oxygenators in garden ponds, but which have begun to 'overwhelm waterways throughout the country'. In the case of Canadian waterweed, such measures are likely to be too little, too late. The plant originally arrived accidentally with the timber trade before being spread by boats, currents and anglers. It is now widespread throughout the country.

Forest ecosystems and change

Forests are not just trees; they form part of ecosystems that underpin life, economies and societies. They are often managed mainly for production. As such, they support such industries as timber, pulp and biotechnology. All forests provide a wide range of ecosystem services, including prevention of soil erosion, maintenance of soil fertility, and fixing carbon from the atmosphere as biomass and soil organic carbon. In addition, forests host a large proportion of terrestrial biodiversity, protect water catchments and moderate climate change. Forests also support local livelihoods, provide fuel, traditional medicines and foods to local communities, and underpin many cultures. The harvesting of forest products and the clearance of large areas of woodland are putting severe stress on the world's forests.

Changes in forest ecosystems are driven by the harvesting of forest products, as well as by natural forest dynamics such as changes in the age, class and structure of species, and natural disturbance. Other drivers include climate change, diseases, invasive species, pests, air pollution and pressures from economic activities, such as agriculture and mining. Demographic trends, including changes in human population density, population movement and growth rates, and urban-rural distribution also have an impact on forest ecosystems. These trends exert pressures on forests through demands for goods such as timber and firewood, and for services such as the regulation of water resources and recreation. On the other hand, in the wealthier nations of the world, social preferences are shifting demands towards cultural services provided by forests.

Exploitation of forests has been at the expense of biodiversity and the natural regulation of water and climate. At the same time, in some regions of the world, exploitation has undermined subsistence agriculture and the cultural values of indigenous peoples. As has already been stated, tropical forest systems are under greatest threat. After a long period of decline, the area of temperate forest has been steadily increasing since the 1990s (see below). There was an annual increase of 30,000 square kilometres between 1990 and 2005. However, the process of deforestation, which began much later in the tropics than in temperate regions, has continued at an annual rate of 130,000 square kilometres over the same period (see figure 1.15 on p23). The largest forest conversions (clearances or replacement of natural forest by commercial forestry) have occurred in the Amazon Basin, South-east Asia, and Central and West Africa. The causes of this land use change have varied over time. For instance, the Amazon Basin was exploited from the late-19th to the mid-20th century to supply rubber to the world market. However, by the second half of the 20th century, large areas were being cleared for cattle ranching. To some extent, this is still the pattern, with continued forest conversion, mainly to farmland, including grassland for beef production.

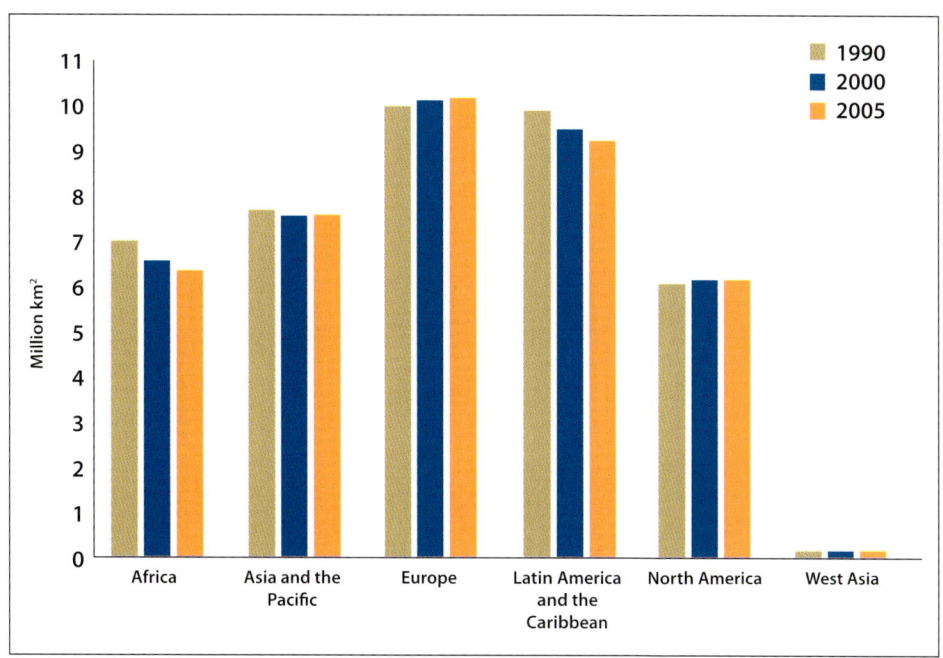

Figure 1.15:
Total forest area by region

See accompanying CD-Rom

Total forest area.ppt

Source: UNDEP, 2007: 39.

The degradation of forest environments is more widespread. For instance, 30,000 square kilometres of forest in the Russian far east have been degraded over the past 15 years by illegal logging and fires. On the other hand, increases in forest area have occurred in the coniferous forests of northern Europe and Asia, and in parts of Asia, North America, and Latin America and the Caribbean, mainly as a result of new planting.

Afforestation in the Lake District

Afforestation, that is to say the creation of newly wooded areas, has a relatively long history in terms of landscape planning in this country. The desires of wealthy Victorians to enjoy the picturesque by creating new landscapes with exotic woodland led to extensive planting of trees during the 19th century. If we take the case of the north-west of England, coniferous plantations occurred on several Lake District estates in the 19th century, as at Grizedale in the Furness Fells, where Montague Ainslie planted 485 hectares of fell land with larch (Winchester, 2006: 236-7).

Later on, the demands of the industrial cities of the north-west led to extensive planting by water companies to ensure the purity of the water in their catchments. For instance, Manchester Corporation planted 810 hectares of conifers to protect the water catchments around Thirlmere. The creation of the Forestry Commission in 1919, to increase the production of home-grown timber, led to further plantings, as with the development of Thornthwaite Forest. A second large forest was created with the purchase of upper Ennerdale in 1925/6.

Attitudes to the planting of coniferous trees have changed in the past 30 years, and there is now a greater stress on the planting of 'native' species, while there has also been a shift in emphasis towards amenity woodland and the creation of woodland on brownfield sites.

The National Forest

An interesting example which illustrates the increasing acreages of temperate forest is the newly created National Forest. The National Forest in the UK is a project to plant 200 square miles of forest across the Midlands of England (figure 1.16). It covers parts of the counties of Staffordshire, Derbyshire and Leicestershire. The aim of the project is to plant woodland across the three counties, and to link two areas of ancient woodland. The planting of the forest has a number of benefits, including providing a valuable habitat, offering recreational and social benefits to local communities, and ultimately counteracting some of the CO_2 emissions from human sources (*www.nationalforest.org*).

Figure 1.16:
The National Forest

See accompanying CD-Rom

National Forest.ppt

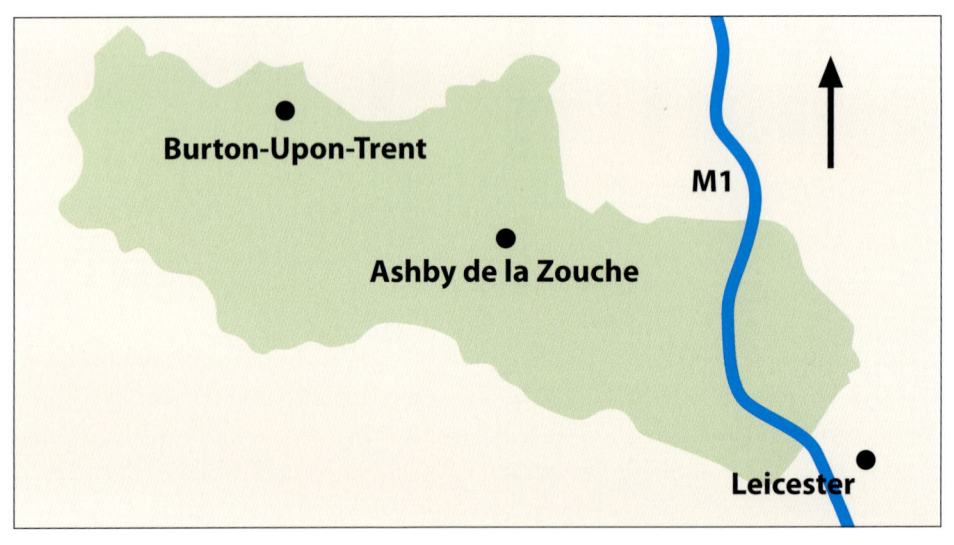

Source: adapted from www.nationalforest.org/forest/whatis/where.php

Teaching idea 1.6

Ask students to investigate an area of recreational planting in their own area. What environmental benefits are claimed for the development? The Forestry Commission website (*www.forestry.gov.uk*) provides details of a range of forestry projects.

See ch 7, Environmental management (176).

The impact of energy usage on biodiversity

As we have already discussed, population growth and increasing levels of affluence around the world, resulting in significantly higher levels of consumption, have been the principal causes of environmental damage over the past 50 years. One key element here has been the rapidly growing demand for energy, in a range of forms, to drive an ever more mobile society, containing an ever-increasing range of energy-consuming devices. Figure 1.17 (on p25) attempts to demonstrate the impacts of this energy usage on biodiversity.

See ch 4, Energy (p99-102).

Figure 1.17: The impact of energy usage on biodiversity

Energy source	Impacts on biodiversity	Subsequent impact on human wellbeing
Fossil fuels Crude oil, coal, natural gas	• Global climate change and associated disturbances, particularly when coupled with human population growth and accelerating rates of resource use, will bring losses in biological diversity. • Air pollution (including acid rain) has led to damage to forests in southern China amounting to US$14bn/year. Losses from air pollution impacts on agriculture are also substantial, amounting to US$4.7 billion in Germany, US$2.7bn in Poland and US$1.5bn in Sweden. • The direct impact of oil spills on aquatic and marine ecosystems. The worst case is the Exxon Valdez, which ran aground in 1989, spilling 37,000 tonnes of crude oil into Alaska's Prince William Sound. • Impacts from the development of oil fields and their associated infrastructure, and human activities in remote areas that are valuable for conserving biodiversity (such as Alaska's Arctic National Wildlife Refuge that may be threatened by proposed oil development).	• Changes in distribution of and loss of natural resources that support livelihoods. • Respiratory disease due to poor air quality.
Biomass Combustibles, renewables and waste	• Decreased amount of land available for food crops due to greatly expanded use of land to produce biofuels, such as sugar cane or fast-growing trees, resulting in possible natural habitat conversion to agriculture, and intensification of formerly extensively developed or fallow land. • Can contribute chemical pollutants into the atmosphere that affect biodiversity. • Burning crop residues as a fuel removes essential soil nutrients, reducing soil organic matter and the water-holding capacity of the soil. • Intensive management of a biofuel plantation may require additional inputs of fossil fuel for machinery, fertilisers and pesticides, with subsequent fossil fuel related impacts. • Monoculture of biomass fuel plants can increase soil and water pollution from fertiliser and pesticide use, with subsequent loss of biodiversity.	• Cardiovascular and respiratory disease from reduced indoor air quality, due to wood-burning stoves, especially among poor women and children. • Decreased food availability.
Nuclear energy	• Water used to cool reactors is released to environment at significantly above local temperatures. • Produces relatively small amounts of greenhouse gases during construction. • Because of the potential risks posed by nuclear energy, some nuclear plants are surrounded by protected areas. For example, the Hanford Site occupies 145,000 hectares in Washington State, USA, providing an important sanctuary for plant and animal populations. • A nuclear accident such as Three Mile Island (1979) or Chernobyl (1986) has grave implications for people and biodiversity.	• Health impacts of radiation include deaths and diseases due to genetic damage (cancers and birth abnormalities).
Hydroelectricity	• Building large dams leads to loss of forests, wildlife habitat and species populations, disrupts natural river cycles, and degrades upstream catchment areas due to inundation of the reservoir area. • Dam reservoirs also emit greenhouse gases due to the rotting of vegetation and carbon inflows from the basin. • On the positive side, some dam reservoirs provide productive fringing wetland ecosystems with fish and waterfowl habitat opportunities.	• Building large dams can result in displacement of people. • Alterations in availability of freshwater resources (positive or negative, depending on the situation) for human use.
Alternative energy sources Geothermal, solar, wind, tidal and wave	• Ecosystem disruption, habitat losses at large wind farm sites, undersea noise pollution. • Tidal power plants may disrupt migratory patterns of fish, reduce feeding areas for waterfowl, disrupt flows of suspended sediments. • Large photovoltaic farms compete for land with agriculture, forestry and protected areas. • Use of toxic chemicals in the manufacture of solar energy cells presents a problem both during use and disposal. • Disposal of water and wastewater from geothermal plants may cause significant pollution of surface waters and groundwater supplies. • Blades for wind and tidal power can cause death for migratory species. • Strong visual impact of wind farms.	• Decreased species populations. • Toxins released to the environment may cause public health problems. • Decreased economic value of lands near wind farms, due to strong visual impacts.

Source: adapted from UNEP, 2007: 179.

See accompanying CD-Rom
The impact of energy usage.doc

The effects of ecosystem change on human health

See Volume 1: Human Geography, ch 9, Geographies of health and environment.

Change is fundamental in ecosystems. Without it the diversity of living organisms cannot be maintained, and yet with change comes a range of pressures which in turn exert stress upon living organisms. Competition and variation, and complexity and organisation, all characterise successful organisms and successful and sustainable ecosystems. Change takes place at a variety of spatial and temporal scales. Micro changes at habitat level may reflect seasonality, the effects of disease, competition between organisms and changes to the abiotic status of the area. Change at the level of biomes will reflect major climate changes such as glaciation. Figure 1.18 shows how biotic change takes place within different timescales and is broadly in tune with major changes to climate. This reinforces the relationship between living organisms, at a range of scales from habitats to biomes, and climate.

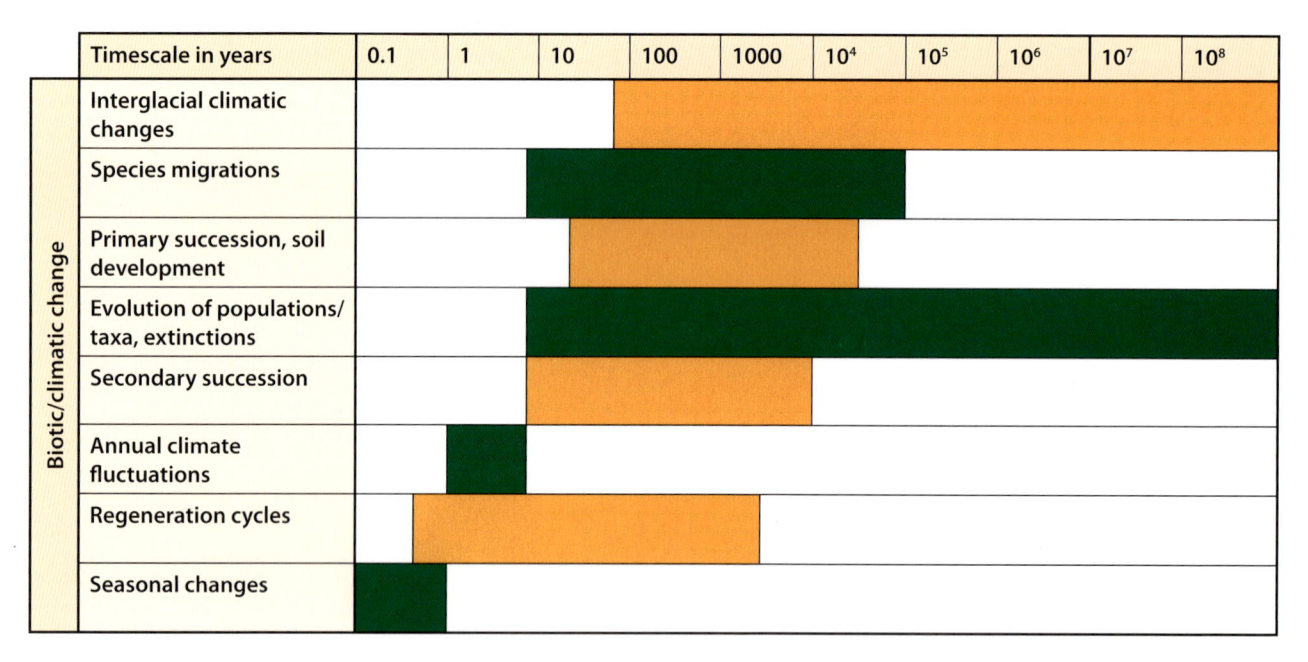

Timescale in years	0.1	1	10	100	1000	10^4	10^5	10^6	10^7	10^8
Interglacial climatic changes										
Species migrations										
Primary succession, soil development										
Evolution of populations/ taxa, extinctions										
Secondary succession										
Annual climate fluctuations										
Regeneration cycles										
Seasonal changes										

Figure 1.18: Time scales for biotic and climatic change

See accompanying CD-Rom

Time scales for biotic and climatic change.ppt

See ch 3, Climate change.

See Volume 1: Human Geography, ch 9, Geographies of health and environment (p192).

The evidence for the impact of human beings upon climate is strong. The debate about the longevity of that impact is current and highlighted by the work of Ruddiman (2005). In addition, there is compelling evidence through pollen analysis about the impact of humans on forest and other ecosystems over long periods of time. We can be certain, then, that the effects human communities have upon ecosystems are considerable and very varied. What is important to consider here is the effect that ecosystem change has upon humans. Given the strong relationship between climate, vegetation and soils described above, it is timely to explore some of the issues around ecosystem stability, sustainability and human health. Where ecosystems are rich in terms of their constituent flora and fauna, where biodiversity is high, and where habitats are relatively stable, the health and economic benefits to human communities are considerable. Where ecosystems are becoming degraded or destabilised, and where biodiversity is falling, then the implications for human health are considerable. It is widely recognised that the importance of ecosystem health and stability is paramount in order to support and sustain human communities. Where degradation occurs, as with desertification in Somalia and Ethiopia, the pressure to provide the resources necessary to support human communities increases, and may lead to conflict, disease, and further environmental

Figure 1.19: Model of ecosystem change

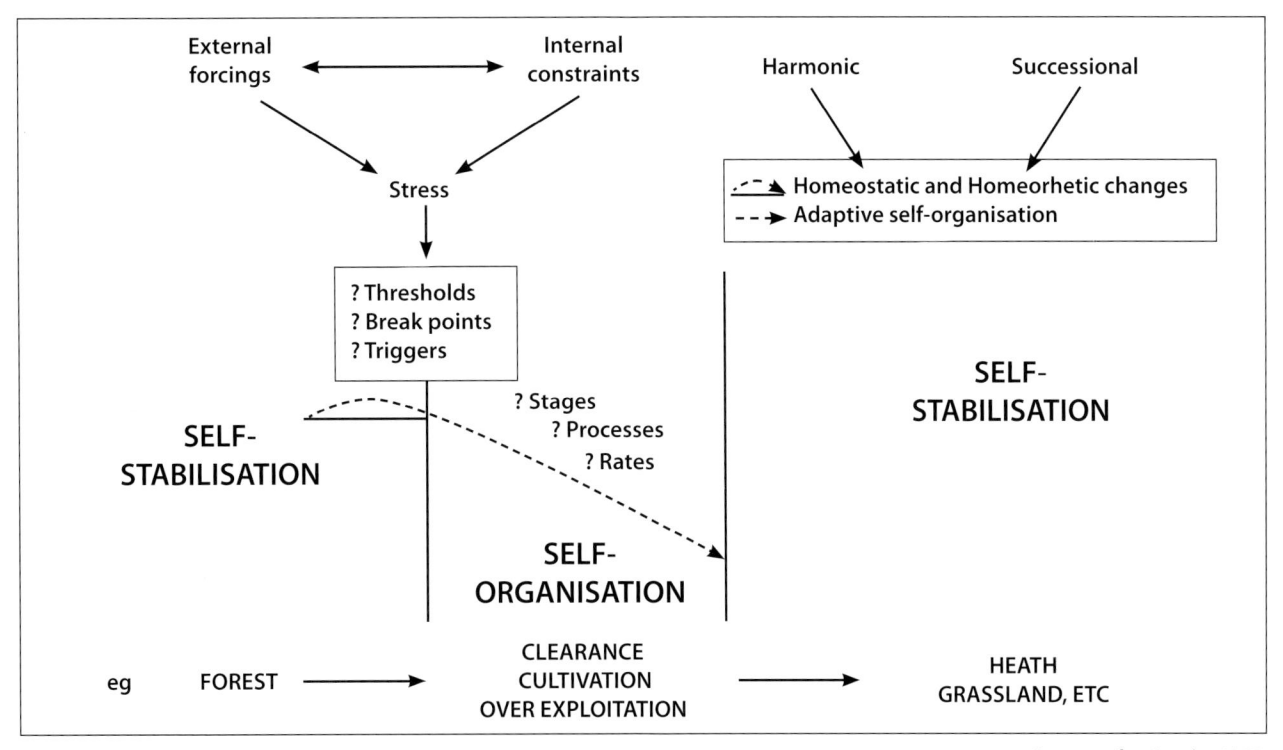

Source: after Laszlo, 1972.

collapse. Of course, not all ecosystem changes lead to land degradation; many also lead to rises in plant productivity and biomass, and thus to increased agricultural output. But what is often misleading is that in some cases increased food production can be short-lived and ultimately cause additional stress to the ecosystem.

In figure 1.19, we see how the ecosystem is characterised by a period of 'self-stabilisation', where vegetation, soils and other environmental factors are stable, and where soil and land degradation are at a minimum. An example of this is the forest ecosystem of montane (highland) Papua New Guinea, dominated by rich tropical rainforest, which is high in biodiversity. With the arrival of Western technologies in the Highlands (metal implements rather than stone axe technologies), forest clearance was increased and this led to instability in soils on the steep mountain slopes. This period of change is described in Laszlo's model as one of self-organisation, and it leads ultimately to a new phase of stability. As yet, in the New Guinea Highlands, such a new phase has not arrived as land degradation, loss of biodiversity and soil erosion are still ongoing [☞]. However, in the UK, our upland moorland ecosystems represent a new phase of stability, albeit that current stability is human-induced. Before human activity expanded and increased, principally during the Bronze Age, the British landscape was defined by its dense, mixed deciduous forests, which extended up to 750 metres above sea level. Extensive clearance of woodland between 4,500 and 2,500 years ago, coupled with a changing climate, saw the almost complete removal of woodlands from the uplands, together with the development of blanket peat. This process led ultimately to the landscape we know today. Empty, heather-clad moorlands are now more typical in upland areas. They represent an interrupted succession from open land to forest, a state which we can identify in Laszlo's model and in SR Eyre's classic diagram of succession (figure 1.20 on p28), human impact and the plagiosere; the plagiosere being where change, development or succession has been interrupted by human activity.

See accompanying CD-Rom
Model of ecosystem change.doc

See ch 6 Sustainability, figure 6.9 and Volume 1: Human Geography, ch 9, Geographies of health and environment, figure 9.18.

**Figure 1.20:
Interrupted succession**

See accompanying CD-Rom

Interrupted succession.ppt

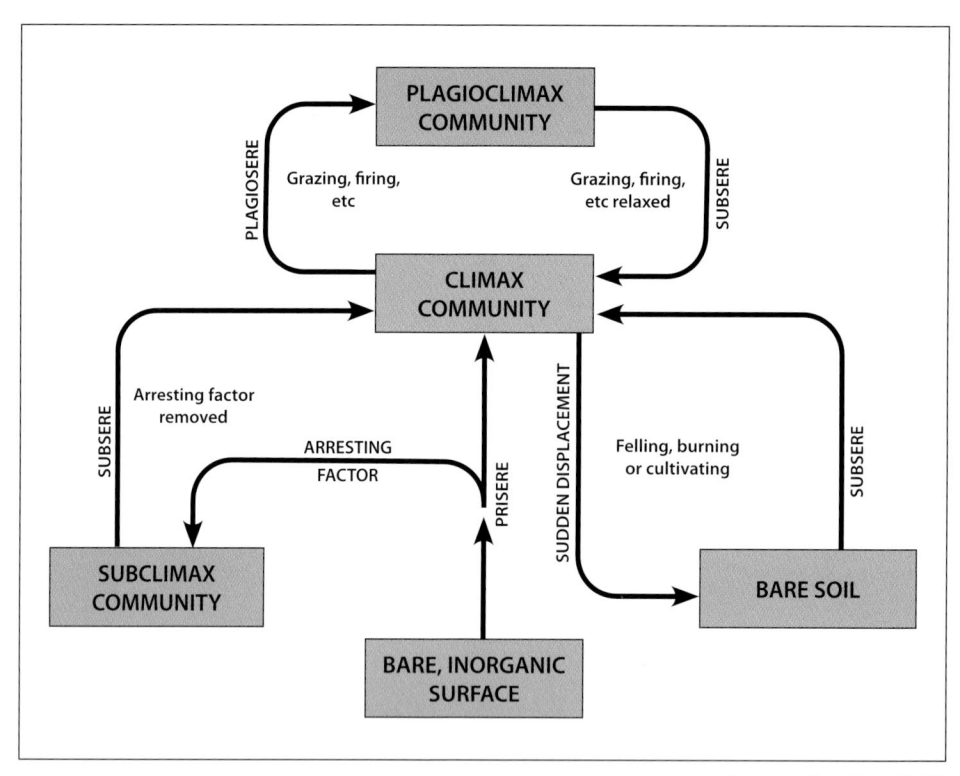

Source: after Eyre, 1968.

While we can see many examples of how human activity affects ecosystems, change within these systems can have considerable impacts upon human communities. The effects can be both positive and negative.

See Volume 1: Human Geography, ch 9, Geographies of health and environment.

See ch 2, Climate and weather (p36).

In the 21st century, human beings are challenged by many interlinked changes in global environments with enormous implications for human health [🔑]. Changes at the global scale, affecting biomes and ecosystems, include global warming, widespread changes to land use due to urbanisation and deforestation, and the depletion of atmospheric ozone. The increased use of fossil fuels is driving climate change, but also of importance is deforestation by slash and burn clearance, especially of tropical rainforests in Brazil, Indonesia and South-east Asia. There are significant associations between the El Niño [🔑] cycle and human health; in 1997 this phenomenon was associated with forest fires, especially in Indonesia, where dramatic increases in hospital admissions, in particular for respiratory problems, were recorded. In addition, across the Pacific in South America, where long-term forest clearances had left landscapes degraded and poor in terms of vegetation (low biodiversity) and soils (thin, nutrient poor), lack of seasonal rains enhanced flooding and led to further landscape degradation. This interconnected sequence of events led ultimately to malnutrition and disease in both Ecuador and Peru.

See ch 8, Globalisation (p198).

Deforestation reduces biodiversity and raises extinction rates. This has led directly to the loss of potential medicines [🔑] for humanity. A survey in the USA showed that of the most frequently prescribed medicines, 57% contained compounds derived from other species. In addition, deforestation is known to cause changes in the incidence of malaria and other vector-borne diseases.

Teaching idea 1.7

Ask students to look at images of a British forest ecosystem, a wetland ecosystem [☞], and upland moorlands. In groups, get them to list the key features of their chosen ecosystem, including what they think is beautiful (or not). List the various uses of the ecosystem's constituents, including plants (eg food output (including animals), herbs for medicines, wood for building, peat for burning, game birds shot for recreation). Then ask them to describe how that environment may be degraded (overgrazing, clearances, draining) and ask them to identify what key features may be lost. What would be the effects of these losses? Would there be any health effects? If so, what might these be?

See accompanying CD-Rom

Wetland ecosystem.ppt

Teaching idea 1.8

Harmful effects of ecosystem changes on health

Using figure 1.14 (see p21), select one major pressure for each student group and ask them to explore, in their groups, what the potential health impacts/effects might be. Ask them to identify direct and indirect impacts on health, and effects that result from changes to the ecosystem but which may be mediated by that system.

Ecosystem thresholds

Most social and biophysical systems are dynamic systems. Feedback loops occur within such systems (figure 1.21). These loops can be described in terms of a pattern of interaction, where a change in one variable, through interaction with other variables in the system, either reinforces the original process (positive feedback) or suppresses the process (negative feedback).

It is becoming apparent that there are major feedbacks in the Arctic systems associated with the rapid changes in the regional climate.

Temperature – albedo feedback
Rising temperatures increase melting of snow and sea ice, not only reducing surface reflectance, but also increasing solar absorption, raising temperatures further, and changing vegetation cover. The feedback loop can also work in reverse. For example, if temperatures were to cool, less snow and ice would melt in summer, raising the albedo and causing further cooling as more solar radiation is reflected rather than absorbed.

Melting of permafrost and methane emissions
Permafrost areas of the Arctic, in particular tundra bogs, contain methane, trapped since the last glaciation. Climate change is resulting in melting of the permafrost, and the gradual release of methane, a gas with warming potential more than 20 times as great as CO_2. This is a positive feedback, which could lead to significant acceleration of climate change.

Figure 1.21: Examples of feedback loops in the Arctic

See accompanying CD-Rom

Ecosystems.doc

Source: adapted from UNEP, 2007: 369.

Where the dynamism within the system results in significant change, this is known as the 'threshold'. Thresholds are sometimes referred to as 'tipping points'. They are common in the Earth system, and represent the point of sudden, abrupt or accelerating and potentially irreversible change, switched on by natural events or human activities. For example, there is evidence to show that a decrease in vegetation cover in the Sahara several thousand years ago was linked to a decrease in rainfall, promoting further loss of vegetation cover, leading to the current dry Sahara. Examples of thresholds being crossed as a result of human activities include the collapse of fisheries, the emergence of diseases and pests, and the introduction and loss of species. Large-scale ecosystem changes (such as savannah to grassland, forest to savannah, shrubland to grassland) clearly occurred in the past during the climatic changes associated with glacial and interglacial periods in Africa. However, these changes took place over thousands of years, allowing ecosystems time to adapt and species to undergo geographical shifts. Changes in the coming decades are likely to produce similar threshold effects in some areas, but over a much shorter time frame. Ecosystems have time lags and inertia. For example, even if greenhouse gas concentrations in the atmosphere were to be stabilised today, increases in land and ocean temperatures due to these emissions will continue for decades, and sea levels will rise for centuries, due to timescales associated with climate processes and feedbacks.

Critical thresholds are the points where activities result in unacceptable levels of harm in terms of ecological change, and demand responses in the form of appropriate management policies. The complexity of both the ecosystems and their relationship with humanity makes it hard to predict precisely where such thresholds lie, and therefore when actions taken are likely to be effective. As a result, society is often left only with the option of damage limitation. Difficulties of prediction also make it challenging to identify measures to pre-empt the crossing of such thresholds. The unprecedented and increasing socio-economic impacts of humanity on ecological systems mean that there are real fears that many ecosystems may be nearing, or have exceeded, some critical thresholds. The crossing of such thresholds may have serious implications for human wellbeing. Catastrophic disruption of societies has occurred in the past as a result of environmental thresholds being crossed. There is no reason to assume this will not be the case in the future.

Summary

This chapter has shown the fundamental importance of understanding the interconnections of fauna and flora with the physical environment. It has also demonstrated both the value and the vulnerability of ecosystems and the crucial nature of biodiversity, both in supporting the sustainability of ecosystems and in terms of supporting human needs. Newer approaches to ecosystems, which conceptualise them in terms of the services they provide, offer some hope that a more inclusive approach to ecosystem management may mitigate some of the environmental damage currently being inflicted on many of the world's ecosystems.

Endnotes

1. This chapter draws heavily on three major reports on the global environment that are available on the internet:

    Millennium Ecosystem Assessment available at: *www.millenniumassessment.org*

    United Nations Environment Programme (2007) *Global environment outlook 4*, available at: *www.unep.org/geo/geo4/media/*

    WWF, *Living Planet Report 2008* available at: *www.panda.org*

2. g carbon m^{-2} yr^{-1} refers to grammes of carbon per metre squared per year. It is a measure of biomass or weight of organic matter in a given unit of area.

Useful website

www.biodiversityhotspots.org – part of the website of Conservation International, providing detailed discussions of biodiversity hotspots around the world.

Climate and weather

Vanessa Holden and Charles Rawding

Introduction

> *'Climate is what we expect, weather is what we get.'*
> (Mark Twain)

It is difficult to overstate the importance of the climate of the planet to all aspects of human life. Variations in climate are critical to all manner of human, environmental and physical developments. This chapter will discuss the principal elements of climate at a global scale before considering aspects of weather with particular reference to the British Isles.

At the simplest level, the distinction between climate and weather is clear. Weather is what we encounter around us every day; it is the rain, the sun, the snow, the fog, the temperature. Climate is the 'average' conditions that occur over a longer time. Reference to the climate of an area is usually based on the average weather conditions experienced over a period of at least 30 years.

The climate of an area, and hence the weather that it experiences, is affected by many different factors. However, in order to understand an extremely complex system, it is necessary to identify the key drivers of climate. These drivers include the energy provided by the Sun, the dynamics between land masses and oceans, variations created by different topographical features on the Earth's surface, and the interactions within the atmosphere consequent on the interplay between the factors mentioned previously.

The role of the Sun

The Sun provides heat and energy to the Earth, but this heat is not provided equally to all areas of the planet. Because the Earth is a sphere, the Sun's rays hit the Earth at differing angles. At the equator (essentially the widest part of the Earth), rays hit the Earth from almost directly overhead, producing a hot climate, with relatively small variations in temperature throughout the year. By contrast, in polar regions, for many months of the year the Sun is not visible at all (it is 'below' the horizon), and even in summer the Sun is very low in the sky. It takes the Earth one year to completely orbit the Sun and, as the Earth's axis is tilted, the angle at which the Sun's rays hit the Earth at any given time varies due to this tilt (see figure 2.1 on p34). The effect of these changes in the Earth's position relative to the Sun is to create seasonal variations in the energy budget of regions. When a part of the Earth is tilted towards the Sun, it is summer in that part of the world; when it is tilted away it is winter. For this reason, seasonal differences increase as we move away from the equator towards the poles. The

Chapter 2: Climate and weather

Figure 2.1:
The tilted Earth's orbit around the Sun

See accompanying CD-Rom

Earths axis.ppt

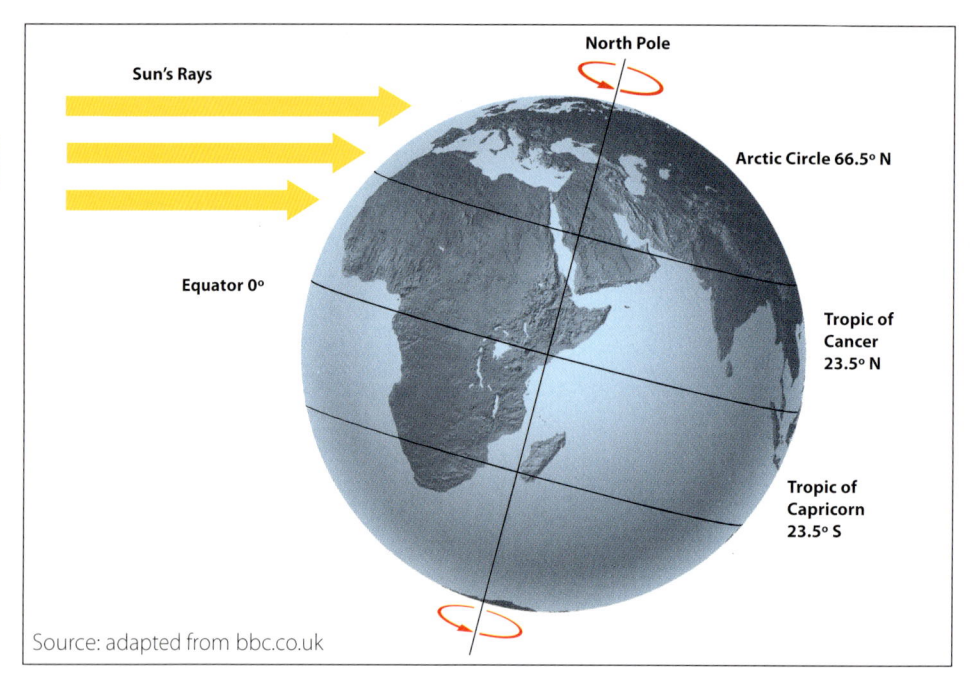

Source: adapted from bbc.co.uk

poles are much more affected by the tilt in the Earth's axis than the equator. Between the equatorial and the polar regions, in both the northern and southern hemispheres, are the 'temperate' or 'mid-latitude' regions. These fall approximately between 30° and 60° latitude, and are where many of the major human centres of populations are to be found, in the northern hemisphere, Europe, and most of North America and Asia.

These differentials in heat and energy are central to the development of climatic patterns. To illustrate this briefly, vegetation is clearly dependent on temperature, and areas of dense vegetation, such as the rainforests, retain more of the heat from the Sun than do polar regions where the Sun's rays are reflected back by the snow and ice. Such responses enhance differences between regions.

The dynamics between land masses and oceans

Climate is strongly affected by the relative positions of land masses and large bodies of water. Quite simply, land both heats up and cools down more rapidly than water. As a result of this, maritime climates tend to experience a lower temperature range than continental climates due to the moderating influence of adjacent water bodies when compared to the absence of such influences at greater distances from the oceans. The most extreme variations in temperature are therefore found in the centres of the continents.

Colder air is more dense (more air molecules for any given area), so exerts a greater atmospheric pressure, with warmer air being less dense, so creating areas of lower air pressure. The speed of change in pressure between different areas – ie the distance over which the change occurs – is the pressure gradient. The differing rates of heating and cooling lead to the creation of pressure gradients with warmer, lighter air sucking in colder heavier air. This means that, during the winter, heavier, colder air pours out from the centres of the continents, while during the summer, the hot interiors of the continent suck in cooler air from the oceans. This reversal of the wind pattern can be seen most obviously in the monsoon wind systems of southern Asia (see figure 2.2 on p35).

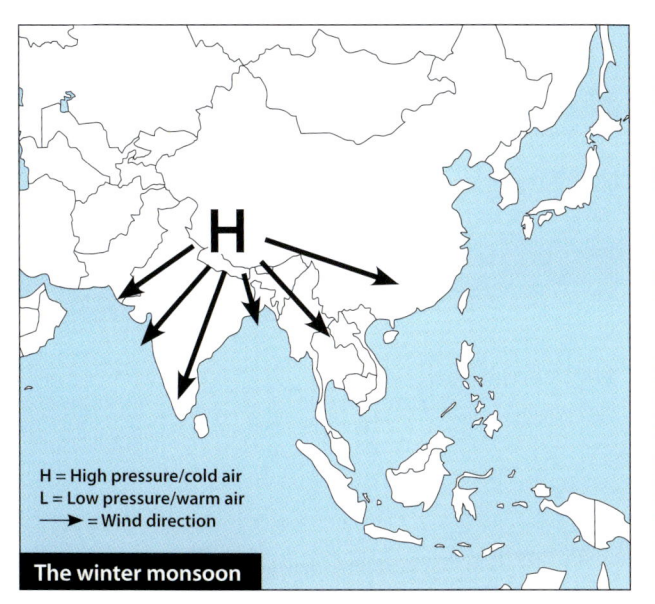

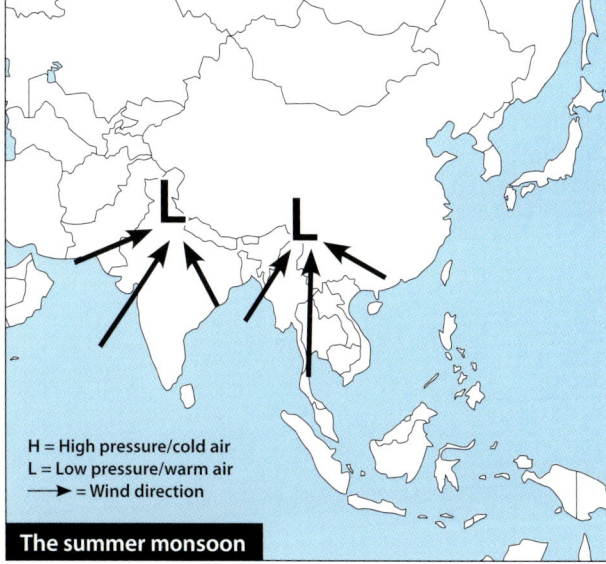

**Figure 2.2:
The monsoon wind system**

Monsoon.ppt

In addition, one might mention here the effects of differential heating of the oceans in creating ocean currents. These currents have a major impact on elements of climate. For instance, coastal deserts [☞] form along the west coasts of continents where air masses have passed over cold ocean currents. These currents have cooled the air mass sufficiently to reduce its capacity to carry moisture. The cold California Current has this effect over much of Baja California, while the Benguela Current has the same effect in South Africa. Coastal fogs often form over the oceans from the moisture left behind, as off the Pacific coast of the Atacama and the Atlantic coast of the Namib deserts.

See Volume 2: Physical Geography, ch 4, Deserts (p92).

In the case of the British Isles, our climate is warmed by the Gulf Stream (specifically its northern extension, the North Atlantic Drift) – a current of relatively warm water that flows northwards off the eastern coast of the United States governed by differing water densities and the action of surface winds (figure 2.3).

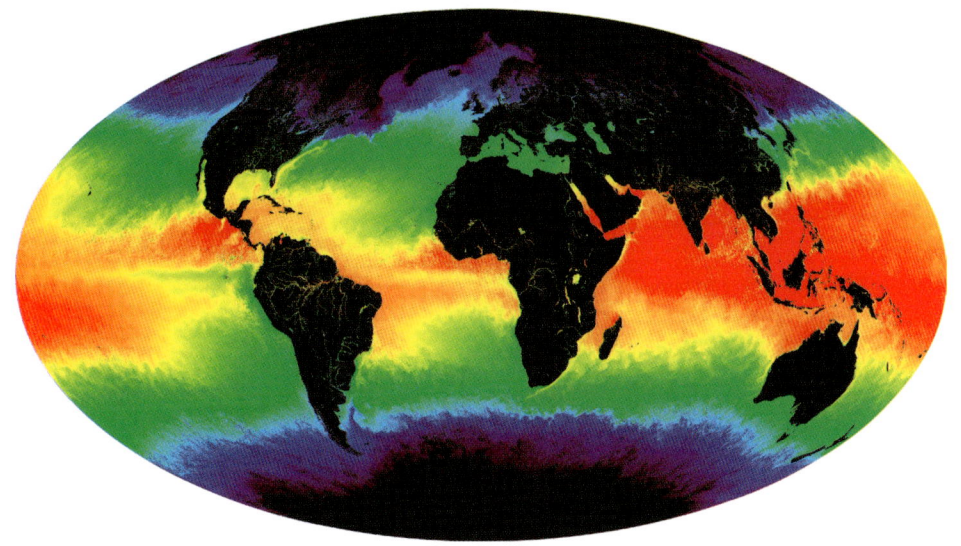

**Figure 2.3:
Global sea surface temperatures**

Ocean currents.ppt

Source: MODIS Oceans Group, NASA Goddard Space Flight Center. www.visibleearth.nasa.gov

Chapter 2: Climate and weather

> **Teaching idea 2.1**
>
> Ask students to investigate climate data for where they live, and for the same latitude on the North American coast of the Atlantic Ocean. What differences do they notice? How might they explain these differences?

Events such as El Niño and La Niña, a cyclical warming and cooling of the tropical Pacific Ocean, have major impacts on weather patterns. El Niño events generally occur every three to seven years, and last for around 12 to 18 months. Average water temperatures can vary by 3°C due to this natural cycle. El Niño is an unusually warm water phase, and La Niña an unusually cool water phase of the cycle.[1] In normal conditions, winds push the ocean waters from east to west, causing an upwelling of colder waters from deeper in the eastern Pacific Ocean. However, during an El Niño, the winds are weaker, so preventing the upwelling of colder ocean waters, leading to warmer ocean temperatures (figure 2.4).

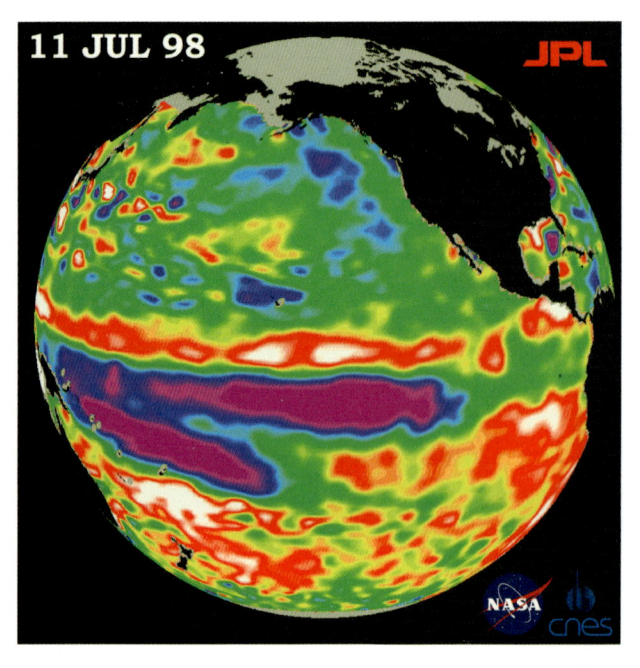

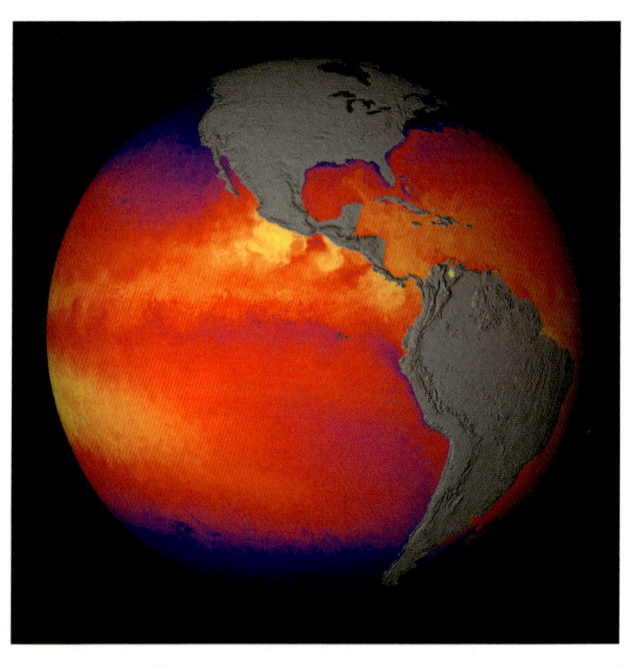

Source: (left) TOPEX/Poseidon, NASA JPL. (right) Jesse Allen, based on data provided by the MODIS OCEAN Team and the University of Miami Rosenstiel School of Marine and Atmospheric Science Remote Sensing Group. *www.visisbleearth.nasa.gov*

Figure 2.4:
Satellite images of warmer (left) and cooler (right) conditions of the Pacific Ocean

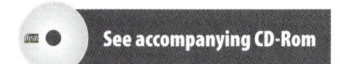

See accompanying CD-Rom

El Niño.ppt

These cycles are extremely important in determining weather conditions, with changes in ocean circulation and temperature leading to changes in primary productivity within the oceans. For example, during a warmer El Niño, the warmer waters are relatively nutrient poor, so sustain less marine life, which results in less food for sea fish, meaning fewer fish survive, so having impacts for fisheries (a decrease in fish stocks). El Niño is also responsible for other weather extremes, with the warmer oceans leading to greatly increased rainfall, and changing patterns in the global jet stream winds. El Niño conditions often lead to flooding in areas such as South America, with corresponding drought in Asia. Very strong El Niño conditions have an even wider impact, resulting in extreme weather in many parts of the world.

36   Contemporary Approaches to Geography Volume 3: Environmental Geography   Chris Kington Publishing

The importance of topographical features

Mountain belts have a significant impact on global atmospheric circulation patterns. Mountain ranges cause air to rise up over them, known as orographic lifting. This rising of the air causes it to cool down, which leads to condensation, and the formation of clouds. These clouds then produce rain, resulting in a wetter climate on the side of the mountain facing the prevailing winds (windward), and a drier 'rain shadow' climate on the other (leeward) side. Where moist, warm air is moving onshore and encountering mountain ranges, such as the Andes or southern Deccan in India, precipitation occurs on the windward side leaving the dry air on the leeward side. If the effect is severe enough, rain shadow deserts such as Patagonia or the Thar in India form. Continental deserts occur where the rain shadow process is repeated by a series of mountain belts or high plateaux. By the time air masses reach the continental interiors, such as the Gobi or central Australia, most of their moisture has gone.

The climate of the British Isles[2] is heavily influenced by topography. The predominance of upland landscapes in western areas, combined with prevailing south-westerly winds, creates similar rainfall patterns to those discussed above. The west of the country, particularly the upland areas, experiences significantly higher levels of precipitation than the east (between 2,300 and 3,900 millimetres annually). Distinctly lower levels of rainfall are experienced across large areas of eastern England (460 to 560 millimetres). These differences can be explained in terms of the rain shadow effect discussed above.

As a general rule, as height above sea level (altitude) increases there is an associated decrease in the density of the atmosphere, resulting in cooler temperatures at altitude (figure 2.5). It is due to altitude that many mountain glaciers [☞] can be found in what are otherwise considered temperate or even equatorial latitudes. The effect of altitude can be seen on any snow-topped mountain (see figure 2.6 on p38), whereby the vegetation gradually changes up the mountain, becoming more adapted to colder climates. Many mountainous areas retain snow on their higher elevations for many months longer than the environment lower down their slopes.

See Volume 2: Physical Geography, ch 5, Ice (p111).

Altitude (feet/metres)	Density (%)	Temp. (Fahrenheit/Celsius)
sea level	100	59.0/15
2,000/610	94.3	51.9/11.1
4,000/1,219	88.8	44.7/7.1
6,000/1,829	83.6	37.6/3.1
8,000/2,438	78.6	30.5/-0.8
10,000/3,048	73.8	23.3/-4.8
12,000/3,658	69.3	16.2/-8.8
14,000/4,267	65.0	9.1/-12.7
16,000/4,877	60.9	1.9/-16.7

Source: adapted from *www.engineeringtoolbox.com*

Figure 2.5:
The relationship between altitude and temperature

The relationship between altitude and temperature.doc

**Figure 2.6:
Effects of altitude**

Effects of altitude.ppt

See Volume 1: Human Geography, ch 2, Geographies of tourism (p47).

Pendle Hill, Lancashire

The Mercantour, inland from the French Mediterranean coast

The Mercantour, inland from the French Mediterranean coast

The Mercantour, inland from the French Mediterranean coast

Atmospheric pressure and winds

The differential heating of the Earth by the Sun sets up convections of warmed air between the equator and the poles but, because the Earth rotates, these air mass movements are deflected to the right in the northern hemisphere and the left in the southern hemisphere. The Earth's surface is rotating fastest (in kilometres per hour) at the equator, and rotates not at all at the poles. This is known as the Coriolis effect. The force of the Coriolis effect is at a maximum around the North and South Poles, with negligible effect at the equator. This force can have a significant effect for long haul aeroplane flights, where an apparently straight flight path will curve off course due to the Earth's rotation if corrections are not made. The Coriolis effect therefore results in the predominant westerly winds in the upper atmosphere of the northern hemisphere, as the warm air from near the equator causes air to rise and subsequently increase in speed as friction forces from the surface are reduced. As the wind speed increases, so does the Coriolis effect. In the upper atmosphere, the effects of pressure gradients and the Coriolis effect combine, producing geostrophic winds that do not flow directly from areas of high to low pressure, but instead follow the patterns of the isobars between pressure differences.

Patterns of global wind systems are produced by the characteristic high and low pressure areas that occur either side of the equator. Globally, there is a standard normal air pressure at sea level of 1,013.2 millibars (mb). The standard is set at sea level, as air pressure reduces with altitude. Although there can be extreme exceptions, the usual range of air pressure from low to high is 980mb to 1,050mb. It is changes in air pressure between different areas that produces wind – the movement of air around the Earth from areas of high pressure to low pressure.

At the equator, there is the equatorial low pressure trough, which, as the name suggests, is an area of low pressure generated by the warming effect on the air of the intensity of the Sun directly over the equator. The drawing up of the warm air leads to the converging of surface winds from both the northern and southern hemispheres. As the rising air cools, the water vapour within it condenses, leading to cloud formation and frequently heavy rainfall. This area is known as the InterTropical Convergence Zone (ITCZ). Movements in the precise location of the ITCZ result in the wet and dry seasons of many tropical countries. The air that is drawn in to the ITCZ comes from the trade winds. In the northern hemisphere these are known as the north-east trade winds,[3] owing to their direction of origin. The course that is made by these winds is known as the Hadley cells (figure 2.7). The Hadley cells are made up of warmed air rising over the equator, cooling as it rises, and depositing its precipitation over the equatorial rainforests, before moving both north and south to sink between 20° and 30° of latitude, and then returning as trade winds to the equator.

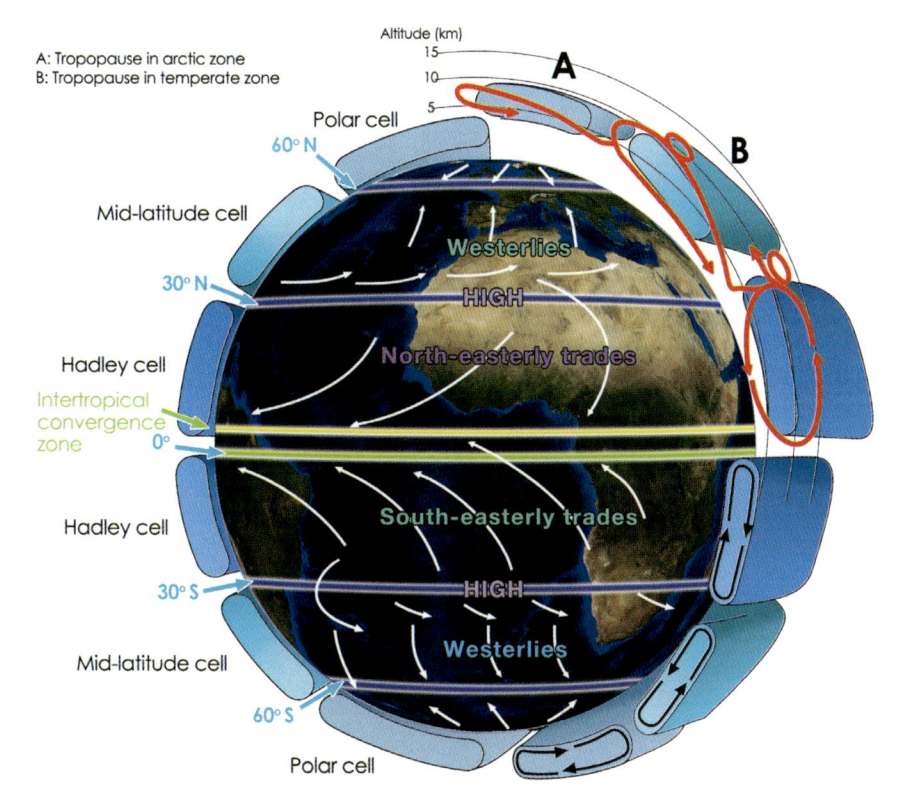

Figure 2.7: Global atmospheric circulation

See accompanying CD-Rom

Global atmospheric circulation.ppt

Source: adapted from NASA. http://sealevel.jpl.nasa.gov/overview/images/6-cell-model.jpg

Poleward of the equatorial low pressure trough can be found the subtropical high pressure cells, generally lying between 20° and 35° latitude. This high pressure zone is associated with hot, dry air, and is responsible for many of the large desert areas of the world (see p40). The dryness is due to large amounts of vapour already being released in the heavy rains of the ITCZ, and the ability of warm air to retain more moisture than cold air. In this zone, the warm air is forced back down towards the surface, with the air then diverging either back into the trade winds, or to the dominant winds to the north of this zone, the westerlies.

The subpolar low pressure cells, between 35° and 60° latitude, are therefore found in the mid-latitude region that includes the British Isles. Where the warm, low latitude air meets the colder, high latitude air is known as the polar front. In winter, the polar front can be found at lower latitudes, moving back to higher latitudes (or disappearing completely) in summer. Large meanders can occur along the front, referred to as Rossby waves. These large-scale air movements in the upper atmosphere result in large areas of cold air being moved further southwards, and warmer air moving north. The warm air is forced up, resulting in condensing water vapour and cloud formation, which often leads to wet weather in Britain. Polar high-pressure cells contain winds that diverge away from the poles in a clockwise direction, resulting in weak, but dry and very cold, winds called the polar easterlies. They blow from the high pressure over the poles out towards the mid-latitude westerlies.

See Volume 2: Physical Geography, ch 4, Deserts (p89).

These patterns of atmospheric circulation have a major impact on the world's climate, as can be demonstrated by a consideration of the location of some of the world's deserts [✍]. The types of desert associated most strongly with atmospheric circulation are both subtropical and polar deserts, which are situated where dry, cool air sinks from the Hadley cells at 20° to 30° latitude and from the polar cells over the poles. These promote stable regions of high pressure dominated by dry air. This dry air in turn produces arid sub-tropical deserts, such as the Kalahari and much of the Sahara, and polar ones, such as much of Antarctica.

Jet streams (figure 2.8) are high-velocity currents of wind between five and ten miles above the Earth's surface, just below the tropopause. They have wavy patterns, generally flowing west to east. The polar jet stream separates masses of cold polar air and warmer mid-latitude air, fluctuating between 30° and 70° latitude. During the winter, the jet stream tends to migrate towards the equator, bringing colder air further south, moving back towards the pole during the summer. Accordingly, the relative position of the jet stream over the British Isles has a significant influence on our seasonal weather patterns. A subtropical jet stream moves between 20° and 50° latitude. These winds can have significant influence over aviation, with east to west flights frequently taking longer than west to east flights due to the jet streams.

**Figure 2.8:
The polar and subtropical jet streams**

See accompanying CD-Rom

Jet stream.ppt

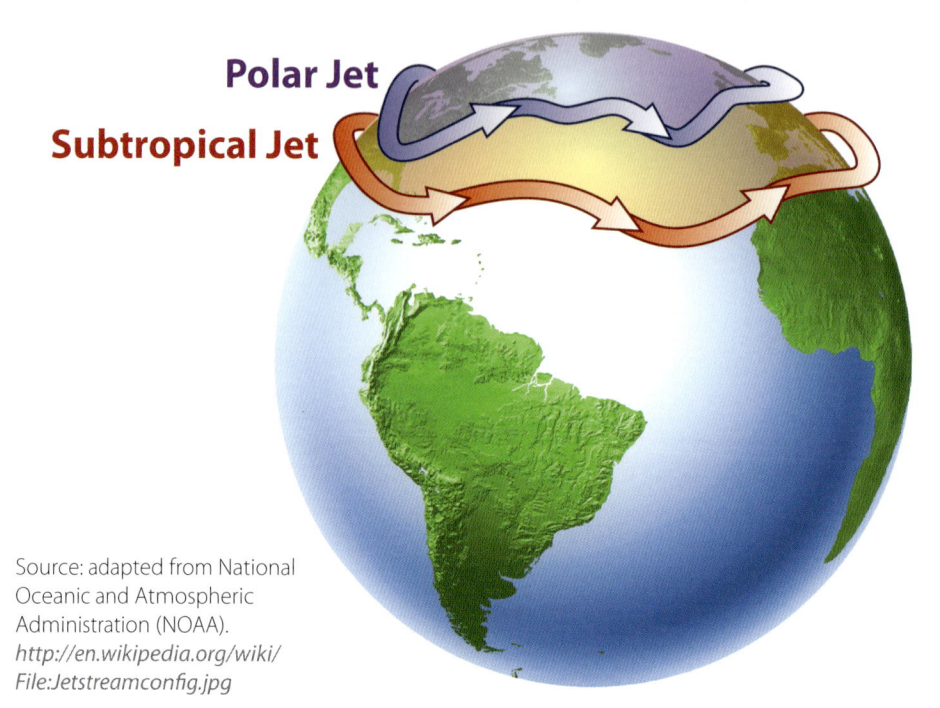

Source: adapted from National Oceanic and Atmospheric Administration (NOAA).
http://en.wikipedia.org/wiki/File:Jetstreamconfig.jpg

Mid-latitude depressions

In mid-latitude regions, when warm and cold air masses meet, a low-pressure depression – 'wave depression' or 'cyclone' – develops. They are found particularly along the polar front. The term 'wave depression' originates as the plan view of the meeting air masses resembles a wave pattern, with crests (higher latitudes) and troughs (lower latitudes) along the path of where the fronts meet, with small low-pressure depressions at the crest of the wave. The initial stage of development of the depression ('cyclogenesis') occurs when warm air from either a Tropical Maritime or Tropical Continental air mass meets colder air from a Polar Maritime or Polar Continental, and the air begins to rise and spiral in an anticlockwise direction (in the northern hemisphere). This leads to the 'mature' or 'open' stage, with the anticlockwise air flow drawing in warm air from the south of the depression along with the colder air from the west and north. However, the cold air behind the warm front is moving more quickly and gradually pushes the warm air upwards, forming an occlusion (the 'occluded stage'). The final 'death' or 'dissolving' stage of the depression occurs when the warm air has been completely undercut by the colder air.

These frontal systems track eastwards across the Atlantic, following the path of the jet streams in the upper atmosphere, and often reach the British Isles when they are in their mature stage, giving rise to much of the characteristic, changeable, damp climate of Britain (see figure 2.22 on p56). The fronts often reach their dissolving stage over the mainland of Europe. The area of low pressure in the centre of the depression can be between 300 and 2,000 miles across, and can last for between four and ten days. Figure 2.9 describes the weather associated with the passage of a depression.

Figure 2.9: Mid-latitude depressions

See accompanying CD-Rom

Mid-latitude depression.ppt

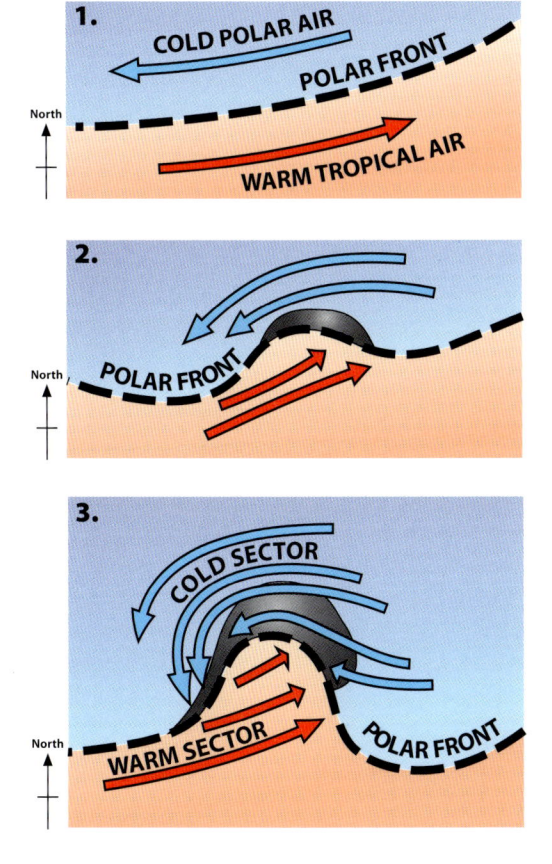

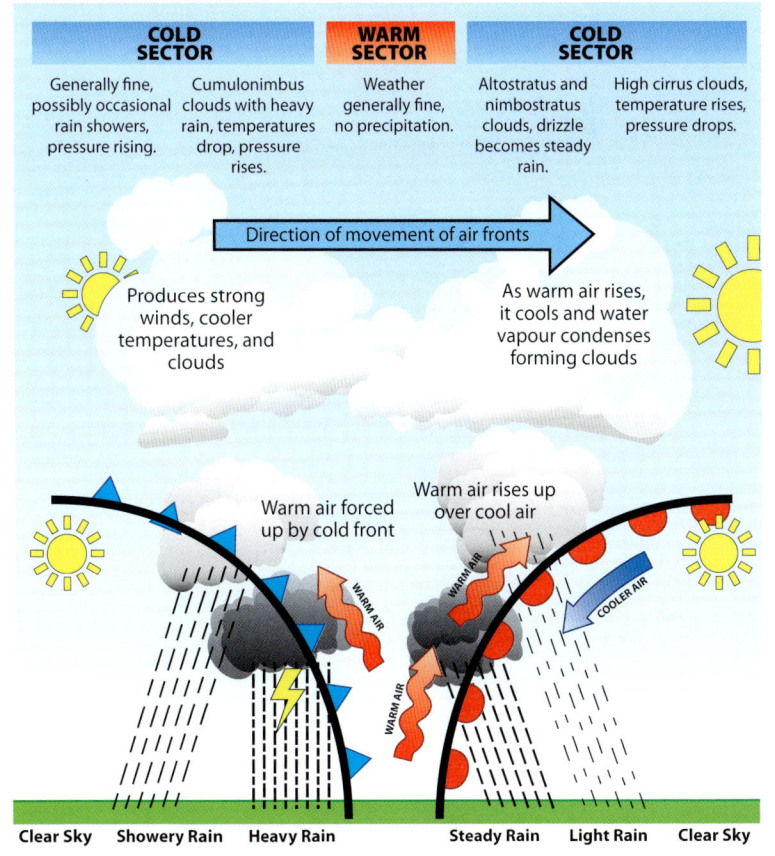

The measurement of wind

As we have seen above, a key element of understanding atmospheric processes is consideration of the concept of atmospheric pressure. Atmospheric – or 'air' – pressure is created by the movement, amount and size of air molecules present in air. This, in turn, is largely dependent upon the density and temperature of the air. Atmospheric pressure is measured using a barometer (commonly an aneroid barometer).

The pressure gradient can be seen on a weather chart showing isobars (lines linking areas of the same pressure) between areas of highest and lowest pressure, in exactly the same way as contour line spacing indicates slope steepness on Ordnance Survey maps. The steeper the pressure gradient – the closer the isobars are – the windier the weather will be. On a weather chart, if the pressure (in millibars) in the middle of the circle is greater than the numbers radiating out, then that represents an area of high pressure; conversely, if the pressure in the middle of the isobars is smaller than the numbers radiating out, then it indicates an area of low pressure.

Figure 2.10: Wind speeds and the Beaufort Scale

See accompanying CD-Rom

Wind speed.ppt

When wind is measured by meteorologists, it is measured at a standard height of 10 metres above the ground. This is because wind speed decreases nearer to the ground, as a result of friction and turbulence, so a standardised height is needed to allow

Wind speed (miles per hour)	Beaufort Scale ('Force')	Description	Characteristic conditions: land	Characteristic conditions: sea
0	0	Calm	Smoke rises vertically.	Sea is smooth.
1-3	1	Light air	Smoke drifts slightly, showing wind direction.	Small ripples on surface.
4-7	2	Light breeze	Leaves start to rustle.	Small wavelets form.
8-12	3	Gentle breeze	Leaves constantly moving. Smoke moves horizontally. Small tree branches start to move.	Large wavelets form.
13-18	4	Moderate breeze	Dust and loose paper raised. Large tree branches sway.	Small waves.
19-25	5	Fresh breeze	Small trees sway. Small waves on inland water bodies.	Moderate waves. Some spray from sea surface.
26-31	6	Strong breeze	Large tree branches sway.	Large waves. Some spray from sea surface.
32-38	7	Moderate gale	Whole large trees sway.	Spray and foam clearly blown in direction of wind.
39-46	8	Fresh gale	Twigs are broken from trees. Difficulty walking.	Long streak of foam on the sea surface.
47-54	9	Strong gale	Slight structural damage to buildings. Large tree branches broken off.	High waves. Spray reduces visibility.
55-64	10	Whole gale	Small trees uprooted. Structural damage.	Very high waves. Sea takes on a white appearance.
65-74	11	Storm	Large trees uprooted. Widespread damage.	Very high waves, small ships hidden in wave troughs.
75+	12	Hurricane	Widespread structural damage.	Storm waves at sea. Almost zero visibility due to spray.

> **Teaching resources**
>
> Surface pressure charts for the British Isles, produced by the UK Met Office, are available at *www.metoffice.gov.uk/weather/uk/surface_pressure.html*

comparisons between data sets. Wind speed is measured using an anemometer. It can be recorded using a number of units, most commonly either in knots (with 1 knot being 1 nautical mile per hour (1.15 miles per hour), or on the Beaufort Scale, where 0 is no wind at all, and 12 represents a hurricane (see figure 2.10 on p42). When wind direction is referred to, this indicates the direction that the wind is coming from, so an easterly wind is blowing from east to west. Direction is measured using a wind vane. The direction of the wind usually provides a reasonable guide as to the weather that can be expected to accompany it.

In the case of the UK, it is not uncommon to experience strong winds. The 'hurricane' of October 1987, which wreaked havoc along the south coast of England as far north as London, was an exceptional event. It was the worst storm to hit England since 1703 and was responsible for the deaths of 18 people in England. The storm had an air pressure equal to that of a category 3 hurricane, and wind speeds equal to a category 1 hurricane on the Saffir-Simpson Hurricane Wind Scale (see figure 2.17 on p50-51). However, winter storms are not unusual in causing disruption to transport and communications systems, occasional damage to buildings or environmental damage (figure 2.11).

Figure 2.11: Storm damage in the Lake District

See accompanying CD-Rom

Storm damage.ppt

Atmospheric moisture and the hydrological cycle

Humidity is the level of water vapour in the air. It is determined largely by air temperature, as warmer air can retain more vapour than cold air: as warm air expands it has a greater water vapour holding capacity. This is often expressed as 'relative humidity', which is the ratio of the amount of water vapour that the air currently holds, compared with the amount of vapour that it could potentially hold at a given temperature, expressed as a percentage. At 100% relative humidity the air is said to be saturated. When air is saturated, if there is subsequently any additional water vapour or a decrease in temperature, condensation will result, either as clouds or precipitation. Changes in humidity due to daily temperature changes are evident from the presence of early morning dew formed when air temperatures drop overnight, meaning relative humidity is high. Satellites are able to sense water vapour content using infrared sensors, which are an important tool for forecasting, enabling meteorologists to determine the level of water vapour that is present, and therefore to forecast the likelihood of precipitation occurring from it.

When open areas of water are warmed by the Sun's rays, the surface of the water evaporates and rises up as water vapour. Evaporation occurs directly from open water bodies, such as the surface of lakes and rivers; evapotranspiration occurs from plants. The water vapour is held in the air until it cools sufficiently to condense and turn back into water droplets. The temperature at which an air mass will become saturated is termed its 'dew point' temperature. Water condenses when it reaches its dew point, which varies depending upon humidity. It is these water droplets that form clouds that can be transported great distances through the atmosphere. Once the precipitation returns to Earth, it gradually flows towards rivers, or through groundwater, and ultimately returns back to the sea or lake, to once again evaporate back into water vapour in the air. The amount of evaporation that occurs from water surfaces depends

**Figure 2.12:
The hydrological cycle**

See accompanying CD-Rom

Hydrological cycle.ppt

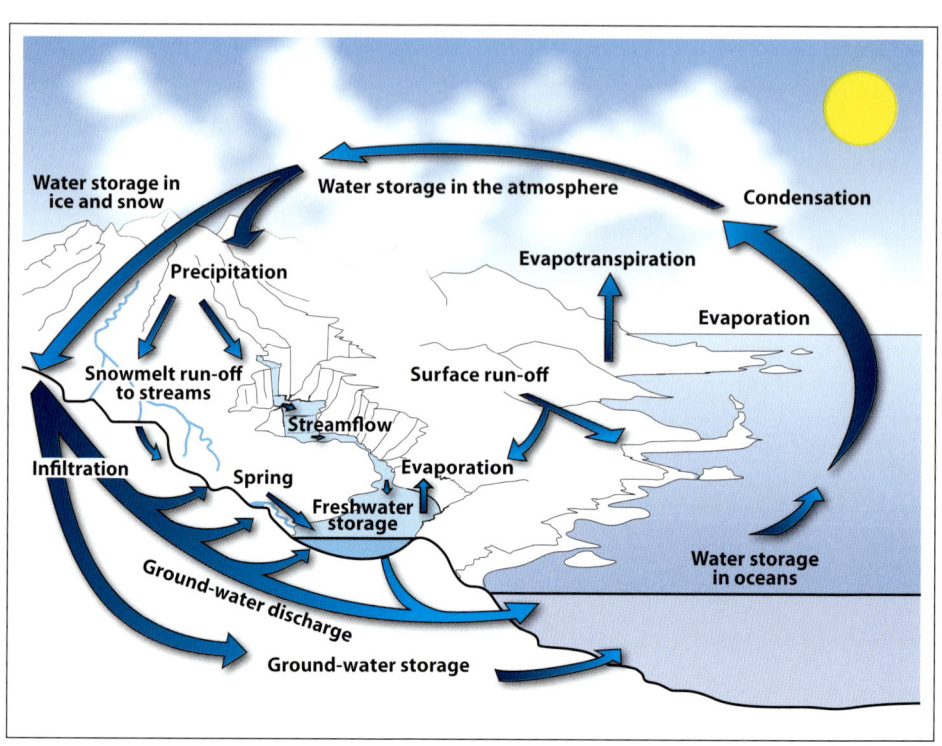

Source: adapted from US Geological Survey. *http://ga.water.usgs.gov/edu/watercycle.html*

on the temperature, the humidity (how much water vapour is already in the air) and the wind speed, with higher wind speeds often resulting in greater evaporation rates as the movement of air prevents it from becoming as humid over the water body. This sequence is known as the hydrological cycle (see figure 2.12 on p44).

Clouds

Clouds are masses of water droplets formed when air cools, usually due to it rising through the atmosphere. The four things that cause air to rise are: convection, which occurs when the Sun warms the ground and the air above it is warmed; convergent lifting, where air flows towards low pressure areas; orographic lifting, due to the presence of mountains forcing air to rise upwards; and weather fronts. As the air rises, it expands, as pressure decreases with height above the Earth. This expansion leads to cooling of the air. If the air eventually becomes saturated, the water vapour will begin to condense, forming water droplets. If the temperature is very cold, around -20°C (such as in very high clouds), the water will freeze into ice crystals, and the clouds will be comprised of ice rather than water droplets. In order for water vapour to condense, cloud condensation nuclei are needed, which are microscopic particles that are present in the atmosphere, such as ash and dust from fires or volcanoes, with the air over cities containing aerosols (a suspension of particulates in a gas, eg smog), while oceanic air is loaded with sea salts.

The water droplets that form from condensation are minute, even compared to raindrops. An average raindrop is 2,000μm,[4] with an individual water droplet being only 20μm, resulting in around 10,000,000,000 droplets per cubic metre (Christopherson, 2005; Pretor-Pinney, 2006). Therefore it takes a huge number of condensed water droplets to form a single raindrop. In mid-latitude regions, the majority of raindrops form through the ice-crystal process, where super-cooled droplets (that are below freezing but still in the liquid state) evaporate near an ice crystal, which then absorbs the water vapour and gradually increases in size until it eventually falls to the ground as rain, snow or sleet. In warmer tropical climates, the tiny droplets condense around cloud condensation nuclei, combining together and growing in size, until they ultimately are too heavy to remain in the air and fall back to Earth as precipitation.

There are numerous different types of cloud, with ten major types, all being a variation of the four main types, named after their characteristics (in Latin). They are: cirrus (meaning a filament); cumulus (a pile); stratus (a layer); and nimbus (rain-bearing) (see figure 2.13 on p46). The ten types can be divided up based upon the height that they are found above the Earth – forming high, medium or low clouds. Figure 2.14 on p46 describes the ten types. Fog is a form of cloud that is simply at ground level. It occurs when the air becomes saturated as the dew point temperature and the air temperature are the same. It can be classified as fog if visibility is less than 1 kilometre. There are a number of different types of fog. Radiation fog occurs when cooling of the ground (such as occurs overnight) chills the air passing over it to its dew point temperature, causing fog to form. Advection fog occurs when an air mass moves to an area where the temperature allows the dew point to be achieved, such as a warm air mass moving over a cold body of water. Similarly, if the reverse happens and cold air moves over a warm water body, evaporation fog will form.

**Figure 2.13:
Images of different types of cloud**

See accompanying CD-Rom

Clouds.ppt

Cumulus

Cirrus

Altocumulus

Cirrocumulus

Source: (top left) Sean Linehan; (top right) Lieutenant Elizabeth Crapo; (bottom) Ralph F. Kresge. NOAA's National Weather Service (NWS) Collection. www.photolib.noaa.gov

**Figure 2.14:
Cloud types**

See accompanying CD-Rom

Cloud types.ppt

High clouds		
Cirrus	Filamentous	Base of clouds between 5,500 and 14,000 metres above Earth. Usually comprised of ice crystals.
Cirrocumulus	Ripples	
Cirrostratus	Sheet	
Medium clouds		
Altocumulus	Rippled, layered	Base of clouds between 2,000 and 5,500 metres above Earth. Comprised of water droplets, sometimes mixed with ice crystals.
Altostratus	Thin grey blanket, allows hazy sun through	
Nimbostratus	Thick, low cloud. Often rain or snow	
Low clouds		
Stratocumulus	Rolls, layered	Base of clouds below 2,000 metres above the Earth. Usually comprised of water droplets (although cumulonimbus can include some ice crystals).
Stratus	Grey blanket, layered	
Cumulus	Individual clouds, vertical rolls with flat base	
Cumulonimbus	Cauliflower-like clouds. Often rain	

Source: adapted from www.metoffice.gov.uk

Biomes

As a result of the processes discussed earlier which create our global climate, climatic regions can be distinguished. These are called bioclimatic regions [☞] (figure 2.15) and have their own characteristic plants and animals living in them. The flora and fauna often have specific adaptations, both physical and behavioural, to optimise their survival in the given environment. In general terms, the major biomes are considered to be: desert, savannah, tropical forest, Mediterranean, temperate grasslands, deciduous forest, coniferous forest, tundra and mountain. The ecosystems [☞] within each biome are very closely linked. On a global scale, the functioning of different types of biomes is often linked to neighbouring biomes, with changes in one biome having consequences in a completely different environment.

See ch 1, Ecosystems (p7).

See ch 1, Ecosystems.

Figure 2.15:
The major bioclimatic regions around the world

See accompanying CD-Rom

Biomes.ppt

Biome	Typical conditions	Example
Desert	Extremely dry and hot areas, and subsequently sustain only very sparse vegetation. Most deserts are found around 20° to 30° latitude, and experience a persistent high pressure. On the edge of this biome desert scrub can be found, where sparse vegetation can just survive.	Sahara Desert, Africa
Savannah (also known as tropical grasslands)	Vegetation is mainly grasses, with only occasional trees. Predominantly hot and dry, but with two seasons: a dry season where there is very little, if any, rain, when much of the vegetation will die back due to the lack of water, and lakes and rivers sometimes completely dry up; a wet rainy season, when the vegetation regrows, and rivers and lakes refill with water.	Northern Australia
Tropical forest	Found near to the equator. They are extremely diverse in terms of the plants and animals that live there. When viewed from satellites, the areas look dark green due to the dense vegetation often found in the regions. This means that they absorb a lot of heat from the Sun's rays, so tend to be very warm and humid.	Central America
Mediterranean	These regions are found between the very hot and very cold regions, so tend to be warm, but not too hot. A distinctive, dry summer.	Mediterranean coastal regions
Temperate grasslands	They have a mild temperate continental climate, with moderate rainfall. The vegetation is characteristically grasses, with sparse trees.	Pampas, Argentina
Deciduous forest	The climate is temperate maritime, which is mild and wet. Trees (and other vegetation) in deciduous forests lose their leaves over winter.	North and Western Europe
Coniferous forest	The climate is cooler than found in temperate deciduous forests, with trees being evergreen, so keeping their leaves all year.	Scandinavia
Tundra	Found on the edge of the polar biome, with very cold temperatures with low annual precipitation. Vegetation is typically very low to the ground. This region often characterises the northernmost extent where trees are found.	Around the North and South Poles, eg northern Russia
Mountain	High areas of mountain will not support the growth of trees. The climate is cold, particularly in winter and overnight.	Canadian Rocky Mountain region

Extreme global weather

The British, perhaps to a greater extent than any other nation, have a serious preoccupation with weather, almost certainly linked to its frequently variable nature. Weather events that make the news around the world are what we might term extreme weather events, although it should be stressed that this does not mean that they are unusual events. Hurricanes have a distinct season (see below), as do monsoon rains.

Hurricanes

Tropical cyclones with maximum winds of 38mph or less are called 'tropical depressions'. Once the tropical cyclone reaches winds of at least 39mph, they are typically called a 'tropical storm' and assigned a name. If maximum sustained winds reach 74mph, the cyclone is called a hurricane (*www.nhc.noaa.gov*). In different parts of the world, they can also be called typhoons. Although classed as extreme forms of weather, there are approximately 80 tropical cyclones each year, around 45 of which are powerful enough to be classed as hurricanes (Christopherson, 2005). Tropical storms begin to form over warm oceans, generally where there is a sea surface temperature of 27°C or more, to a depth of about 60 metres, combined with humid air above the warm sea. The number of category 4 or 5 hurricanes (see figure 2.17 on p50-51) has almost doubled in the past 30 years as sea temperatures rise [✋]. They form from waves of low pressure moving westwards in the region of the trade winds. The warm air rapidly rises in the region of low pressure, leading to huge cloud formation and heavy rain. The very low pressure causes air to be drawn in near the surface, producing spiralling strong winds,

See ch 3, Climate change (p68-69).

Figure 2.16: Hurricanes

See accompanying CD-Rom

Hurricanes.ppt

Hurricane Dennis | Hurricane Floyd
Hurricane Floyd | Hurricane Andrew

Source: (top left) Jesse Allen, NASA GSFC SV; (top right) Liu, Hu, and Yueh, NASA Jet Propulsion Laboratory; (bottom left) Marit Jentoft-Nilsen, NASA GSFC Visualization Analysis Lab; (bottom right) NOAA's National Weather Service (NWS) Collection.
www.visibleearth.nasa.gov; www.photolib.noaa.gov

> **Teaching idea 2.2**
>
> Ask students to investigate a series of hurricanes of varying strengths that followed different tracks (preferably choosing one hurricane that landed on mainland USA and one that landed on a poorer Caribbean island). How did the hurricanes vary in terms of their impacts? Why was this the case? See the US National Weather Service for more information www.srh.noaa.gov. The five most costly hurricanes to date are: Katrina (2005) (see below), Andrew (1992), Wilma (2005), Charley (2004), and Ivan (2004). Note: hurricanes are named alphabetically each year, with the first one at the start of the season beginning with the letter A and so on.

with the air flowing out aloft, leading to more air being drawn in at the surface. These hurricane areas of low pressure are frequently immense formations, being in the region of 300 miles across, with an eye – the centre of the low pressure – being 30 miles across. Due to prevailing global winds (see p38), hurricane winds spiral anticlockwise in the northern hemisphere and clockwise in the southern hemisphere (see figure 2.16 on p48), which means that they usually travel in a generally westerly direction across the ocean, ultimately towards land.

Tropical storms (cyclones in the Indian Ocean, typhoons in the Pacific, hurricanes in the Atlantic) are particularly destructive when they hit land and are combined with strong surface winds and heavy rain. Much of the destruction can stem from erosion caused by tidal surges in coastal areas, particularly low-lying land that is dependent upon sea defences which may not be sufficient to cope with such extreme events. As hurricanes travel relatively slowly, taking days to move across oceans, forecasting and monitoring of hurricanes is possible, with advances in monitoring leading to reduced loss of life as a result of the storms. However, their economic cost continues to increase due to infrastructure development in susceptible areas. Hurricanes are classified into five categories according to the Saffir-Simpson Hurricane Wind Scale (see figure 2.17 on p50-51).

Hurricane Katrina and New Orleans

Hurricane Katrina hit the south-eastern United States, specifically the coastal city of New Orleans, in August 2005 (see figure 2.18 on p52) [☞]. The city was largely built below sea level, and was protected from coastal flooding by large sea walls called 'levées'. However, when Hurricane Katrina hit, the extremely strong onshore winds, the low pressure, heavy rainfall and the extreme wave heights pushed up by the winds caused the complete failure of many of the levées, leading to almost 80% of the city being flooded, with flood waters being up to 6 metres deep in some areas. As a result, more than 1,500 people were killed, largely due to the flooding. It is estimated that an area the size of the British Isles was directly affected by the hurricane.

See ch 7, Environmental management (p171).

Other consequences included destruction of thousands of homes and businesses, with associated loss of employment for thousands of people, loss of vital agricultural land and crops, destruction of infrastructure, such as roads, power networks, water supply, with damage to oil refineries and rigs. This latter effect had global implications, with the price of oil rising around the globe. The flood waters also led to a concentration of toxic pollutants within the waters.

Figure 2.17:
The Saffir-Simpson Hurricane Wind Scale

See accompanying CD-Rom
Saffir-Simpson.doc

Category	Wind speed (mph)	Comment	Damage (comments relate to USA)
5	>155	Catastrophic damage	Very high risk of injury or death from flying or falling debris.
			Almost complete destruction of all mobile homes, a high percentage of frame homes will be destroyed, with total roof failure and wall collapse. Extensive damage to roof covers, windows, and doors will occur. Large amounts of windborne debris will be lofted into the air. Windborne debris damage will occur to nearly all unprotected windows and many protected windows. A high percentage of industrial buildings and low-rise apartment buildings will be destroyed.
			Nearly all windows will be blown out of high-rise buildings resulting in falling glass, which will pose a threat for days to weeks after the storm.
			Nearly all trees will be snapped or uprooted and power poles downed. Fallen trees and power poles will isolate residential areas.
			Power outages will last for weeks and possibly months. Long-term water shortages will increase human suffering. Most of the area will be uninhabitable for weeks or months.
			Examples: Hurricane Mitch (1998) was a category 5 hurricane at peak intensity over the western Caribbean. Hurricane Gilbert (1988) was a category 5 hurricane at peak intensity and is the strongest Atlantic tropical cyclone on record.
4	131-155	Catastrophic damage	There is a very high risk of injury or death to people, livestock and pets due to flying and falling debris.
			Nearly all older (pre-1994) mobile homes will be destroyed. A high percentage of newer mobile homes also will be destroyed. Poorly constructed homes can sustain complete collapse of all walls as well as the loss of the roof structure. Well-built homes also can sustain severe damage with loss of most of the roof structure and/or some exterior walls.
			Large amounts of windborne debris will be lofted into the air. Windborne debris damage will break most unprotected windows and penetrate some protected windows.
			There will be a high percentage of structural damage to the top floors of apartment buildings. Steel frames in older industrial buildings can collapse.
			Most windows will be blown out of high-rise buildings resulting in falling glass, which will pose a threat for days to weeks after the storm.
			Most trees will be snapped or uprooted and power poles downed.
			Power outages will last for weeks and possibly months. Long-term water shortages will increase human suffering. Most of the area will be uninhabitable for weeks or months.
			Examples: Hurricane Luis (1995) was a category 4 hurricane while moving over the Leeward Islands. Hurricanes Felix and Opal (1995) also reached category 4 status at peak intensity.

Chapter 2: Climate and weather

Category	Wind speed (mph)	Comment	Damage (comments relate to USA)
3	111–130	Devastating damage will occur	High risk of injury or death to people, livestock and pets due to flying and falling debris.
			Nearly all older (pre-1994) mobile homes will be destroyed. Most newer mobile homes will sustain severe damage with potential for complete roof failure and wall collapse. Poorly constructed frame homes can be destroyed by the removal of the roof and exterior walls. Unprotected windows will be broken by flying debris. Well-built frame homes can experience major damage involving the removal of roof decking and gable ends.
			There will be a high percentage of roof covering and siding damage to apartment buildings and industrial buildings. Isolated structural damage to wood or steel framing can occur. Complete failure of older metal buildings is possible, and older unreinforced masonry buildings can collapse.
			Numerous windows will be blown out of high-rise buildings resulting in falling glass, which will pose a threat for days to weeks after the storm.
			Many trees will be snapped or uprooted, blocking numerous roads.
			Electricity and water will be unavailable for several days to a few weeks after the storm passes.
			Examples: Hurricanes Roxanne (1995) and Fran (1996) were category 3 hurricanes at landfall on the Yucatán Peninsula of Mexico and in North Carolina, respectively.
2	96–110	Extremely dangerous winds will cause extensive damage	There is a substantial risk of injury or death to people, livestock and pets due to flying and falling debris.
			Older (mainly pre-1994 construction) mobile homes have a very high chance of being destroyed and the flying debris generated can shred nearby mobile homes. Newer mobile homes can also be destroyed. Poorly constructed frame homes have a high chance of having their roof structures removed, especially if they are not anchored properly. Unprotected windows will have a high probability of being broken by flying debris. Well-constructed frame homes could sustain major roof and siding damage.
			There will be a substantial percentage of roof and siding damage to apartment buildings and industrial buildings. Unreinforced masonry walls can collapse.
			Windows in high-rise buildings can be broken by flying debris. Falling and broken glass will pose a significant danger even after the storm.
			Many shallowly rooted trees will be snapped or uprooted and block numerous roads.
			Near-total power loss is expected with outages that could last from several days to weeks. Potable water could become scarce as filtration systems begin to fail.
			Examples: Hurricane Bonnie (1998) was a category 2 hurricane when it hit the North Carolina coast, while Hurricane Georges (1998) was a category 2 hurricane when it hit the Florida Keys and the Mississippi Gulf Coast.
1	74–95	Very dangerous winds will produce some damage	People, livestock and pets struck by flying or falling debris could be injured or killed.
			Older (mainly pre-1994 construction) mobile homes could be destroyed, especially if they are not anchored properly, as they tend to shift or roll off their foundations. Newer mobile homes that are anchored properly can sustain damage involving the removal of shingle or metal roof coverings, and loss of vinyl siding, as well as damage to carports, sunrooms or lanais. Some poorly constructed frame homes can experience major damage, involving loss of the roof covering and damage to gable ends as well as the removal of porch coverings and awnings. Unprotected windows may break if struck by flying debris. Masonry chimneys can be toppled. Well-constructed frame homes could have damage to roof shingles, vinyl siding, soffit panels and gutters.
			Some apartment building and shopping centre roof coverings could be partially removed. Industrial buildings can lose roofing and siding especially from windward corners, rakes and eaves. Failures to overhead doors and unprotected windows will be common.
			Windows in high-rise buildings can be broken by flying debris. Falling and broken glass will pose a significant danger even after the storm.
			Large branches of trees will snap and shallowly rooted trees can be toppled.
			Extensive damage to power lines and poles will likely result in power outages that could last a few to several days.
			Examples: Hurricanes Allison (1995) and Danny (1997) were category 1 hurricanes at peak intensity.

Source: adapted from www.srh.noaa.gov

Figure 2.18:
The impact of hurricanes – Hurricane Katrina

See accompanying CD-Rom

Katrina.ppt

Source: (top left) Collection of Gretchen Imahori, NOAA/NOS/Office of Coast Survey; (top right) Lieutenant Phil Eastman, NOAA Corps/NMAO/AOC; (bottom left) Collection of Wayne and Nancy Weikel, FEMA Fisheries Coordinators; (bottom right) Lieut. Commander Mark Moran, NOAA Corps, NMAO/AOC. NOAA's National Weather Service (NWS) Collection. *www.photolib.noaa.gov*

Although Hurricane Katrina occurred in a more economically developed country (MEDC), with all the forecasting technologies and education and emergency services in place, it still led to massive-scale destruction, with significant environmental and social consequences. There has subsequently been significant controversy regarding how the impacts of the hurricane were handled by US government agencies, from the mass evacuations of communities with reports of significant violence and disturbingly serious assaults within refuge shelters, to the rebuilding of the city. In addition, once the flood waters eventually subsided – taking months in some cases – many residents were unable to claim on insurance policies to rebuild their homes, as the majority of the damage was due to water damage and not wind (flood damage was not covered on many insurance policies). So, with no employment due to the destruction of businesses, people cannot afford either to rebuild their homes or to move elsewhere, and have to live in government-provided trailers. There are also the emotional issues faced by residents and relief workers, such as the fate of thousands of pets, and the attempts to rescue, provide shelter and ultimately reunite rescued animals with their owners. It is unlikely that anyone studying the impacts of Hurricane Katrina will not be moved in some way by the experience.

Tornadoes

Tornadoes are columns of air that rotate rapidly while in contact with both the Earth's surface and the base of a cloud, usually a cumulonimbus (see figure 2.14 on p46). For a tornado to develop, strong winds are required high in the troposphere with weaker winds at ground level, which leads to a rotating motion of the winds parallel to the ground. When the rotating air encounters activity associated with the development of a thunderstorm, with strong updrafts, it forces the rotating air into a vertical rotation. This rotating column of air then forms a mesocyclone within a supercell cloud (a particularly large thunderstorm cloud), with characteristic weather of heavy rainfall, strong winds, and hail storms. As a mesocyclone matures, a supercell tornado can develop, with the characteristic funnel of air travelling from the cloud down to the ground. Tornadoes can measure anywhere from a few metres to many hundreds of metres across, frequently travel in excess of 100mph, and can travel many miles before dispersing. Tornadoes are commonly classified according to the Fujita Scale (figure 2.19b), which was designed by meteorologist Theodore Fujita to be a continuation of the Beaufort Scale used to classify winds. Since 2007 the Enhanced Fujita Scale has been used in the United States, which has been further developed in terms of the wind speeds experienced, and the degree of damage caused based upon the type of structure. However, in the majority of other countries, the original scale is still commonly used. The proportion of tornadoes that are extremely destructive is relatively low. Tornadoes are experienced on many continents, but they are often associated with the United States in particular due to its topography and latitudinal position, with 'Tornado Alley' in the central US experiencing the highest number of tornadoes anywhere in the world (see figure 2.19c on p54). Their average life span is around five minutes, but they can last up to an hour.

Figure 2.19a (left): Tornadoes

Tornadoes.ppt

Figure 2.19b (below): The Fujita Scale linked to damage-causing wind speeds

Tornadoes.ppt

Source: (left) Harald Richter; (right) Sean Waugh. NOAA's National Severe Storms Laboratory Collection. www.photolib.noaa.gov

Damage f scale		Little damage	Minor damage	Roof gone	Walls collapse	Blown down	Blown away
		f0	f1	f2	f3	f4	f5
Windspeed F scale		17m/s 32 50 70 92 116 142						
		| F0 | F1 | F2 | F3 | F4 | F5 |						
		40mph 73 113 158 207 261 319						
		To convert f scale into F scale, add the appropriate number						
Weak outbuilding	-3	f3	f4	f5	f5	f5	f5
Strong outbuilding	-2	f2	f3	f4	f5	f5	f5
Weak framehouse	-1	f1	f2	f3	f4	f5	f5
Strong framehouse	0	F0	F1	F2	F3	F4	F5
Brick structure	+1	–	f0	f1	f2	f3	f4
Concrete building	+2	–	–	f0	f1	f2	f3

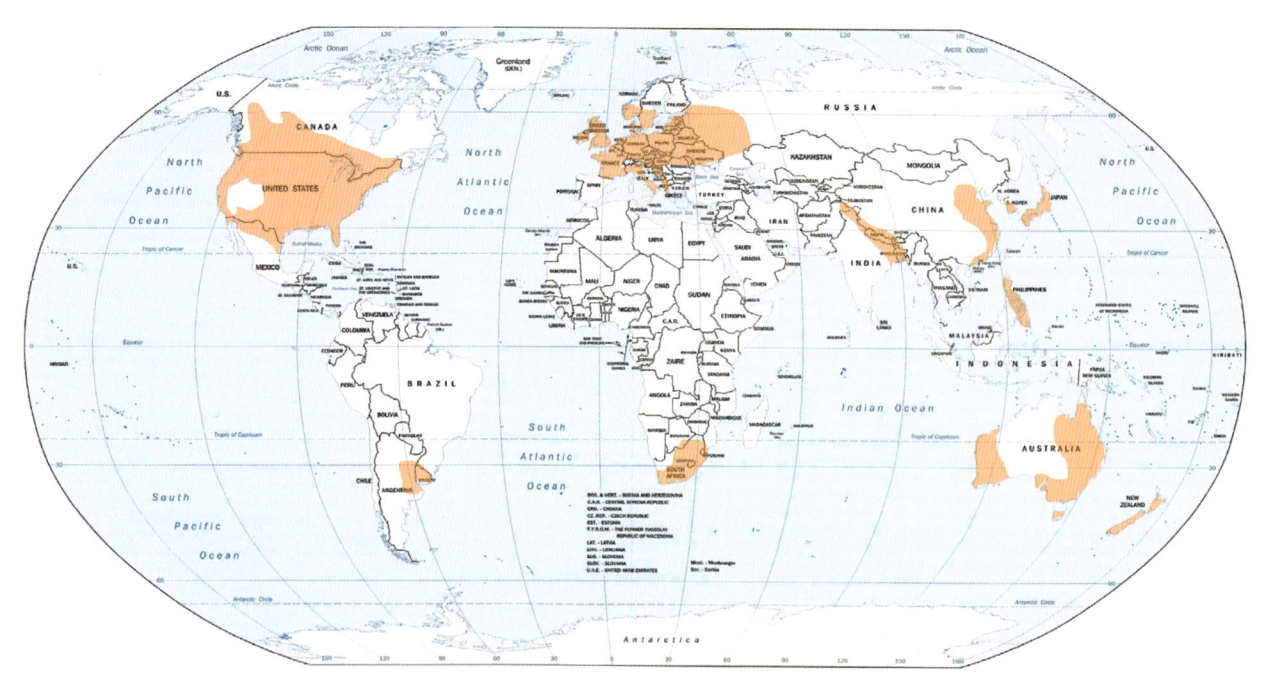

Source: National Oceanic and Atmospheric Administration.

**Figure 2.19c:
Distribution map of likely occurrence of tornadoes**

See accompanying CD-Rom

Tornadoes.ppt

Thunderstorms

Thunderstorms are caused by unstable air, as a result of warm air rising, for example as in a weather front, or when the ground becomes very warm during the summer, or due to orographic lifting at mountains. The warm air rising cools as it gains altitude, with the water vapour contained within it gradually condensing to form cumulus clouds. The clouds frequently become so large that the water vapour within their upper limits forms ice. At this point, the action of the wind causes a characteristic anvil shape to the thunder clouds. The condensation of the water vapour releases latent heat, causing highly localised warming of the air, which results in the warmed air having a lower density than the surrounding air, leading to updrafts of air. However, as the condensed raindrops fall through the cloud, they create a downdraft. This mixture of updrafts and downdrafts leads to significant turbulence within the air mass, producing strong winds. If the wind shear (differing wind speeds and directions at different layers of the atmosphere) is slight, the downdraft will push down through the base of the thunderstorm and dissipate. This produces a phenomenon known as downbursts, which can be particularly hazardous to aircraft due to rapid change in wind speed and direction.

The very large clouds associated with thunderstorms are part of the cause of lightning. Lightning occurs when electrons (negatively charged particles) in an atom move about from one place to another. As the electrons reposition, their movement produces a spark, which is the flash that is seen during lightning (see figure 2.20 on p55). In the high (icy) parts of the cloud, atoms collide, with larger particles gaining negative electrons, while smaller particles lose them. The larger particles gradually start to fall through the cloud, so that eventually the base of the cloud will have an overall negative charge. This process results in the ground underneath the cloud becoming positively charged, until the gradient between the negative cloud and positive ground becomes big enough to overcome the resistance of the air in between. When this occurs, a large, rapid transfer of the negatively charged electrons, discharging hundreds of millions of volts of electricity that superheats the surrounding air to temperatures up to 30,000°C, causes the flash of lightning. The thunder that accompanies lightning is caused by the expansion and heating of the air that the lightning is passing through. The sound of the thunder takes longer to travel through the air than the lighting flash, hence thunder lasts longer than lightning. For this reason, thunder and lightning occur almost simultaneously when a thunderstorm is directly overhead. By counting the number of seconds between a flash of lightning and the start of the accompanying thunder, and then dividing by three, it is possible to calculate roughly how far away the centre of the storm is in kilometres.

Source: C. Clark. NOAA Photo Library, NOAA Central Library; OAR/ERL/National Severe Storms Laboratory (NSSL). *www.photolib.noaa.gov*

Local climatic variations

The factors that have already been discussed play the major role in determining weather and climate patterns across the globe. However, within the climate of an area there will be numerous 'micro-climates'. These are small variations in the average climate over a relatively small area. For example, the south-facing (adret) slope of a hill will receive sunlight during the day, and so can be warmed by the Sun's rays. However, on the other side of the hill, the north-facing (ubac) slope will never receive any direct Sun's rays, and will be permanently in shade. This will result in the north-facing slope being slightly cooler than the south-facing side. This also affects the structure and properties of soils, which in turn affect plant habitats and the rate at which plants can grow. We thus often see distinctive variations in plants communities on north- and south-facing slopes.

Distinctive farming patterns can be identified in areas of viticulture, where vines are grown on well-drained, south-facing slopes, even in surprisingly northerly locations (see figure 2.21 on p56). Equally, many gardeners favour south-facing gardens, as the direct sunlight produces a warmer climate, more favoured by many species of plant.

Figure 2.20: Lightning

See accompanying CD-Rom

Lightning.ppt

Teaching idea 2.3

Ask students to investigate micro-climates around their school – which areas are warmest, coolest, most exposed, most sheltered? How does the micro-climate of the school grounds influence student behaviour during lunch and break times?

Figure 2.21: Viticulture in north Lincolnshire

Viticulture.ppt

The British Isles

The British Isles[2] can be approximately divided into four climatic regions that are subtly different (figure 2.22). As we have already seen (p37), in general terms, the west receives more rain than the east, and the mountainous regions receive more rain than the lowlands. Similarly, average temperatures are lower in higher latitudes (ie Scotland rather than southern England), and are lower at higher altitudes, such as in mountainous regions.

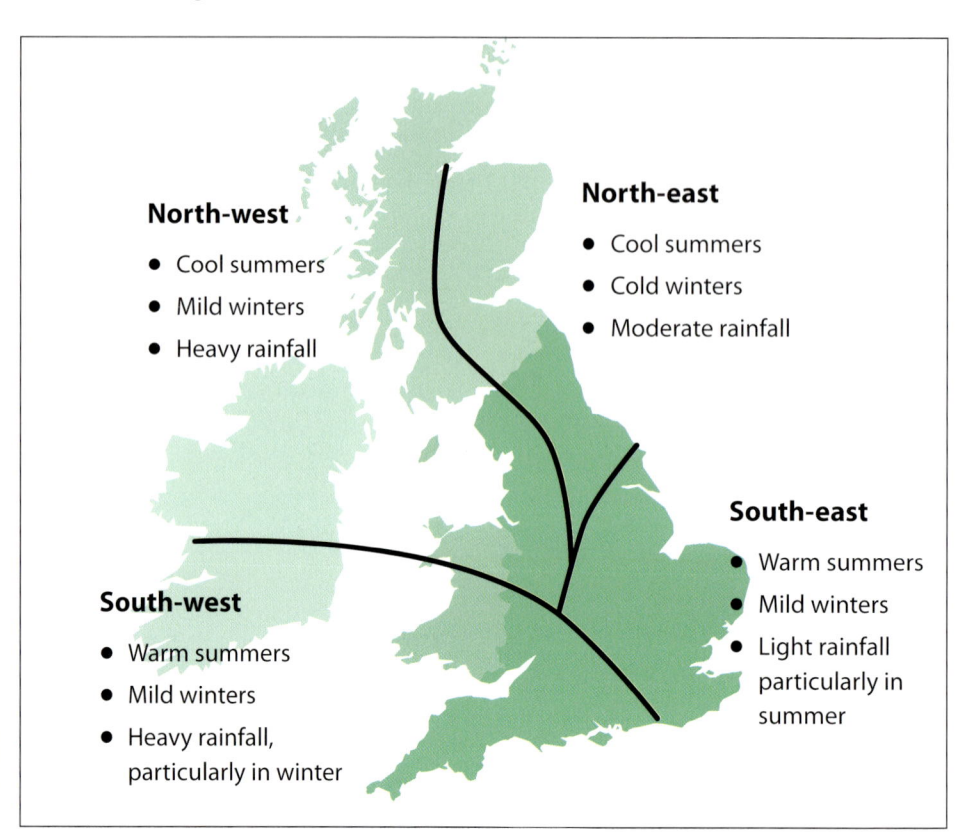

North-west
- Cool summers
- Mild winters
- Heavy rainfall

North-east
- Cool summers
- Cold winters
- Moderate rainfall

South-west
- Warm summers
- Mild winters
- Heavy rainfall, particularly in winter

South-east
- Warm summers
- Mild winters
- Light rainfall particularly in summer

Figure 2.22: Climatic regions of the British Isles

Climatic regions.ppt

Air masses

An air mass is an individual parcel of air that has characteristics dependent upon the region from where it originated and its route of travel across continents and oceans. Vertical changes in temperature and humidity within the mass are relatively small. As changes in temperature within an air mass can be very slow, for an air mass to take on cool or warm properties requires it be stationary in an area for a relatively long time (eg weeks). Therefore, the areas where air masses tend to remain static are termed air mass source regions, and tend to be the high pressure regions of either the tropics or the polar regions. In the British Isles, air masses arrive either by passing over continental areas, and hence tend to be dry, or by travelling over oceans, which result in very moist air masses. There are six types of air mass that shape the weather of the British Isles (see figure 2.23 on p58); they are:

- Polar Continental (Pc)
- Polar Maritime (Pm)
- Tropical Continental (Tc)
- Tropical Maritime (Tm)
- Returning Polar Maritime (rPm)
- Arctic Maritime (Am)

Polar Continental air has its source in eastern Europe, where there are significant winter snows. This type of air mass only occurs during the winter, when the interior of the continent is significantly colder than the coastal areas and, as a result, heavier colder air flows out of the interior towards the British Isles. During the warmer summer months, the temperature differential is reversed as continental land masses heat up more rapidly than the coastal margins. In this case, the interior draws in air masses from the same direction and would be classed as Tropical continental. If this air mass reaches the southern coast of Britain – and so only crosses a relatively very small body of water – the resulting weather will be cold and dry. If, however, the air mass affects higher latitudes further up the British Isles where a larger expanse of sea needs to be crossed, there may be showers associated with it due to the moisture that has been picked up from the sea.

From the north-west, Polar Maritime air originates from northern Canada and Greenland. This very cold air travels over the northern Atlantic Ocean, which warms the air mass, leading to very moist unstable air. As the air warms it is forced to rise, forming cumulus clouds, thereby bringing the cold, rainy weather that is characteristic of north-westerly winds. In the summer, the east of Britain will experience more showers, due to heating of the air mass by the land mass, whereas during the winter, the north and west will receive more of the precipitation.

Tropical Continental air originates from North Africa and the Sahara, and brings dry weather, often with the highest annual temperatures. Visibility, however, can be poor, due to dust and pollutants picked up while the air is travelling over continental Europe. This often results in a fine layer of orange Saharan dust being deposited out of the air over cars and static objects, particularly if there is any rain associated with it, as there can be occasional thundery showers.

Chapter 2: Climate and weather

**Figure 2.23:
Air masses influencing
the British Isles**

British air masses.ppt

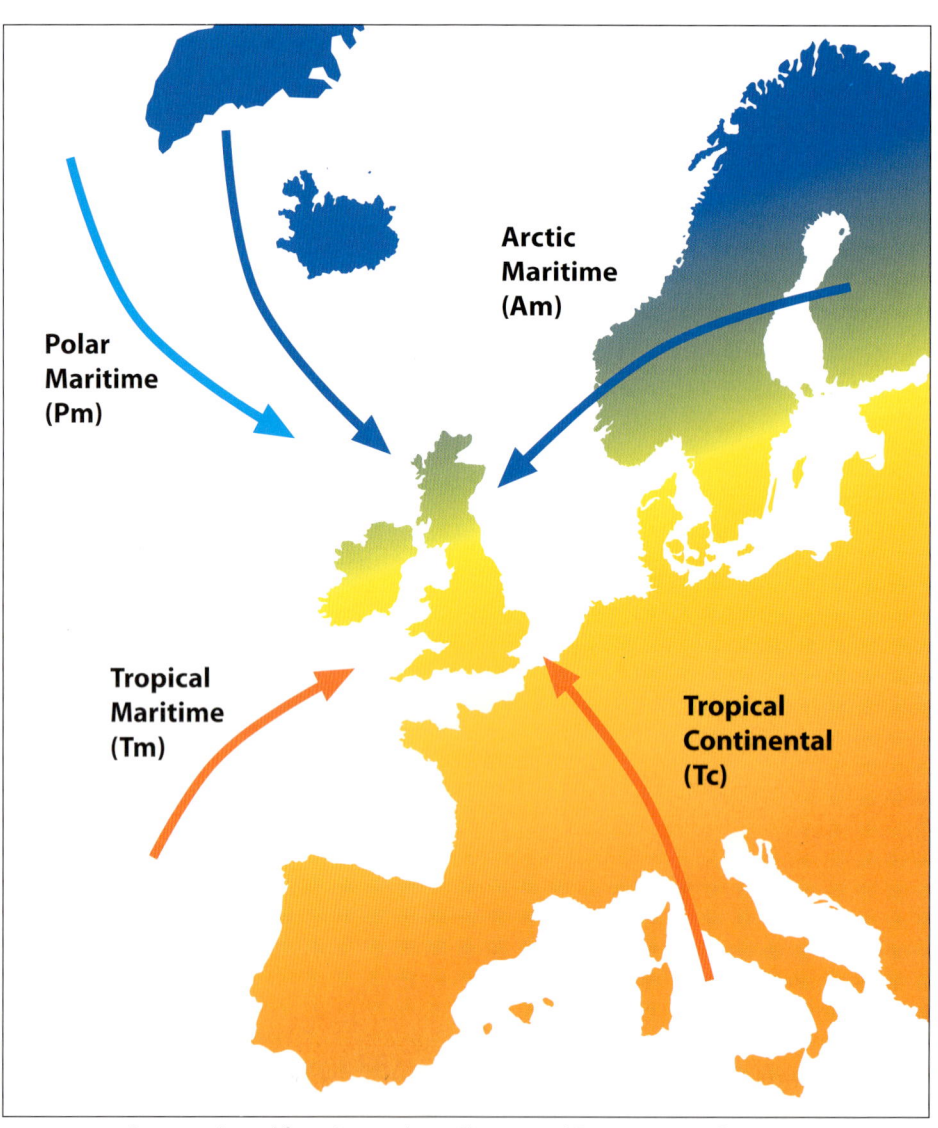

Polar Maritime (Pm)

Arctic Maritime (Am)

Tropical Maritime (Tm)

Tropical Continental (Tc)

Source: adapted from Atmosphere, Climate and Environment Information programme, Manchester Metropolitan University.

	Tropical Continental (Tc)		Polar Continental (Pc)		Tropical Maritime (Tm)		Polar Maritime (Pm)	Arctic Maritime (Am)	Returning Polar Maritime (rPm)
	Summer	Winter	Long sea stack	Short sea stack	Exposed	Sheltered			
Temperature	Very warm or hot	Average	Cold	Very cold	Near sea temperature	Warm	Rather cold	Cold (colder than Pm)	Warm (warmer than Pm)
Humidity	Relatively dry	Rather moist	Moist in lowest layers	Very dry	Very moist	Moist	Moist	Fairly moist (not as moist as Pm)	Fairly moist (not as moist as Pm)
Weather	Clear, occasional thundery showers	Clear	Rain or snow showers	Clear	Low cloud, drizzle	Broken cloud, dry	Variable cloud showers	Showers (mainly coastal)	Showers (mainly coastal)
Visibility	Moderate or poor	Moderate or poor	Good	Moderate or poor	Often poor with coastal fog	Moderate	Good	Very good	Very good

Source: adapted from the Met Office, 2007.

Air originating from the Tropical Maritime sources is relatively warm but, due to travelling across the Atlantic Ocean, it becomes cooler as the air travels north and the air becomes saturated. Therefore, this air mass is associated with mild seasonal temperatures, but often with rain, drizzle and sometimes fog in coastal regions.

Arctic Maritime air masses originate in the Arctic region, and subsequently produce the coldest temperatures during winter in Scotland. However, for the rest of Britain, as the air mass is travelling in a southerly direction from the north, Arctic Maritime air masses are not as cold as Polar Continental air masses. Although the air mass travels across the sea, it is a much shorter distance than is covered by Tropical Maritime air masses, so they tend to possess less moisture.

A Returning Polar Maritime air mass is one that has the same source as Polar Maritime air (Greenland and northern Canada), but has travelled further south across the Atlantic Ocean, and has then diverted back towards the north-east to cross the British Isles. As it has spent longer over the Atlantic Ocean than the Polar Maritime air, it is warmer and contains more moisture.

Weather fronts

The boundary between two air masses is called a 'front'. Each of the air masses will have its own temperature, humidity, wind speed and direction, and atmospheric pressure; therefore the fronts where the air masses meet are areas of significant weather activity. There are three types of weather fronts: (i) cold fronts; (ii) warm fronts; and (iii) occluded fronts. A cold front occurs where colder air displaces warmer air. As the cold air of the front pushes underneath the warm air, it is often associated with rain, which can be heavy, a shift in the wind direction and a drop in pressure. The pressure rises again as the front passes, with cooler temperatures following. A bank of cloud can often be seen as a cold front approaches. Cold fronts are shown on weather charts as a solid line with blue triangles on the side of the warmer air, pointing in the direction of movement of the air mass.

A warm front occurs when warm air gradually displaces cooler air. As the warmer air is less dense than the cooler air, the warm air rises over the cooler air, pushing it into a wedge shape. It is often associated with sheets of flat stratus cloud that form as a result of the water vapour in the warm air condensing as it rises up and cools. Temperature and dew point within the cooler air mass underneath the warm front will rise, while atmospheric pressure will fall. There can also be rain associated with the passing of a warm front, which usually stops once the front has passed. Warm fronts are shown on synoptic charts as a solid line, with red solid semi-circles on the cold air side, pointing in the direction of movement. As the warm front passes over the cooler air mass, there will be a point when the warm air is no longer in contact with the ground, and at this point an occluded front will result.

An occluded front occurs when a cold front 'catches up' with a warm front, and either undercuts the warm front (a 'cold occlusion'), or rises over the warm front (a 'warm occlusion') (see *Mid-latitude depressions* on p41). An occluded front is associated with changeable weather conditions, often with heavy rain and storm conditions. It is represented on weather charts by a solid line, with alternate semi-circles and triangles next to each other, often coloured red and blue respectively, or as both symbols coloured purple or yellow.

Forecasting weather

Agencies such as the UK Met Office produce forecasts of the weather across a huge range of timescales, from just a few hours ahead, to long-range planning over a century ahead. All predictions of future weather are based upon past and current weather observations. The main sources of such weather data are from surface and marine data, aircraft, weather balloon-mounted radiosonde and meteorological satellites. Satellites effectively provide 'photographs' of very large areas. They provide a means for meteorologists to track weather systems across countries, with satellites that have infrared allowing temperature also to be recorded.

> **Teaching resources**
>
> The latest infrared and visible radiation satellite images of the UK, updated every hour, are available from geostationary satellites at *www.metoffice.gov.uk/satpics/latest_uk_ir.html* and *www.metoffice.gov.uk/satpics/latest_uk_vis.html*

Short-range weather forecasts are often produced using 'ensemble forecasting'. This process involves considering the current weather conditions, and calculating how the current conditions could change over time. The initial data is taken from thousands of weather observation points. This data is then processed by highly complex computer models, running the same data sets (but with very slight difference to allow for variations in the original data) many times, to produce a range of possible forecast outcomes. This method of forecasting not only predicts the possible weather events that may occur, but also the confidence of such an event occurring based upon the multiple model runs.

Long-range forecasts are based upon current weather conditions to provide a basis on which to predict future weather. Although current weather conditions are a sound starting point on which to make predictions, if there are any anomalies in the weather data set, these have an impact on the ultimate prediction that is made. Therefore, if long-range forecasts can be based on the largest data sets possible, this improves the accuracy of the end prediction. Long-range modelling involves computer models being run repeatedly to produce as many potential outcomes as possible based upon each starting data set. This ensures the greatest possible chances of various outcomes being considered.

Synoptic charts

Weather charts that show the weather conditions at a particular time are called 'synoptic charts'. Although there are many types of weather chart, all generally use standard symbols (see figure 2.24 on p62). The charts record a number of atmospheric and weather conditions at a particular weather station:

- Temperature: the temperature in °Celsius.

- Current weather: taken at the time of recording, eg rain, snow, fog.

- Weather since last recording: using the same symbols as current weather.

- Air pressure: the pressure in millibars at time of recording.
- Wind speed and direction: the tail of the symbol shows the wind direction, with speed being shown by smaller lines at the end of the tail, to the nearest 5 knots.
- Cloud cover: shown by the amount of shading in a circle. To record cloud cover, the sky needs to be divided in eight – no shading means a clear sky, with complete shading reflecting complete cloud coverage.

Each of these parameters is plotted on a map, showing the location of the weather station.

Teaching idea 2.4

Ask students to keep a spreadsheet-based 'weather diary'. Measure: air temperature with thermometer; rain with rain gauge; wind speed with anemometer or assess wind speed in terms of Beaufort Scale; wind direction (can measure by holding a flag or piece of light fabric, with a compass). If students do not have access to this equipment, the UK Met Office provides the latest weather conditions online, searchable by postcode at: *www.metoffice.gov.uk/weather/uk/uk_latest_weather.html*

Or ask students to record and listen to the shipping forecasts over a week. They can then, with help, draw their own synoptic weather charts in order to predict the weather.

Alternatively, the US National Oceanic and Atmospheric Administration provides a summary of weather conditions each hour for the previous 24 hours for a huge number of weather stations around the British Isles, accessible at: *http://weather.noaa.gov/weather/GB_cc.html*. This data can then be related to prevailing weather conditions – is the area experiencing cyclonic or anti-cyclonic weather? Students could plot this data on synoptic charts for a few adjacent stations (including drawing isobars) and then 'forecast' weather for the next 24 hours.

Teaching resources

Climographs are graphs of average temperature and precipitation each month over the course of an average year at a particular location. They show temperature as a line graph, with rainfall (or precipitation) as a bar graph. Temperate climate averages for cities around the world are available on the UK Met Office website at: *www.metoffice.gov.uk/education/teachers/temperate_climate_averages.html*

Tropical climate averages for cities around the world are also available on the UK Met Office website at: *www.metoffice.gov.uk/education/teachers/tropical_climate_averages.html*

Chapter 2: Climate and weather

Cloud cover	
Clear sky	○
One okta (1/8 of the sky covered)	◔
Two oktas	◔
Three oktas	◔
Four oktas	◑
Five oktas	◕
Six oktas	◕
Seven oktas	◕
Eight oktas	●
Sky obscured	⊗

Precipitation	
Drizzle	▪
Shower	▽
Rain	●
Snow	✶
Hail	△
Thunder	⚡
Heavy rain	⋰
Sleet	•✶
Snow shower	✶▽
Mist	═
Fog	≡

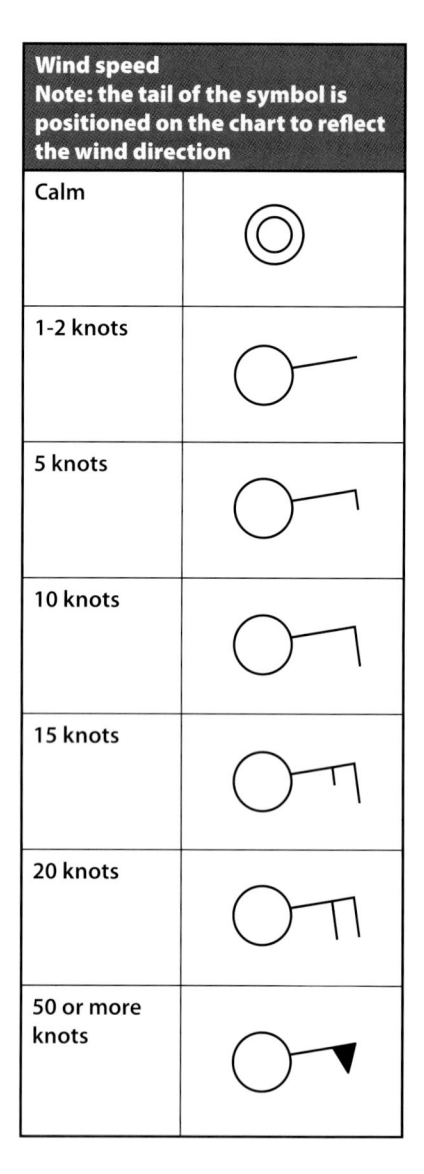

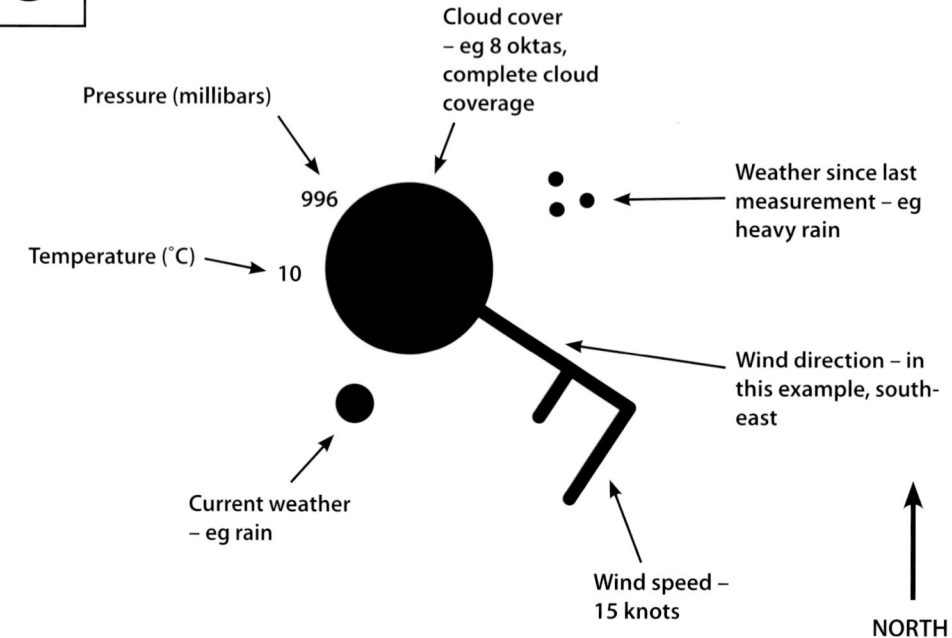

Wind speed Note: the tail of the symbol is positioned on the chart to reflect the wind direction	
Calm	◎
1-2 knots	○—
5 knots	○—\
10 knots	○—\\
15 knots	○—\\\
20 knots	○—\\\\
50 or more knots	○—▶

Figure 2.24:
Synoptic charts and standard weather symbols

See accompanying CD-Rom

Synoptic charts.ppt

Pressure (millibars) → 996

Temperature (°C) → 10

Cloud cover – eg 8 oktas, complete cloud coverage

Weather since last measurement – eg heavy rain

Current weather – eg rain

Wind direction – in this example, south-east

Wind speed – 15 knots

NORTH

Summary

This chapter has shown how the climate of the Earth is a consequence of a wide-ranging set of interconnecting variables. It is impossible to understand climatic patterns fully without taking into account the role of the Sun in its differential heating of the planet, the juxtaposition of land masses and oceans and the rotation of the Earth on its tilted axis. It then becomes possible to focus on local examples of both climate and weather and to identify the role that such elements play in the development of environment and livelihoods. The immediacy of the weather and the importance it plays in our daily lives enables us to make direct links between the known world of the student and the geographies of weather and climate; as such it becomes possible to make a potentially difficult topic much more accessible and relevant.

Endnotes

1. El Niño is the name given to the phenomenon of warmer waters by South American fishermen who first noticed it due to its effects on fish stocks. It means 'Christ child' or 'the little boy' and it acquired its name due to the phenomenon generally being evident just before Christmas.

2. For a wide range of data on UK climate see: *www.metoffice.gov.uk* – for specific references see 'Useful websites' below.

3. The trade winds were named due to their importance from the 14th century onwards when merchant sailing ships relied on prevailing winds to sail around the world. Much political geography can be linked to the early patterns of trade around the world determined by the direction of the trade winds.

4. 1μm (micron) equals 1/1000 of a millimetre, hence 2,000μm is equivalent to 2mm.

Useful websites

El Niño and La Niña
Numerous excellent diagrams and animations illustrating El Niño and La Niña are available to download at the Tropical Atmosphere Ocean project website: *www.pmel.noaa.gov/tao/proj_over/diagrams/index.html*

Hurricanes
Comprehensive information regarding Hurricane Katrina and its aftermath is covered on the special report page of the BBC website at: *http://news.bbc.co.uk/1/hi/in_depth/americas/2005/hurricane_katrina/default.stm*

A wealth of information regarding the most extreme hurricane events in the United States is available as a paper from NOAAs National Hurricane Center, downloadable as a PDF or MS Word document from: *www.nhc.noaa.gov/dcmi.shtml*

The tracks of all historical hurricanes can be seen over a base map at NOAAs Coastal Services Center website: *http://csc-s-maps-q.csc.noaa.gov/hurricanes/viewer.html* by selecting the storm name.

UK weather data
Long-term UK weather data for the 37 UK Met Office ground weather stations are available at: *www.metoffice.gov.uk/climate/uk/stationdata/index.html*. This excellent resource provides data on temperature, frost, rainfall and sunshine hours for every month of every

year. The start date of the data collection varies depending on the station (eg 1873 for Stornoway, through to 1959 for Eastbourne).

The UK Met Office produces excellent weather presenting kits – 'hard copy' and interactive versions available, which can be ordered (one copy per school) from:

www.metoffice.gov.uk/education/teachers/resources-weather-presenting-kit.html

www.metoffice.gov.uk/education/teachers/resources-interactive-weather-presenting-kit.html

Climate change

Vanessa Holden

Introduction

Climate change is one of the foremost issues of the last few years. It is mentioned in all areas of the media, at various levels of complexity. Very few political debates fail to mention climate change and how our every move is 'contributing to climate change'. Because it has become such a significant issue (and some would say rightly so), there is an incredible amount of information, facts, figures and, of course, confusion about what the whole concept is actually about and what the implications of the change are. Therefore, this chapter is aimed at setting out the basic facts behind climate change, to then allow the reader to be able to follow up more detailed information in some of the major areas of climate change as they wish.

While climate change was first described by Swedish scientist Svante Arrhenius in the 19th century, a more general awareness of climate change became apparent during the 1980s, with phrases such as 'global warming' increasingly used to describe the phenomenon (Weart, 2008, *www.aip.org/history/climate/co2.htm*). However, 'the greenhouse effect is leading to global warming' is a very misleading statement. The term 'greenhouse effect' does not accurately represent what is happening, and global warming implies a pleasant general warming-up of the temperature (to which people often respond that they'd like it a bit warmer!). Such simplicities fail to mention the other aspects of climate change, such as increasing frequency of storms and more extremes of weather, and the implications of these developments, such as more flooding.

The Earth's climate changes naturally over seasons, decades, centuries and millennia. This is shown by the occurrence of Ice Ages [☞], and the warming of the Earth in between. Natural changes can occur due to solar variations, ocean cycles, and events such as volcanic eruptions. However, while solar inputs to the Earth have remained fairly stable over the past few decades, temperatures have increased significantly. Therefore, the magnitude of the temperature increases seen is highly unlikely to be related entirely to solar (sunspot) activity. Similarly, volcanic eruptions emit carbon dioxide gas (CO_2), although it has been calculated that volcanoes are responsible for less than 1% of the emissions from human activities (Royal Society, 2008). When volcanoes erupt, they emit significant amounts of particulates into the atmosphere. These particulates act as cloud condensation nuclei (encouraging the formation of clouds), and scatter incoming solar radiation, both of which act as cooling mechanisms. However, the current concern over climate change is the speed and amount of change that have been recorded since the beginning of major industrial activity by humans. In conjunction with this, the outputs of carbon dioxide and other gases from human activities have increased dramatically. It is this change in climate in relation to human influences that is the cause of such concern for the future.

See Volume 2: Physical Geography, ch 5, Ice.

There is significant debate about whether the changing climate that we are currently experiencing is due to natural variations in the global climate or to human influences. This chapter aims to provide the current evidence and scientific thinking on the topic, but will ultimately leave the reader (and their students) to form their own conclusions as to the nature, severity and importance of the implications of climate change as we currently understand it.

How climate works

The greenhouse effect (figure 3.1) is essential to life on Earth. It provides us with enough warmth to survive. We receive ultraviolet (UV) and visible light from the Sun, and emit infrared (IR) radiation (heat) back out into space. The presence of certain gases with heat-trapping ability in our atmosphere (called 'greenhouse gases') allows some of the IR radiation to be trapped, so keeping some of the heat within our atmosphere. It has been calculated that although these gases only constitute a tiny 0.5% of the atmosphere, they keep our planet 30% warmer than if they were absent (Met Office, 2009).

Carbon dioxide (CO_2) is the greenhouse gas that is most commonly associated with climate change, as it is released into the atmosphere in significant quantities by many human activities. CO_2 is also increasing in concentrations due to deforestation [💾], which has reduced global acreages of forests which had previously absorbed large amounts of the gas. Records show that before industrialisation, the quantity of CO_2 in the atmosphere was around 280 parts per million (ppm); in 2005 it was at 379ppm – this apparently small increase has already led to an average rise in temperature of 0.74°C (IPCC, 2007; Royal Society, 2008). Scientific evidence can show that much of the increase in CO_2 is due to burning fossil fuels [💾]. Other greenhouse gases include methane (from human activities such as landfill sites, and from the digestive processes of livestock) and nitrous oxide (from fertilisers used in agriculture). However,

See ch 1, Ecosystems (p18).
See ch 4, Energy (p86).

Figure 3.1:
The greenhouse effect

See accompanying CD-Rom

The greenhouse effect.ppt

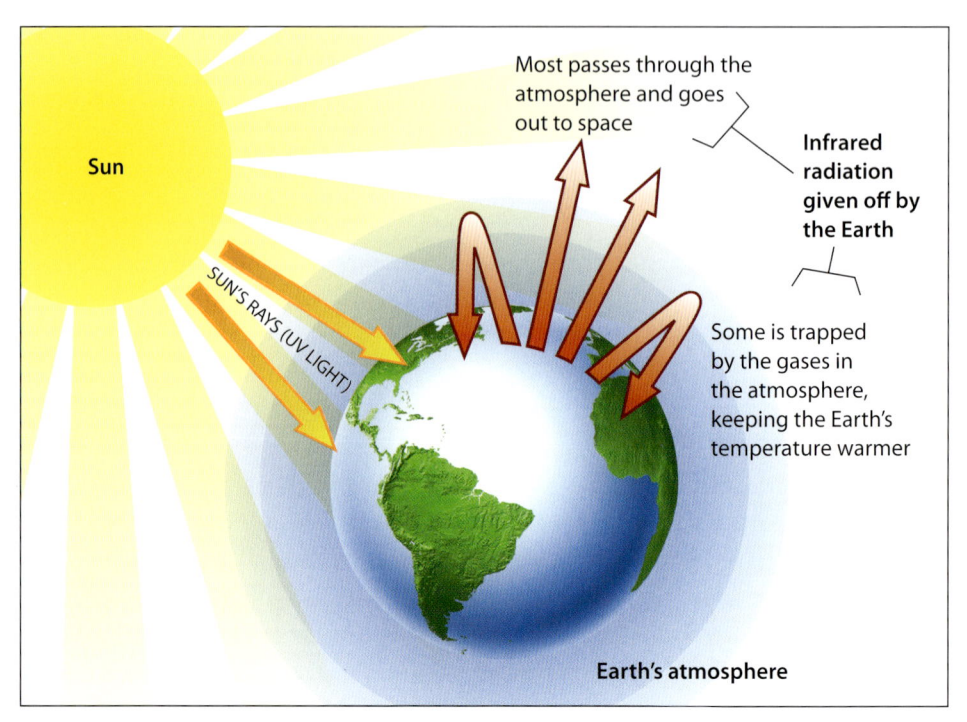

these other gases are not released in such large quantities as CO_2. Ozone and other halocarbons (such as CFCs [☞], from aerosols and domestic refrigerators, that were prominent in the news during the 1980s) are also commonly referred to as greenhouse gases. They trap heat in the same way as CO_2 but remain in the atmosphere for a much shorter time. The most abundant greenhouse gas is actually water vapour. With a warming of the climate, so the levels found in the atmosphere will rise due to increased evaporation from the oceans (Royal Society, 2008).

See ch 8, Globalisation (p184).

With increased summer temperatures, so temperate climates such as the UK may experience lengthier summer droughts, with bursts of intense rainfall, leading to localised flooding. It is intense rainfall that caused the disastrous floods in the villages of Boscastle and Crackington Haven in Cornwall, UK, in August 2004. Many other factors led to the severity of the damage caused by the flood, but it was the intensity of the rainfall that was the precursor to the floods.

Climate change does not necessarily mean that every year will be progressively warmer than the last one – there will still be natural variations. It does mean, however, that the long-term trend will be one of increasing temperatures.

Evidence of short-term changes: direct evidence

Weather stations

Direct evidence of climate changes can be derived from observations taken from weather stations around the globe. These have been used since the mid-19th century, so providing in some cases around 150 years of direct recorded data (figure 3.2). Weather stations can gather information such as wind speed, air temperature and amount of rainfall (see figure 3.3 on p68). Early weather observations were obtained

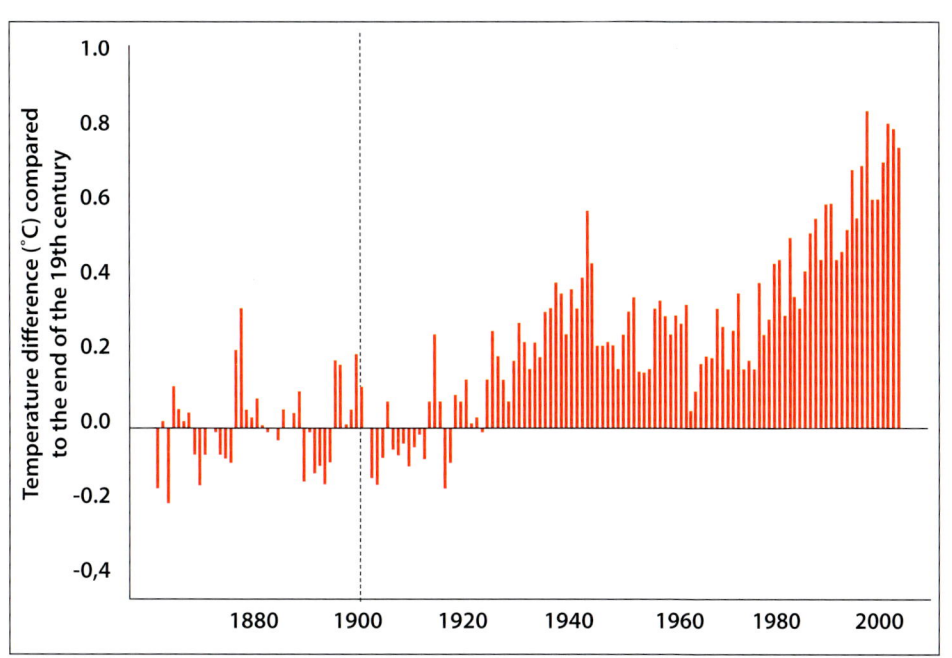

Figure 3.2: Global average temperatures, 1861-2004

Global temperatures.ppt

Source: adapted from Met Office Hadley Centre, 2005.

Sources: Kathryn Coffey (left) and NOAA's National Weather Service (NWS) Collection www.photolib.noaa.gov incl. Brent French (right).

Figure 3.3:
Weather stations

See accompanying CD-Rom

Weather stations.ppt

manually, with rainfall being collected in containers, and the levels being read by a human operator. As the technologies have advanced, so increasingly measurements are taken automatically by electronic devices, and relayed to computers for analysis. This results in more frequent measurements being taken, often more precisely, and in more remote areas.

Teaching idea 3.1

Long-term weather data (up to 140 years, depending on location) is available for 37 weather stations around the UK at www.metoffice.gov.uk/climate/uk/stationdata/index.html. Ask students to collect current local weather data and to compare it with past weather. Can they identify any major changes that have occurred over time in their local area?

Satellite measurements

Since 1979, satellites orbiting the Earth have been recording global atmospheric temperatures (see figure 3.4 on p69). With increasing CO_2 concentrations, so the temperatures of the lower levels of the atmosphere also undergo warming. Although initial analysis of these measurements indicated that the global warming was not occurring as rapidly as was suggested by the land-based temperature measurements, advances in the methods of data analysis now show a much stronger correlation between the increases in temperatures shown by both land-based and satellite measurements.

Sea levels

Coastal flooding in many areas across the globe has resulted in an increased awareness of the trend of rising sea levels since the mid-20th century. Extreme predictions during the 1980s acted as a springboard for scientific research, with the result that the science of predicting sea-level rise has developed into a significant multi-disciplinary

Figure 3.4:
Satellite measurements

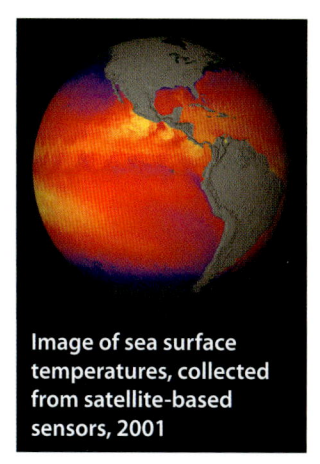

| Historic radar image of hurricane, Florida, 1946 | Satellite Image of Hurricane Floyd, Florida, 1999 | Satellite image of clouds over Ireland, 2003 | Image of sea surface temperatures, collected from satellite-based sensors, 2001 |

Sources (left to right): NOAA's National Weather Service (NWS) Collection *www.photolib.noaa.gov*; Marit Jentoft-Nilsen, NASA GSFC Visualization Analysis Lab *www.visisbleearth.nasa.gov*; Jacques Descloitres, MODIS Rapid Response Team, NASA/GSFC *www.visisbleearth.nasa.gov*; Jesse Allen, based on data provided by the MODIS OCEAN Team and the University of Miami Rosenstiel School of Marine and Atmospheric Science Remote Sensing Group *www.visisbleearth.nasa.gov*

body of data, models and forecasts. Such research is often led by governmental and international organisations, directed at determining the most accurate range of sea-level rise scenarios, in order to develop more well-informed management strategies. An excellent example of such an organisation is the UK's Permanent Service for Mean Sea Level (PSMSL) (*www.psmsl.org*).

The causes of sea-level rise are generally accepted, and widely reported (eg Pugh, 2004; Valiela, 2006). Sea levels are rising due to a number of processes, with the major ones being:

- **Thermal expansion.** As water heats up, so it expands and physically takes up more space. Therefore, the height (or 'level') of the sea rises in relation to the level of the adjacent land.

- **Melting of ice.** Ice is 'permanently' found at the North and South Poles, in glaciers, and in areas of permafrost. As the temperature of the Earth increases, so the ice is melting, with the melt water flowing into the sea.

- **Crustal deformation.** Following the last Ice Age, the Earth's crust is still rebounding from the release of the weight of the ice, so resulting in continued movement of the crust. For instance, the landmass of the north-west of Scotland is rising above present sea level, while the south-east of England appears to be sinking.

- Changes in meteorological forcing factors such as increased wind strength.

There are decadal scales of variation in sea level, notably the 18.6-year nodal modulation of the lunar tides, along with annual variations, such as maximum annual sea levels experienced around September (in the northern hemisphere), following heating and expansion of the water during the summer months (Pugh, 2004). Accordingly, by analysing long-term trends, the Intergovernmental Panel on Climate Change (IPCC) reported in 2007 that global average sea level had risen, since 1961, at an average rate of 1.8 millimetres per year (mm/yr) and since 1993 at 3.1mm/yr (although it is unclear whether the increase in rate since 1993 is due to climate change or natural variation) (see figure 3.5 on p70).

See accompanying CD-Rom

Satellite measurements.ppt

**Figure 3.5:
Rate of average global sea-level rise**

Global sea levels.ppt

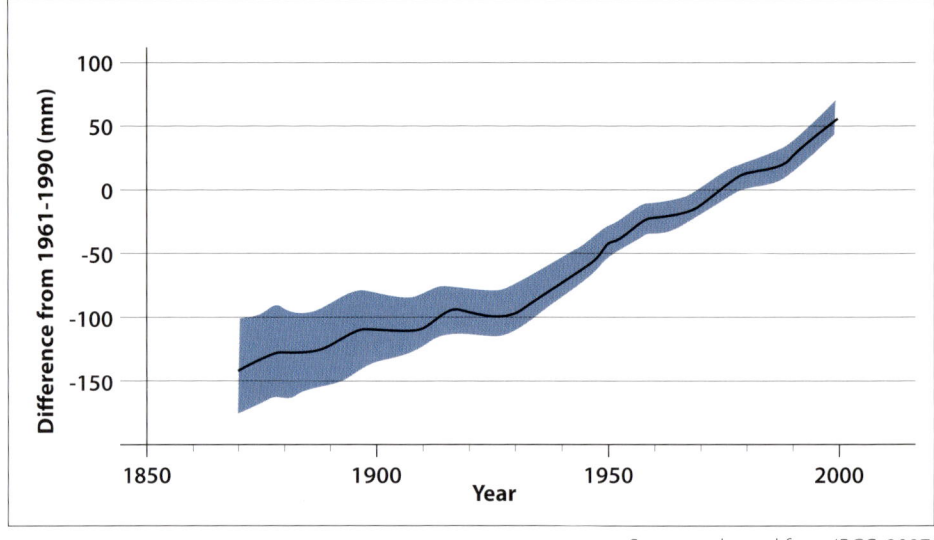

Source: adapted from IPCC, 2007.

Some records of sea levels are based upon significant records of observations. For example in Liverpool, UK, it has been established that the rate of sea-level rise is of the order of 1 to 2mm per year, based upon a 200-year record of tidal heights. This record is the second-oldest in the world (Amsterdam has data from 1682) (Woodworth, 1999). A combination of data held by the Royal Society on tide heights from the 19th century, along with data recorded by the Mersey Docks and Harbour Board and the Proudman Oceanographic Laboratory, means that there now exists an almost complete record of all of the high waters at Liverpool for the past 200 years.

See Volume 2: Physical Geography, ch 5, Ice.

Melting of global snow and ice stores

Global snow and ice stores can be found either in polar ice caps or in mountainous glaciers. By using satellite imagery to map the extent of Arctic sea ice during the summer months, the IPCC (2007) has calculated that volumes of ice have reduced by 2.7% per decade since 1978. This method of monitoring the polar ice caps provides a continual basis for gathering direct evidence that the coldest environments are reducing in their extent as a result of climate change.

**Figure 3.6:
Glacier retreat**

Glacier retreat.ppt

Bergsetbreen, September 1998

Bergsetbreen, September 2008

PHOTOS: STEVE SUGGITT

Similarly, many glaciers on land are reducing in size (often referred to as 'retreating'), which is often shown from aerial photography or fixed-point photography (see figure 3.6 on p70). Although glaciers can appear to be advancing due to an increase in snow during the winter months, the general trend is for mountainous glaciers to be decreasing in size, with their related environments being found at steadily higher altitudes.

Permafrost occurs where soil is always below freezing, often in sub-arctic conditions or high in mountainous regions. Permafrost is a store for CO_2 and methane (CH_4). Subsequently, with increasing air temperatures due to climate change, areas of permafrost are thawing, releasing the CO_2 and methane back into the atmosphere. This therefore further contributes to the concentrations of greenhouse gases in the atmosphere.

Evidence of long-term changes: proxy evidence

Long-term changes in the climate can be determined by using proxy evidence. This form of evidence is obtained from the natural environment (such as ice cores or lake sediments) and provides vital historic information about the condition of the climate at a given time. Different types of proxy evidence allow determination of climatic conditions at different spatial scales, from the highly local and specific through to the global.

Long-term changes in climate, over hundreds of thousands of years, can be demonstrated by using ice cores (see British Antarctic Survey *www.photo.antarctica.ac.uk* or US Pacific Marine Environmental Laboratory *www.pmel.noaa.gov/foci/visualizations/images/iceCores/* for images of ice cores). Ice cores also provide important evidence for the link between CO_2 and increasing temperatures. The major ice sheets of Antarctica and Greenland provide an ideal environment for the collection and study of these cores.

An example of the information that can be contained within the core, is the presence of 'heavy isotopes'. (Isotopes are atoms of the same element – such as oxygen or hydrogen – that have the same number of protons, but different numbers of neutrons). For example, the isotope deuterium, when found in higher concentrations in the ice, means the temperature was warmer when the ice was deposited. Conversely, when the climate becomes really cold (even for the Antarctic!), the heavy isotopes are absent from the cores.[1]

Concentrations of atmospheric gases can also be measured in ice cores. As snow and ice accumulate on the ice sheets, tiny pockets of air become trapped within the ice. As the ice builds up over time, so the air is held within the tiny pockets, as a permanent record of the components of the air at the time in which the ice accumulated. This analysis of the changes in atmospheric gases over such long timescales provides evidence that the currently high levels of CO_2 are a very new occurrence. Levels are now 35% higher than they have been for the last 650,000 years (Royal Society, 2008).

Lake sediments

Cores taken from the sediment that collects at the bottom of lakes is a further valuable source of information about past environments (see figure 3.7 on p72). A straightforward indicator of past climate is the colour of the sediment in a core: a light beige-grey layer indicates mainly inorganic matter (eg particles of rock and soil), suggesting a cold

**Figure 3.7:
Lake sediments**

See accompanying CD-Rom

Lake sediments.ppt

Upland lake in south Cumbria

Lake sediment core

climate; whereas a dark brown, almost black layer is produced by a high content of organic matter (from plants), which indicates a warmer climate and more stable soils.

Fossil pollen grains are also found within the cores of lake sediments. These pollen grains allow the reconstruction of the types of vegetation that were present at the time that the sediment accumulated in the lake. Types of vegetation are closely linked to climate; so changes in vegetation relate to changes in climate. Further fossil evidence from lake sediment cores is also possible through the study of chironomids (tiny non-biting midges) (figure 3.8). The larvae of these midges start life in the shallow water and lake sediments. A large proportion of the larvae do not make it to adulthood, with the body of the larvae decomposing. However, the head capsule is composed of a substance called chitin, which does not decompose, and so remains to become

**Figure 3.8:
Chironomids**

See accompanying CD-Rom

Chironomids.ppt

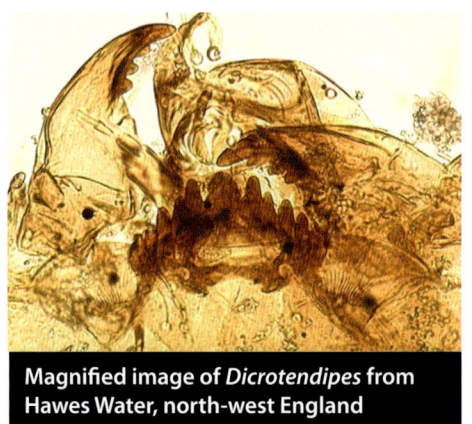

Magnified image of *Cricotopus* from Hawes Water, north-west England

Magnified image of *Dicrotendipes* from Hawes Water, north-west England

preserved in the sediment. Different species of chironomid have different shapes of head capsule, and so can be identified. These different species live in different temperatures of water, so by identifying which species have been present over the time shown in the sediment core, the changing temperature of the water that was present (and hence the climate) can be reconstructed.

Peat bogs

Peat bogs are wetland environments where dead vegetation can build up over time, with very little decomposition occurring. This build-up of plant matter forms peat. Ombrotrophic peat bogs are a specific environment where the raised peaty bog obtains all its water and nutrients from rainwater or dry deposition from the atmosphere (Proctor, 2003). These bogs do not receive any surface water from streams or through the groundwater. They are therefore low in nutrients and tend to be acidic environments, and as such have specific types of vegetation that can survive in these conditions. The peat bog is made up of a mixture of micro-environments, from relatively dry raised hummocks, through to waterlogged pools (figure 3.9). As the dead plant matter undergoes little decomposition, parts of the plants are preserved in the peat as 'macrofossils' (fossil remains that are large enough to be seen without a microscope, such as leaves and stems). Therefore, any different types of plants that have grown on the bog over time are preserved as a record down through the layers of peat. In this way, changes in vegetation can be studied over timescales of thousands of years. Also, by studying the different layers or bands that can be found through a core of peat (its 'stratigraphy'), different colours of peat can be identified that relate not only to the different species of vegetation, but also to the different amounts of decomposition that have occurred. These differences indicate past levels of wetness

Figure 3.9: Peat bogs

Peat bogs.ppt

of the bog surface at the time that the vegetation initially started to decompose. Therefore, a wet bog surface in the past suggests a wet climate (more rainfall), with a dry bog surface indicating a drier climate (less rainfall).

What's wrong with climate change?

See ch 8, Globalisation (p189).

A changing climate has global implications [🔗]; nowhere on Earth will fail to feel some effect of the changes. The degree of impact around the globe will vary, but all human societies will require some form of adaptation to adjust, and in some cases, to survive. In terms of natural ecosystems, the impacts could be critical, through loss of habitat and food sources, and through an inability to adapt to new conditions. The implications of climate change will be seen through all aspects of life – from the food we eat, to where we can live, to the effects on our own health. The UK Met Office Hadley Centre (on behalf of the UK government) has produced a map of impacts that are predicted as likely to occur if the global average temperature rises 4°C above the pre-industrialisation average. This very useful interactive map can be seen at: *www.actoncopenhagen.decc.gov.uk/content/en/embeds/flash/4-degrees-large-map-final*

> **Teaching idea 3.2**
>
> Ask students to identify the areas predicted to experience the greatest levels of temperature change from the UK Met Office map cited above. Then ask students to choose one or two of those areas in order to investigate in more depth the impacts of climate change on environment, agriculture and ecosystems.

Biodiversity and ecosystems [🔗]

See ch 1, Ecosystems.

There is no simple formula for understanding how 'natural' systems will be affected by climate change. Some animals and plants will flourish with the changes, while others will be lost through extinction. Significant losses in biodiversity are anticipated in highly specialised and climatically very sensitive areas such as coral reefs, which are home to highly specialised marine life, and are seriously threatened by climate change. This will have significant 'natural' knock-on effects through loss of species and reduction in food and shelter for many marine species, while also having 'human' effects, such as a reduction in tourism to areas such as the Great Barrier Reef. This, in turn, will have economic implications for those communities dependent upon tourism. Similar issues face tropical rainforests, which are incredibly diverse environments (see figure 3.10 on p75).

Forests and mountain regions are particularly susceptible to climate change, due to the predicted decline in rainfall in Mediterranean and tropical areas (IPCC, 2007).

Agriculture and food supply [🔗]

See ch 5, Food supply.

Initially, an increasing global temperature may allow for longer crop-growing seasons, resulting in greater crop yields. However, this benefit is likely to be short lived. Such a scenario would only benefit the currently cooler temperate parts of the world, where there are generally fewer deficiencies in food availability. In the longer term, with rising sea levels triggered by increasing temperatures and more frequent stormy weather, much of the agriculturally productive land that is currently found in low-lying areas will be

**Figure 3.10:
Threatened environments
– coral reefs and tropical
rainforests**

See accompanying CD-Rom

Coral reefs and rainforests.ppt

Satellite image of the Great Barrier Reef, Australia

Species diversity on coral reef

Tropical rain forest, the Amazon Basin

Tropical rain forest, the Amazon Basin

Source: (top left) NASA/GSFC/LaRC/JPL, MISR team; (top right) David Burdick, NOAA's Coral Kingdom Collection; (bottom) Janet Holden.

vulnerable to flooding. This will result in reduced crop yields, or even complete crop failure in those areas most at risk. Conversely, in more arid climates, there will be issues of increased occurrence of drought and desertification [☞]. Desertification is a process whereby dry arid soils are farmed more intensively to try to meet growing demands for crop yields. This intensification leads to stripping of the nutrients from the soils, breakdown of the soil structure and erosion of the soil. As the soil becomes less productive, so the farming is forced to further increase in intensification, so eventually degrading the soil to the point where it is virtually impossible for it to produce any crops. The reduction in yield of crops, whether by increased extreme rainfall and occasional flooding, or through increasingly scarce water supply, coincides with a time when the global population is expanding at an unprecedented rate, further heightening the demand for food. It is estimated that with a 4^0C rise in temperature there will be a 10 to 20% increase in the number of people at risk from hunger, predominantly in southern Asia, Central America and sub-Saharan Africa (IPCC, 2007). In addition, with greater frequencies of intense precipitation, it can be anticipated that there will be considerably more damage to crops, and increased rates of soil erosion (IPCC, 2007). Livestock productivity is also very likely to come under threat, particularly in regions such as Central and South America, with fewer feedstock crops available to rear animals, and reduced water availability.

See ch 7, Environmental management (p158).

The survival and biodiversity of insects is important to the growing of food crops in many parts of the world. Insects improve the structure and fertility of soil. However, where climate change results in hotter, drier summers, this is likely to affect the types and numbers of insects found in soils, with consequences for subsequent fertility. At the same time, certain diseases and pests that affect UK crops are less likely to be killed off during warmer winters, with implications for agrarian management and crop yields.

Soils are one of the UK's largest CO_2 sinks. This is particularly the case with the peats found in the north and west of Britain (UK Biodiversity Partnership, 2007). Therefore, their continued existence is important to keep the CO_2 held within the soil, rather than being released back into the atmosphere. In warmer temperatures, the organic matter in soil breaks down more quickly, which releases CO_2 back into the atmosphere at a greater rate.

Rising sea levels

At the beginning of the 21st century, 600 million people worldwide live less than 10 metres above the present sea level. In South and East Asia in particular, huge populations live in low-lying deltas and on small islands that are only marginally above sea level. Such deltas are highly populated due to the availability of flat, fertile agricultural land.

The impacts of sea-level rise are numerous. Coastal land is generally of high value, both economically and socially. The extensive urbanisation of coastal margins has also resulted, perhaps ironically, in a greater awareness of potential habitat infringement and loss, due to human manipulation of the coastline in so many areas. The highly specialised habitats of salt marsh and mangrove coasts are particularly at risk from climate change (IPCC, 2007). They are found in specific zones within the tidal frame, with the vegetation being adapted to tolerate certain frequencies of high tides and subsequent salinities. As sea level rises, the salt marsh or mangrove (the tropical version of a salt marsh) will try to roll back landwards to stay within the same tidal zone, or elevation. If, however, as is the case along many human-altered coastlines, there are structures such as sea walls, this will prevent the landward movement of the salt marsh, resulting ultimately in the salt marsh environment being eroded away and the habitat lost. This process is termed 'coastal squeeze'. Specific coastal habitats such as these are extremely important for the survival of both plants and animals, particularly wild birds that use the coastline as winter feeding sites (see figure 3.11 on p77). Furthermore, salt marshes are stores for carbon, as the plants absorb CO_2 from the air. If the marshes erode, this store of carbon is once again released into the environment.

See Volume 2: Physical Geography, ch 3, Coasts (p160).

In addition to the direct effects of sea-level rise, other consequences of climate change have clear implications for coastal regions. Increased storminess and rainfall can have significant impacts upon the coastal system in terms of tidal and wave action. With wetter, stormier winters predicted, storm surges are likely to become more frequent. Storm surges occur when high tides coincide with strong onshore winds. This combination effectively pushes the tide even higher towards land. This leads to an increase in coastal erosion and exacerbates the impacts of coastal flooding [🖱].

The consequences of rising sea levels can be critical, not only in terms of the natural environment, but also in terms of the human environment. Many UK electricity-generating power stations are situated in the coastal zone, in particular a number of nuclear power generation plants. Expansion on the site of several of these plants is being considered, requiring consideration of coastal defence from tidal inundations and erosion for at least the next 150 years to cover operation and decommissioning.

**Figure 3.11:
Salt marsh in the Ribble Estuary, UK**

Salt marsh.ppt

Many coastal locations are important for tourism, recreation, agriculture and industry. Alongside each of these factors are the associated issues of transport networks, buildings and infrastructure. As such, many locations require proactive management to balance the requirements of humans, the natural environment and the changing coastline (figure 3.12).

**Figure 3.12:
Coastal flooding**

Coastal flooding.ppt

Sources: (top) images courtesy of Sefton Metropolitan Borough Council; (bottom) images copyright of North West and North Wales Coastal Group.

> **Teaching idea 3.3**
>
> The Permanent Service for Mean Sea Level (PSMSL) holds electronic archives of sea-level data from hundreds of tide gauges from around the world. This data is available to download as both raw data (sea-level heights in millimetres) and plots of sea levels for each gauge from *www.psmsl.org/data/*. Ask students to investigate the database for a location of their choice. Can they identify any significant changes in mean sea level over time? What implications do these changes have for the local community, and for coastal management practices?

Marine ecosystems

See ch 7, Environmental management (P169).

Growth in CO_2 concentrations is increasing the acidity of the world's oceans. There has already been a decrease in the pH by 0.1 units since 1750, with projections from the IPCC (2007) estimating a continued reduction in pH of between 0.14 and 0.35 units in the next 100 years. This acidification of the oceans has major implications for marine life, particularly species highly sensitive to their environment, such as coral reefs. In 2005 the Royal Society produced a comprehensive report on the acidification of oceans due to CO_2 (*http://bit.ly/ocean_acidification*).

See ch 7, Environmental management (p171).

In marine systems, plankton and algae are responsible for one third of the Earth's primary production (conversion of solar energy and carbon from the atmosphere into biomass) (UK Biodiversity Partnership, 2007). Plankton are sensitive to light levels and turbulence in the ocean water, both of which are affected by changes in the climate. As plankton forms a highly important basis of the marine food chain, so the impacts are felt right through the food chain, through fish and higher mammals, and potentially as far as humans via the fishing industry with changing fish distributions. Therefore, every aspect of the marine system is being affected by variations in the global climate.

Human health

See Volume 1: Human Geography, ch 9, Geographies of health and environment (p185).

Some greenhouse gases that contribute to climate change are also directly linked to human health. For example, ozone is vitally important in certain parts of the atmosphere for the functioning of the climate system, but it is a respiratory irritant, and is frequently recorded in urban areas, with aerosols found in particulate matter contributing to respiratory and cardiovascular disease (Met Office, 2008). In addition, it is anticipated that there will be an increase in allergenic pollen in northern latitudes with significant consequences for allergy sufferers (IPCC, 2007).

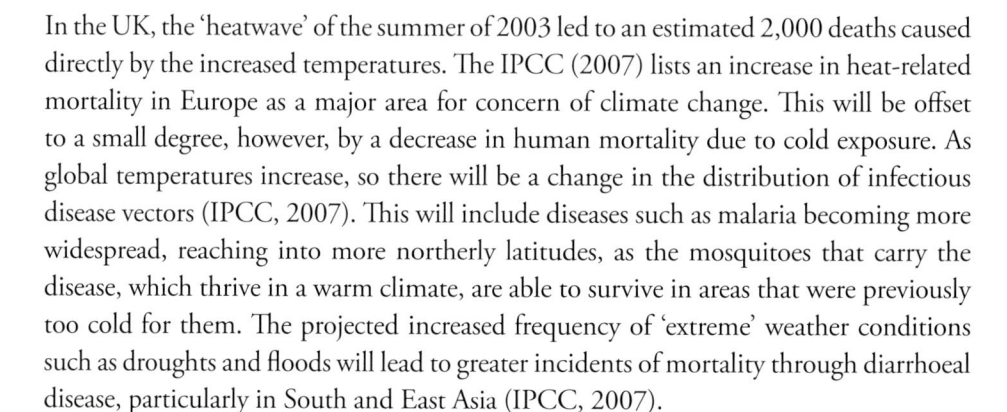

In the UK, the 'heatwave' of the summer of 2003 led to an estimated 2,000 deaths caused directly by the increased temperatures. The IPCC (2007) lists an increase in heat-related mortality in Europe as a major area for concern of climate change. This will be offset to a small degree, however, by a decrease in human mortality due to cold exposure. As global temperatures increase, so there will be a change in the distribution of infectious disease vectors (IPCC, 2007). This will include diseases such as malaria becoming more widespread, reaching into more northerly latitudes, as the mosquitoes that carry the disease, which thrive in a warm climate, are able to survive in areas that were previously too cold for them. The projected increased frequency of 'extreme' weather conditions such as droughts and floods will lead to greater incidents of mortality through diarrhoeal disease, particularly in South and East Asia (IPCC, 2007).

> **Teaching resources**
>
> A good source of information regarding the impacts of climate change on human health is the 2008 publication by the UK Department of Health, *Health Effects of Climate Change in the UK 2008*, which can be accessed at *http://bit.ly/ ClimateChangeHealthEffects*. This document outlines the health impacts related to waterborne diseases from flooding, impacts of drought, the direct effects of increased UK temperatures, health effects of UV light levels, vector-borne disease and increased disease occurrence, such as food poisoning.

Water availability

For many animal and plant species, including humans, freshwater is fundamental to survival. However, with climate change, the availability of freshwater will come increasingly under threat. Rising sea levels will result in increased occurrences of saline (seawater) intrusion into freshwater areas. In addition, increasing temperatures will lead to less river run-off, reducing the amount of water within river systems. A reduction in freshwater has implications for agricultural crop yields, which may already be under strain (see *Agriculture and food supply* on p74).

With reduced supplies of water, any available resources will be placed under increasing stress for other uses, resulting in less clean drinking water being available. It is highly likely that this will lead to a significant increase in disease spread via unclean water and poor sanitation in those countries of the world least able to afford to introduce preventative measures.

Policies relating to water resources in regions such as the US and northern Europe will require significant adaptation to enable decreasing resources to be utilised for essential requirements. It is likely that alternative options will need to be employed for non-essential use, for example the use of greywater[2] recycling for watering gardens.

How can human-induced changes be stabilised?

Internationally

The United Nations Framework Convention on Climate Change (UNFCCC) was agreed at the United Nations Conference on Environment and Development (commonly called the 'Rio Conference') in 1992, and came into force in 1994 as a result of increasing recognition of human-induced climate change. The main objective of the treaty was to control greenhouse gas emissions. In 1997 a protocol to the treaty (known as the 'Kyoto Protocol') was adopted, whereby many developed countries agreed to a legally binding commitment to reduce their emissions of certain greenhouse gases. More information can be found at: *http://unfccc.int/essential_ background/items/2877.php*

The Intergovernmental Panel on Climate Change (IPCC) is one of the most widely cited and respected authorities on climate change. It is a scientifically based, multi-governmental body, organised originally by the United Nations to investigate and evaluate the impacts of climate change. This is done via the analysis of scientific reports and publications. Subsequently, the IPCC has published a series of 'Assessment Reports' on the risks from climate change based upon the latest scientific understanding. The first IPCC report was published in 1990, with subsequent reports published in 1995, 2001 and 2007. A fifth report is planned for 2014.

The Copenhagen Climate Change Summit (referred to as COP15) was convened by the United Nations in December 2009, and was aimed at setting CO_2 emission reduction targets and encouraging decarbonisation and/or the adoption of low carbon technologies. The summit was intended to develop further the aspirations of the Kyoto Protocol by establishing politically firmer, more definite targets for reducing emissions, while drawing in a greater number of countries. The outcomes of the summit were mixed. Positive responses reflected the acceptance of the need for action to stem the effects of human activities on the climate, while negative comment was made about the absence of legally binding targets to reduce greenhouse gas emissions. Concerns are now being expressed that the lack of definite targets and plans for future reductions in emissions will allow climate change to continue to dangerous levels. The outcome of the conference was the 'Copenhagen Accord', with the main agreement by many countries (but not all) being to try to keep increases in temperature to a maximum of 2°C higher than pre-industrial level. The summit confirmed that climate change is now very much on the agenda for political issues, and generated unprecedented media coverage to the 'general public'. In addition, a Green Climate Fund will be established to provide financial assistance to developing countries.

Much of the adaptation by humans will be forced by the problems created by climate change. Such scenarios include adapting to declining food crop production and reduced availability of fresh water. The capacity of a community to adapt is highly variable across the globe. In general terms, more economically developed countries (MEDCs) are in a stronger position to adapt. They have access to the necessary technologies and capital available to invest, along with the necessary infrastructure and communications to raise awareness. However, in less developed areas of the world, the ability to adapt is far less straightforward. Even if the desire is there, the means to do so may not be available. There may be no alternative technologies for water usage, or there may be no higher ground on which to move a community. In such cases, the issues relating to climate change are going to have a much bigger impact on these societies.

United Kingdom

Even if major reductions in the amount of CO_2 emissions are made straight away, there will still be inevitable temperature increases for at least the next 30 years, as a result of the CO_2 that has already been released remaining in the atmosphere, and the time it will take the climate to respond. To keep temperature increases to the lowest possible levels, CO_2 emissions need to be reduced dramatically immediately. The Met Office calculates that if emissions can be reduced by 3% per year, then temperatures will rise by 1.7°C by 2050, and by 2°C by 2100 (Met Office, 2008).

Local authorities are being encouraged to take the 'political' lead in adapting to climate change. In recognition of this, the UK Department for Environment, Food and Rural Affairs (Defra) established the National Indicator 188 (NI188) Adapting to Climate Change performance indicator. Each local authority reports annually on its progress towards NI188. The indicator has four levels, ranging from the basic recognition of priority areas for adaptation, through to maintaining an adaptation action plan. Also at a local level, and as a means of authorities achieving the first stage of NI188, the UK Climate Impacts Programme (UKCIP) has developed the Local Climates Impact Profile (LCLIP), designed to help authorities assess their local climate impacts (UKCIP, 2009) (*www.ukcip.org.uk/images/stories/LCLIP/LCLIP_guidance.pdf*). High-profile examples of the development of local authority strategies include the 'Low Carbon London' project (*www.lowcarboneconomy.com*).

> **Teaching idea 3.4**
>
> Ask students to investigate the approach of their own local authority towards NI188. Do they agree with the authority's approach or can they suggest alternative strategies that might be pursued in their local area?

Under the Climate Change Act, the UK is required to produce an Adaptation Programme by 2012. The Adapting to Climate Change Programme is being coordinated by Defra. This aims to raise awareness of climate change and its effects across all sectors of the public, and to develop a sound evidence base of the impacts that climate change will have. In the longer term, it will provide a means of encouraging and monitoring adaptation to inevitable climate change (*www.defra.gov.uk/environment/climate/programme/index.htm*).

> **Teaching resources**
>
> The UK Climate Projections (UKCP09) have prepared a range of resources, including maps and graphs of the impacts of climate change across the UK, depending upon different emissions scenarios. These can be accessed at: *http://ukclimateprojections.defra.gov.uk/content/view/865/521*

A key strategy in mitigating the impact of climate change, and in reducing the causal factors such as CO_2 emissions, will be that the underlying principles of emissions reduction need to become integrated in all new policy and regulation development. Climate change cannot be a stand-alone issue – its implications are global and affect every aspect of life.

> **Teaching idea 3.5**
>
> Ask students to brainstorm ways of reducing emissions in order to mitigate the effects of climate change. This might be done at two levels; firstly, 'painless' reductions which do not have a significant impact on lifestyle, such as switching off a light bulb; and secondly, reductions that will require changes in lifestyle. What changes in lifestyle may have to happen to reduce emissions?

Summary

The fact that climate change is a reality is now accepted almost universally. The debate is centred on the degree to which changes are due to human activities, and increasingly, how the changes can be minimised by human influence, to reduce the impacts on global societies and the natural environment. The phenomenon of climate change cannot be considered as a unique issue. It needs to be considered as an over-arching theme in every area of human activities, particularly in government policy. This acceptance was demonstrated globally during the Copenhagen Summit in December 2009. Increasingly, the acceptance of some degree of impact from climate change is being acknowledged, with discussion developing around the concept of 'adaptation' by societies to climate changes.

Endnotes

1. Water molecules are made up of oxygen and hydrogen atoms. Oxygen has three naturally occurring stable isotopes, hydrogen has two. As water molecules evaporate, the lighter versions of the isotopes evaporate before the heavier isotopes (which contain more neutrons) due to the latter having a lower vapour pressure. So, when the air subsequently cools, the molecules condense out in reverse order, heavier molecules first. It therefore requires much more cooling to take place for the lighter molecules to condense out and fall as precipitation. Hence a greater concentration of heavier molecules is associated with warmer temperatures.

2. Greywater is the term used to describe water that originates from domestic activities, such as dishwashing and bathing. It is water that is not drinkable but does not have the high concentrations of toxins that would be expected in sewage.

Useful websites

Climate resources for teaching in the classroom:

www.climate4classrooms.org – teaching resources from the Royal Meteorological Society.

www.metlink.org – further resources from the Royal Meteorological Society.

www.yourclimateyourlife.org.uk – teaching resources from the Royal Geographical Society.

The Intergovernmental Panel on Climate Change. An excellent, scientifically reasoned, clear explanation of the current understanding of the impacts and future scenarios for climate change. If you download just one document, make it this one!
www.ipcc.ch/pdf/assessment-report/ar4/syr/ar4_syr_spm.pdf

The UK Meteorological Office (Met Office) is a leading voice in the debate about climate change, and into the research behind it: *www.metoffice.gov.uk*

Met Office Hadley Centre (2005) *Climate Change and the Greenhouse Effect*. Available to download at: *www.metoffice.gov.uk/publications/brochures/2005/climate_greenhouse.pdf*

Met Office (2008) *Avoiding Dangerous Climate Change*. Available to download at: *www.metoffice.gov.uk/publications/brochures/cop14.pdf*

Met Office (2009) *Warming: Climate change – the facts*. Available to download at: *www.metoffice.gov.uk/climatechange/guide/downloads/quick_guide.pdf*

Government and policy resources

The UK government's Department of Energy and Climate Change (DECC) is responsible for developing UK policy on energy usage: *www.decc.gov.uk*

The UK government's Department for Environment, Food and Rural Affairs: *www.defra.gov.uk*

Adaptation

Act on CO_2 is a UK government-led initiative to encourage changes in daily life to reduce CO_2 emissons: *www.direct.gov.uk/actonco2*

The Commission for Architecture and the Built Environment has produced a downloadable guide to holding a 'Green Day' in your school. The leaflet provides many teaching ideas around the subject of climate change: *www.cabe.org.uk/files/green-day-second-edition.pdf*

Environment

The Permanent Service for Mean Sea Level (PSMSL), based at the National Oceanographic Centre in Liverpool, England, has been responsible for the collection, analysis and interpretation of data from a network of several hundred tide gauges around the world and has been operating since 1933. Archives of data are available from the PSMSL at: *www.psmsl.org/data/*

Hundreds of excellent images of all aspects of coral reefs from around the world are available to download at: *www.photolib.noaa.gov/reef/index.html*

Climate Change and Marine Ecosystems: Eur-Oceans is a programme of collaborative work between European aquaria and multi-disciplinary scientists with the aim of raising awareness of the impacts of climate change on the marine environment: *www.eur-oceans.info/EN/home/index.php*

Royal Society (2008) *Climate Change Controversies: A simple guide*. The Royal Society, London. Available to download at: *http://bit.ly/ClimateChangeControversies*

Energy

Charles Rawding

Introduction

Over the past 20 years, global energy production has grown at a staggering rate. The world economy currently produces about 12 billion oil equivalent tonnes of primary energy annually, a 30% increase over 1990 figures. By 2030, it is estimated that primary energy supply should have grown by another 50%, largely driven by increasing energy consumption in the rapidly industrialising countries of the developing world, such as India and China. Of this supply, 80% currently comes from fossil fuels (Garcier, 2009: 198).

The provision of adequate and appropriate sources of energy is likely to be one of the most important environmental considerations for policy makers in the coming years. Concerns over the effects of fossil fuels on greenhouse gas emissions and climate change, when combined with worries over dependence upon energy supplies from countries that are regarded as politically unreliable, will ensure that energy remains at the top of the policy agenda for governments in the developed world. By 2020, the UK will be importing the majority of its gas and more than half of its oil.

It is important to realise that energy dependency has very wide-ranging implications. For instance, the modern food chain [☞], from the production of fertiliser through to the preparation of food, is highly dependent on energy, mostly from fossil fuels. The shift from carbon-based energy sources that is required to tackle climate change [☞] will be a major challenge to current food systems.

See ch 5, Food supply (p109).
See ch 3, Climate change.

Historical geographies of energy

A brief glance at school textbooks from the 1970s shows just how dramatically the topic of energy has changed. If we take the best-selling *A Course in World Geography* (Young and Lowry, 5th Ed, 1979), the discussion focuses almost exclusively on fossil fuels, detailing the changing fortunes of the British coal mining industry, the discovery of oil and gas in the North Sea and the importation of oil and gas, principally from the Middle East. Nuclear power and hydroelectricity are mentioned only briefly (with no discussion of the environmental issues surrounding these two sources), while there is no mention of biofuels or other alternative sources of energy. Nor is there any discussion of the effects of carbon emissions in the atmosphere. Indeed, the use of petroleum in transport is discussed without any reference to environmental issues.

Over the past 30 years, there have been shifts in perceptions of energy production and consumption. In the case of the nuclear industry, the disasters of Three Mile Island (1979) and Chernobyl (1986) led to widespread disenchantment with the potential of nuclear power. However, the realisation that the nuclear industry does offer the prospect of reduced carbon emissions has led to some reconsideration of the future role of nuclear power stations (see p93). Interestingly, the 1979 O Level textbook warns students that the map of UK production may well be out of date by the time they see it; a caveat that can be applied equally today to almost any considerations of energy production and consumption.

The current situation

> **Point for consideration**
>
> Per head of population, the UK (followed by the USA and Germany) has put more CO_2 into the atmosphere than any other country. Are we in a position to tell China or India that they cannot burn coal?

Current policy initiatives are focused on the seemingly irreconcilable priorities of sustaining growth while reducing emissions. As such, the focus has shifted towards improving vehicle efficiency (through a shift to a taxation system based on the levels of pollutants emitted) and developing fuels that might be considered carbon-neutral. In many ways, patterns of energy production and consumption have been governed by the prevailing market price (or level of subsidy) for different methods of production, which on the one hand has enabled governments (through taxation and subsidy) to influence energy markets, but on the other hand has also resulted in consumer resistance to higher prices (as with the failed fuel price escalator, which was effectively dropped after the UK fuel protests in 2000).

Energy production from fossil fuels

Fossil fuels – coal, oil and gas – meet about four-fifths of the world's energy needs today (figure 4.1). The International Energy Agency expects that this proportion will only drop to about two-thirds of the world's energy by 2030. Countries such as China, India and Russia have large remaining reserves.

Figure 4.1:
World energy production by source, 2006

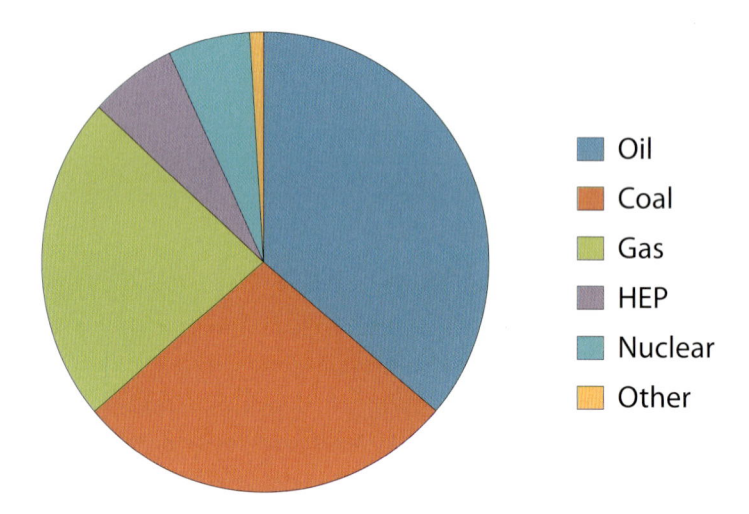

See accompanying CD-Rom

World energy production.ppt

Legend: Oil, Coal, Gas, HEP, Nuclear, Other

Source: data from US Energy Information Service at *www.eia.doe.gov/iea/overview.html*

Coal

See Introduction (p1).

Coal is the world's major source of electricity, generating 41% of the world's power supply. Even in technologically advanced nations such as the USA, coal provides almost half of all electricity generated. In the case of China, 80% of its energy comes from coal. China is now the world's largest emitter of CO_2. However, per capita [🔑], the Chinese emit less than half the amount that Britons do, and a quarter that of Americans (Bromilow, 2009: 219). Indeed, it has been pointed out that in the richest nations of the world, people have the equivalent of 100 servants working for them, thanks to the use of oil, gas and electricity (*Financial Times*, 4 November 2009)!

Coal poses special environmental problems. It is a dirty fuel that not only adds to the accumulation of greenhouse gases in the atmosphere, but also pollutes the world's oceans and streams with mercury, arsenic and other dangerous chemicals. It also releases pollutants that cause acid rain. In addition, it is a much less efficient fuel than gas or oil, producing less heat and therefore requiring greater amounts to produce equivalent levels of energy. Having said this, coal, at a global level, remains plentiful and relatively cheap. Supplies are expected to last for hundreds of years, while oil and gas are likely to run out during this century. Indeed, although the British mining industry is a mere shadow of its former self, it is still estimated that Britain has more than 100 years of coal supply yet to be mined (figure 4.2). The largest mining group in the UK is UK Coal, which currently has five deep mines in northern and central England. In 2009, the company produced 6.2 million tonnes of coal from its deep mines and 1.4 million tonnes from its surface operations.

Figure 4.2:
UK Coal – deep mines

See accompanying CD-Rom

UK Coal.doc

Daw Mill in Arley, near Coventry in the West Midlands, is the single largest coal-producing mine in the UK, mining a five-metre thick section of the Warwickshire Thick seam some 750 metres below the ground. The present mine shafts, 558 metres and 556 metres deep, were sunk between 1957 and 1959 and 1969 and 1971 respectively. The company expects to be able to continue to mine coal at Daw Mill by accessing further resources until 2028.

Kellingley, located at Knottingley, Yorkshire, is the largest remaining deep mine in Yorkshire. Production began in April 1965. Kellingley's two main shafts are each almost 800 metres deep. Kellingley supplies local power stations and also produces some housecoal quality coal (larger sized coals of higher calorific value for use on, for example, open fires and stoves). Mining of the new Beeston Seam is expected to start during 2010. This reserve is expected to extend the life of the mine until at least 2015. Further reserves are also expected to be accessible in the Silkstone Seam thereafter, which will extend the life of the mine to 2019.

Thoresby, Edwinstowe, Nottinghamshire dates back to 1925. Linked underground with the neighbouring Welbeck colliery, the group's intention is for Thoresby to concentrate production in a new area of reserves in the Deep Soft seam at approximately 750 metres below ground. Mining at the Parkgate seams at the Thoresby mine has suffered from poor mining conditions with the main problem being interference from previous mine workings undertaken approximately 120 metres above the current mining area. However, increased preparatory work and mine replanning have allowed the group to access the final face in the Parkgate seam, which was expected to be concluded by March 2010. Mining was then to commence at the Deep Soft Seam, which is being accessed as part of the investment programme costing approximately £55 million, which is expected to extend the life of the mine to 2017.

Welbeck, Meden Vale, Mansfield, Nottinghamshire, dates back to 1912, when two shafts were sunk to 635 metres below ground. The Welbeck colliery is planned to cease operations in the first quarter of 2010, after the last of its current reserves capable of economic exploitation has been mined.

Harworth Colliery, Bassetlaw, Nottinghamshire. Currently closed but being maintained with the possibility of future reopening to extract an estimated 54 million tonnes of resources.

Source: adapted from *www.ukcoal.com*

In addition to its deep mines, the company operates a number of surface mines. In these instances, operations take place over a much shorter period of time and involve restoration of the landscape [☞] at the end of the project (see figure 4.3 on p88).

See ch 7, Environmental management (p177).

Location	Dates	Size of mine (hectares)	Amount of coal (tonnes)	Planned restoration
Steadsburn	2007-11	69	350,000	Significant new woodlands, species-rich hay meadows, water bodies and high quality arable agricultural land.
Lodge House	2008-12	122	1,000,000	A significantly diverse wildlife habitat area compared to that which currently occupies the site. The restoration scheme will generate new areas of woodland, species-rich hay meadows, wetland habitats, as well as vastly improved and increased public access. It will also make improvements to some poor quality, post-war land restoration.
Cutacre	2006-10	322	900,000	The creation of over 100 hectares of amenity woodland and wetlands as well as an area for industrial development.
Long Moor	2007-11	70	750,000	A mixture of agricultural land, mixed deciduous woodland, wet carr woodland, species-rich hay meadow, reed beds and an area of open water.

Source: www.ukcoal.com/sm-restoration-sites

Figure 4.3:
UK Coal – surface mines

See accompanying CD-Rom

UK Coal.doc

Teaching idea 4.1

Ask students to investigate a local deep or surface mine operation. This might be in the form of an historical study of previous industry or an environmental assessment of current activities. What impacts have the operations had on the local area? (Information on current mining activities is available at *www.ukcoal.com*)

Oil production

Future levels of oil production and consumption are likely to have a massive impact on both the global economy and global political activity. Currently, concerns regarding security of supply are being heightened by a combination of fears over future levels of oil production as 'peak oil' (see p91) is reached, while the political instability of major suppliers, particularly in Central Asia and the Middle East, is a significant concern to Western politicians at a time when China is expanding its links with Asian producers, as it strives to find appropriate supplies for its rapidly growing demands, both for industrial production and for transport (see figure 4.4 on p89). China's use of energy doubled between 1990 and 2006 and is expected to double again by 2025.

Teaching idea 4.2

Ask individual students to investigate energy production within one of the countries supplying China that are shown in figure 4.4. Students can then present their findings to the rest of the group. What similarities and differences are identified between countries?

The exploitation of fossil fuel reserves, particularly oil and gas, is heavily dependent on the prevailing price of oil. The most easily accessible resources have already been developed, leaving more expensive and risky developments to be exploited. A collapse in oil prices from US$147 per barrel in July 2008 to only US$40 in February 2009 highlights the problems facing the industry when planning its longer-term investments (see figure 4.5 on p89). The Falkland Islands provide a good example of the influence of oil prices on exploration. Geological surveys suggest there could be up to 60 billion barrels beneath the seabed around the islands. During 2010, four companies (Desire Petroleum, Rockhopper, BHP Billiton and Falkland Oil and Gas) plan to drill in the North Falkland basin. This will be the first drilling in Falkland waters since Shell suspended exploration in 1998 after oil prices slumped to US$12 a barrel (*The Guardian*, 7 Feb 2010).

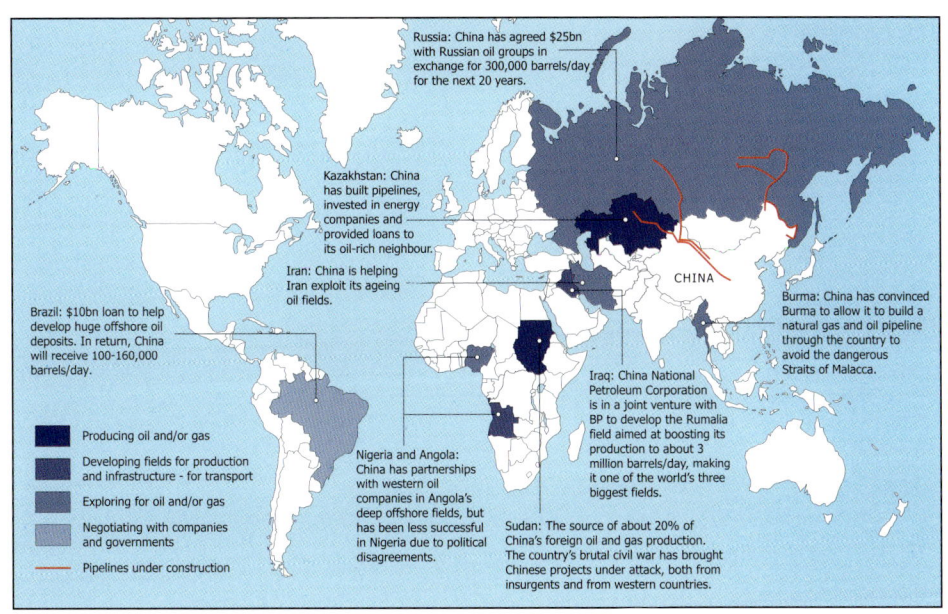

Figure 4.4: Chinese oil links

See accompanying CD-Rom

Chinese oil links.ppt

Source: adapted from *Financial Times*, 4 November 2009. Drawn by Ann Chapman.

Figure 4.5: Variations in world oil prices, 1987-2009

See accompanying CD-Rom

Oil price.ppt

Source: adapted from wikimedia.org.

Teaching idea 4.3

Ask students to investigate an oil producer through its website. What exploration is currently being undertaken? What plans does the company have for the near future? Where is most of their current production occurring? An example of a small-scale company which operates a range of fields, including Lincolnshire, UK, is Europa Oil & Gas (*www.europaoil.com*).

Oil prices are vulnerable to a range of factors, such as market demand and levels of supply. For instance, the Gulf of Mexico supplies 2% of the world's crude oil, and the damage caused to its oil refineries by Hurricane Katrina in 2005 slowed production. This slowdown resulted in crude oil prices jumping to more than US$70 a barrel (UNEP, 2007).

Oil can also be produced from tar sands. Large-scale developments have been undertaken in northern Alberta, Canada, where there are estimated reserves of 173 billion barrels of oil. However, the extraction of oil can only be achieved with expensive filtering technology. It is estimated that the oil price needs to remain above US$80 per barrel to enable the Canadian deposits to be sufficiently profitable for continued investment to take place. While these tar sand developments have produced boom towns in northern Canada (figure 4.6), they have also had environmental consequences. Vast quantities of water are needed to produce the steam used to extract deep oil sands deposits. The upgraders that turn the tar sands into crude oil produce significant levels of greenhouse gases, while the nine new upgraders planned for the region will consume ten times as much water as the 750,000 residents of Edmonton, the capital of Alberta. At the same time, the landscape has become pock-marked with unsightly open-pit mines, which have also resulted in environmental disasters such as the poisoning of 1,600 ducks that landed in a waste pond of bitumen and muck.

Figure 4.6:
Fort McMurray and the Canadian oil rush

See accompanying CD-Rom

Fort McMurray.doc

Fort McMurray has grown from an isolated community in a wooded valley to a city almost overnight. Population has been rising at 9% per annum as oil companies have moved in to tap the oil sands. Its current population is 65,000 people, but the rapid growth of the city has caused a range of problems. Average house prices are £437,000 despite a very difficult climate (average January temperatures peak at -15°C). Sewage treatment, schools, parks and transport are stretched. Major traffic jams occur on the main road to Edmonton, the provincial capital of Alberta, while the two-lane road is being upgraded. In many ways the town resembles the gold prospecting towns of the US and Canada in the 19th century. A transient population of 20,000, mostly men, live in out-of-town work camps and come into town to eat, drink, gamble and shop, but few are intending to stay for any length of time. On the other hand, the high wages mean that there is plenty of money coming into the town, enabling the development of social services and provisions.

Source: adapted from 'Tar boom hits a sticky patch' *The Guardian*, 7 February 2009.

Teaching idea 4.4

Ask students to study the extract in figure 4.6 and to investigate the development of Fort McMurray in more detail using online information. What effects does the exploitation of energy resources have on the economic development of a region?

See ch 8, Globalisation (p193).

The issue of tar sands exploitation has become much more high profile in recent times with groups such as Friends of the Earth campaigning against their exploitation. Pressure is now being exerted on corporations such as Shell and BP to review their activities. In this instance, pressure is being brought to bear through the objections of pension fund investors at shareholders' meetings, an interesting example of the globalisation of environmental activism [✍] (see *www.countingthecost.org.uk* for this campaign).

Peak oil?

The term 'peak oil' refers to the high point of oil output prior to stocks becoming steadily depleted. While the actual date at which peak oil will occur is hotly debated, it is clear that large new finds will be needed at a time when other major production areas such as the Gulf of Mexico, the Middle East and the North Sea are beginning to run dry, while new fields such as the Tiber field in the Gulf of Mexico (BP) and the Santos Basin of Brazil (BG) are in much deeper water and therefore will be much more expensive to exploit. Other possible areas for exploitation are in environmentally sensitive areas such as the Barents Sea off Norway and the waters around Alaska.

The drop in oil demand due to the world economic downturn, combined with recent discoveries of new deposits in Brazil, the USA and West Africa, have reduced fears that the world is running out of oil. However, at an economic level, there is a very real risk that prices will rise dramatically again when demand outstrips supply (as occurred in summer 2008 when oil prices reached US$147 per barrel). However, renewed economic growth and the increasing demands of China and India suggest that unless the most optimistic projections for future oil production are met, then oil prices will rise significantly with potentially severe consequences for the global economy.

At the same time, as we saw in chapter 3, the burning of fossil fuels has resulted in steadily increasing concentrations of greenhouse gases in the atmosphere (figure 4.7). The unprecedented recent rise in concentrations of CO_2 has resulted in a current level of 380 parts per million (ppm), much higher than the pre-industrial (18th century) level of 280ppm. Since 1987, annual global emissions of CO_2 from fossil fuel combustion have risen by about one-third, and the present per capita emissions clearly illustrate large differences between regions (see figure 4.8 on p92).

In the context of well-founded fears over rising future energy prices, questions of reliability over the security of supply for future energy needs, and a host of undesirable environmental impacts, it becomes clear why policy initiatives are focusing on alternatives to oil.

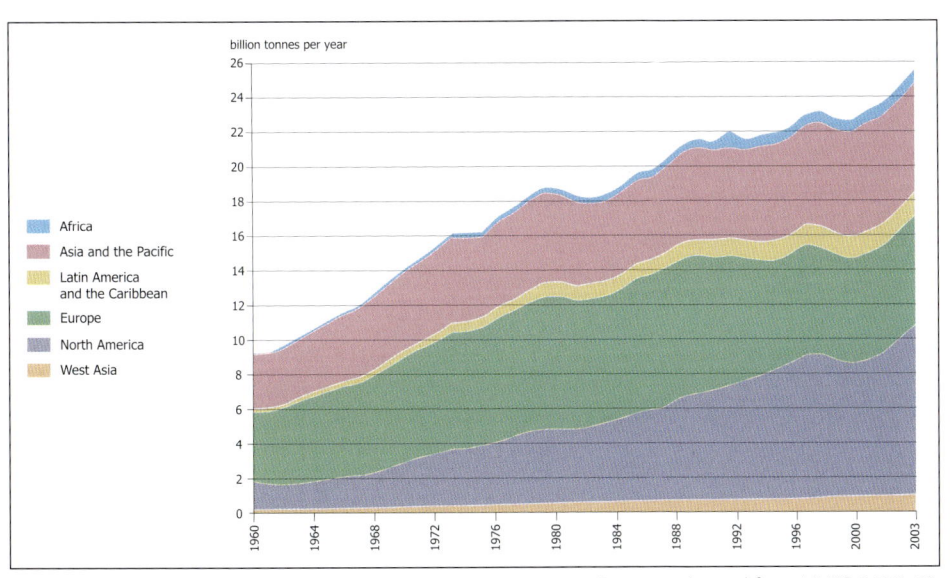

Figure 4.7:
CO_2 emissions from fossil fuels

CO_2 emissions.ppt

Source: adapted from UNEP, 2007: 60.

Figure 4.8:
Per capita CO₂ emissions

CO₂ emissions.ppt

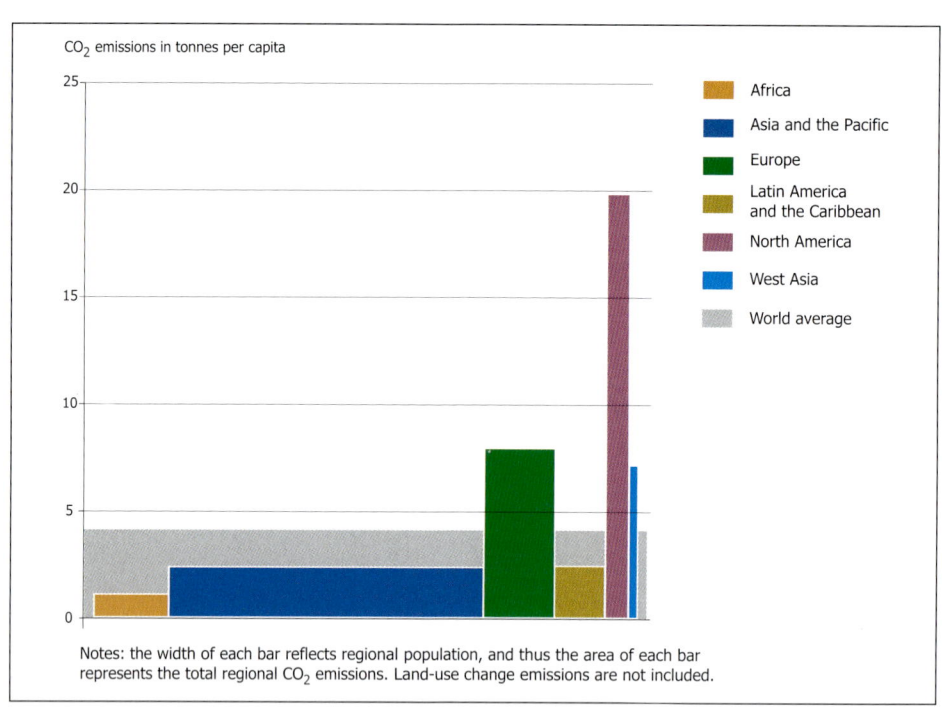

CO₂ emissions in tonnes per capita

Legend: Africa; Asia and the Pacific; Europe; Latin America and the Caribbean; North America; West Asia; World average

Notes: the width of each bar reflects regional population, and thus the area of each bar represents the total regional CO₂ emissions. Land-use change emissions are not included.

Source: adapted from UNEP, 2007: 61.

Energy from wood and deforestation

The burning of wood is broadly carbon-neutral, since the carbon consumed by the tree during growth is returned to the atmosphere through burning. Where the wood being burnt is being replaced by new woodland in a sustainable fashion, a chemical balance can be maintained (although, of course, the timber may have to be transported from its place of production to its location for consumption).

Deforestation, on the other hand, is thought to account for 18% of global greenhouse gas emissions. Deforestation is a major issue in many less economically developed countries (LEDCs), which retain significant amounts of their original forest cover. Increasing population pressures in countries such as Tanzania have resulted in serious environmental degradation. Between 1970 and 1998, Tanzania lost 24 million acres of national forest, and subsequent attempts to reduce environmental damage in forest areas and reinstate woodlands have met with limited success.

Carbon capture and storage (CCS) and decarbonisation

Carbon capture and storage is the process by which carbon dioxide is extracted from fossil fuels before it reaches the atmosphere and is then stored safely to help offset the build-up of CO_2 in the atmosphere. There are three main techniques that have been developed: *pre-combustion capture*, where coal particles are mixed with steam to produce hydrogen and carbon dioxide, with the hydrogen being burned to drive turbines and the carbon dioxide buried; *post-combustion capture*, where the coal is burned normally and the carbon dioxide produced is then extracted and stored; and *oxy-fuel combination*, where the coal is burned in pure oxygen, triggering high temperature reactions that produce fewer polluting by-products.

There have been objections to the storage of carbon in locations close to residential areas, and it is probable that future storage is more likely to occur in depleted underwater oil and gas fields where leakage cannot affect towns and cities. An example of such storage in practice is the Sleipner East platform in the North Sea, where a million tonnes of carbon dioxide a year have been pumped into an old gas field over the last decade. It is the world's longest-running carbon storage experiment. If the technology can be adopted successfully on a wide scale, then there is a possibility that the world can continue to burn fossil fuels without creating dangerous levels of emissions. Pumping gas into depleted oil fields also helps to push out the last reserves of oil (ironically, adding to greenhouse gases but also assisting the cost-effectiveness of the practice). However, we are still some way from being able to demonstrate carbon capture technology that is pursuable on a commercial scale. For instance, the fitting of carbon capture technology currently makes power stations twice as costly to build as conventional plants.

> **Point for consideration**
> How can developed countries that experienced extensive deforestation during the Industrial Revolution expect LEDCs to respond differently to pressures for development and resource extraction?

Decarbonisation is the progressive reduction of the proportions of energy generated by fossil fuels. This process is likely to continue in the future as energy production is switched to electricity generated from a range of less environmentally damaging sources. It is much easier to cut carbon dioxide emissions from power generation than from transport fuels. Indeed, the European Union's leading power companies have set themselves the goal of making their electricity carbon-free by 2050 by using a mix of renewable, such as wind and solar power, nuclear power stations and coal and gas-fired plants that capture carbon dioxide.

Carbon-neutral energy production

There is a strong political will to shift towards alternatives to carbon-based energies. Renewable energy must account for 20% of Europe's energy usage by 2020, according to EU targets, while China is committed to generating 15% of its energy from low carbon sources by that date. Most American states have goals for renewable energy production. Currently, about 18% of world energy production comes from renewable sources. However, 15% is provided by large hydroelectric dams. Future provision of such dams is highly restricted by the lack of suitable locations for such installations.

Opposition to renewable energy comes from a range of sources. Countries with large fossil fuel reserves, such as Russia and Saudi Arabia, have tended to side with oil and coal companies, although in both cases stances have been softening as the evidence for climate change strengthens. In developed countries, 'nimbyism' can also be a problem, where people may protest against the installation of wind farms and solar plants on aesthetic grounds.

Carbon footprints

In simple terms, a carbon footprint [☞] is the total set of greenhouse gases emitted by an organisation, event or individual. Increasingly, large organisations and government bodies have begun to address this issue. For instance, the Carbon Trust (see p94) has worked with UK manufacturers on a range of products, introducing a CO_2 label in March 2007. The label is intended to comply with a new British public available specification (ie not a standard), PAS 2050. The intention here is to develop a holistic approach to the issue of carbon footprints. While much media attention has focused

See ch 5, Food supply (p124).

See Volume 2: Physical Geography, ch 5, Ice (p138).

on emissions from transport, it is also necessary to consider industrial production. Manufacturing industry is responsible for 25% of total UK CO_2 emissions, largely through energy use in the manufacturing process. For instance, aggregates [💿], animal feeds and plastic bottle manufacturing together produce 3.62 million tonnes of CO_2 annually. In the case of aggregates, over one-third of emissions relate to the transport of aggregates from the quarry to the construction site, while one-quarter comes from asphalt manufacture (figure 4.9).

Figure 4.9: Carbon trust accelerator findings and the aggregates industry

See accompanying CD-Rom

Carbon trust.doc

> There are 1,300 quarries in the UK producing £3 billion of aggregate products every year. The industry produces 2.6 million tonnes of CO_2 accounting for about 1.7% of UK industry carbon emissions.
>
> - Transport accounts for 35% of CO_2 emissions.
> - Asphalt production is responsible for 25% of emissions.
>
> Proposals:
>
> - To develop a market for lower temperature mixed asphalt – which could save 80% of the energy required for a traditional hot asphalt mix.
> - Heat recovery – 12% of the input energy is wasted on relatively low-grade heat which can also contain polluting particulates.
> - Advanced burner controls on the asphalt plant.
> - The use of low carbon vehicles in the quarry environment.

Source: The Carbon Trust. *The Observer*, 22 November 2009.

See ch 5, Food supply, figure 5.15.

As the government drives the UK towards decarbonisation, industry will have to cut back emissions by 21% by 2022, reducing the carbon footprint of everything, from the roads we drive on to the pint of milk we buy. Such practices are now spreading, as with the decision by Tesco [💿] in summer 2009 to begin adding carbon footprint information to its dairy products.

> **Teaching idea 4.5**
>
> Ask students to calculate their carbon footprint. There are several online ways of doing this (see for instance: www.carbonfootprint.com). Having calculated their carbon footprint, ask them to identify ways in which they might reduce it.

Nuclear power

Nuclear power provides about 15% of the world's electricity and about 6% of world energy production. Following several decades of uncertainty, after the nuclear disasters mentioned at the beginning of the chapter, the risk of nuclear disaster seems to have receded, and nuclear power appears more attractive as policy makers aim to tackle the dangers of climate change. However, this does not mean that the safety issues relating to nuclear power have gone away (see figure 4.10 on p95).

In 2009, 50 new nuclear reactors were being built, and 60 more were in an advanced state of planning, adding to the 436 existing reactors worldwide. The country with the most ambitious plans for nuclear expansion is China; of the 50 new reactors under

Figure 4.10: Sheep farming and Chernobyl

On 26 April 1986, an accident at the Chernobyl nuclear power complex in the Ukraine led to an explosion that released a plume of radioactive smoke into the atmosphere. Subsequent heavy rain released high concentrations of caesium-137 from this cloud, dropping radioactive fallout over many European countries, including parts of the UK. Instead of being 'locked' in soil, it was taken up by grass and plants in certain upland areas. Once sheep grazing on this land ate these plants, they became radioactive too. As a consequence, the government introduced tight restrictions on the sale and slaughter of affected sheep. These restrictions were expected to last for only a few months, but in 2004 they remained on 14 farms totalling 16,300 hectares in Scotland, 359 farms totalling 53,000 hectares in Wales, and 9 farms totalling 12,000 hectares in England. They are still required 'to ensure that no significant amounts of caesium-137 from Chernobyl enter the food chain'. In 2000, it was estimated that they may be needed for 'another 10 to 15 years', illustrating the length of time environmental damage can persist. While the restrictions have helped maintain public confidence in the affected meats, they had cost UK taxpayers around £13 million in compensation payments by 2003.

Source: Defra, 2006: 67.

See accompanying CD-Rom

Sheep farming and Chernobyl.doc

construction, 16 are in China. Many countries have revised their nuclear strategies, with the industry now being presented as an essential element of sustainable, carbon-free development, as well as being a rational and secure option to assist with growing energy demands. However, it is extremely difficult to calculate the actual cost of nuclear power, given that the very high initial costs of building nuclear power stations have to be combined with the decommissioning costs at the end of their life. Without support in the form of high carbon taxes on fossil fuels or government subsidies, the extent to which nuclear power can be considered an alternative to lower-cost alternative fuel sources remains a point for debate. At the same time, unlike other fuels, nuclear power is subject to far greater political scrutiny as a result of its dual use of uranium, for energy production and weapons manufacture. There is a clear political conflict between the desire to expand a supposedly 'clean' energy source, and an unwillingness to allow the dissemination of nuclear technologies because of the possible use of this technology for military purposes. The highly politicised nature of nuclear power means that in many countries its progress will be delayed.

Point for consideration

'If we want to curb greenhouse gas emissions by 50 to 80% by 2050, and we don't use nuclear power for base load electricity generation, what can we use instead?' (H Rogner, International Atomic Energy Agency, quoted in *Financial Times*, 8 September 2009).

Renewable energy

Hydroelectric power

Water has been used to generate electricity for more than a hundred years, and for centuries prior to that was used to turn waterwheels for industrial processes such as the grinding of corn. Worldwide, just over 20% of electricity generation is from hydroelectricity. The economic generation of hydroelectric power (HEP) requires locations with specific geographical attributes [☞]. It is estimated that about three-quarters of all such locations in Europe and North America have already been developed. However, huge potential remains, particularly in some areas of Asia and Africa. The proposed Grand Inga project in the Democratic Republic of Congo will restore an existing HEP plant and create a new, bigger dam with a total capacity of 40 gigawatts, making it the world's biggest hydroelectric project.

See Volume 2: Physical Geography, ch 5, Ice (p136).

In Norway, which is geographically ideal for the production of hydroelectric power, almost 100% of the nation's electricity comes from hydro. Approximately 85% of the electricity in Brazil is provided by hydroelectric power derived from its river systems. However, in the case of Brazil, in both 2001 and 2002, electricity had to be rationed after mismanagement and low rainfall exposed the danger of relying so heavily on one type of generation. There are currently two major HEP stations under construction on the Madeira River in the Amazon Basin, although neither has been without controversy, particularly in relation to environmental issues. The first plant, Santo Antonio, is expected to enter service in 2012.

See Volume 1: Human Geography, ch 4, Urban geographies (p95).

The generation of hydroelectricity has created both environmental and social concerns. For instance, the Three Gorges Dam in China, although it provided electricity for the first time for approximately 10 million people, resulted in the displacement of 1.5 million people with allegations of intimidation and violence. In similar vein, the Ilisu Dam project in Turkey will flood the ancient city of Hasankeyf and, according to human rights groups, displace tens of thousands of local Kurds.

Figure 4.11: The Hoover Dam

Hoover Dam.ppt

Other tensions and contradictions may be apparent as well where the provision of environmentally friendly energy occurs. In the case of the city of Las Vegas [👁], much of its electricity is drawn from the hydroelectricity produced by the Hoover Dam (figure 4.11). Vegas consumes vast amounts of electricity, most obviously through the array of neon that makes the Strip so distinctive. However, overconsumption of water from behind the dam, triggered by huge increases in population in the area, means that, at current rates, by 2017, the water levels will have fallen to the point where HEP production becomes problematic. As a result of the security situation that has arisen since the terrorist attack on the Twin Towers in New York (9/11), major constructions, such as the Hoover Dam, have been deemed targets for possible terrorist attack. Security is now very tight for traffic crossing the dam, and a new road and suspension bridge are being built at enormous expense to divert traffic away from the dam.

Alongside large-scale HEP projects, there is now also considerable interest in smaller-scale projects, such as adding an HEP plant to existing water reservoirs. This process is happening to a significant level in China.

Wind power

Wind power capacity has been increasing rapidly. It is the fastest-growing renewable energy source. Economically, wind power would seem to be the most likely renewable energy to be able to compete with fossil fuels, particularly where carbon taxes are introduced. Modern wind turbines are bigger, more powerful, lighter and cheaper than their predecessors. Both China and India are rapidly developing their own capacity for wind power. Indeed, China has built the biggest solar and wind industries in the world.

In many of the more developed countries, opposition to wind farms by local residents has forced governments to rethink planning legislation to enable national considerations to overrule local objections, although at the same time, partly as a consequence, there has been a greater focus on offshore developments. The role of planning policy and objections from residents can be seen clearly in the development of wind farms in the north-west of England. The region's exposure to winds blowing in from the sea attracted the attention of energy companies during the 1990s. However, existing planning controls in the National Parks and Areas of Outstanding Natural Beauty [☞] meant that wind farms could not be sited on much of the uplands. As a result, clusters of wind turbines are located in two distinct environments: on moorlands outside the protected zones of upland landscape, such as the West Pennine Moors to the south of Burnley and Blackburn (see figure 4.12 on p98), and on former industrial 'brown belt' land on the coast, as in the Liverpool dock area and along the Cumbrian coast from near Workington in the north to Askam in Furness in the south (Winchester, 2006: 237).

See Volume 1: Human Geography, ch 2, Geographies of tourism (p50).

Nevertheless, in January 2010, the UK government announced an ambitious plan to build 6,500 wind turbines around the coasts of Britain designed to generate 25% of the country's electricity (see figure 4.14 on p98). The proposed wind farms will be further away from the coast and in deeper waters than existing offshore projects. The offshore development of wind farms benefits from greater wind speeds and fewer planning objections, but these developments are roughly twice as expensive to construct (see figure 4.13 on p98). The UK has more offshore wind projects installed or in planning than any other country in the world.

Chapter 4: Energy

Figure 4.12:
Onshore wind turbines in north-west England

See accompanying CD-Rom

Onshore wind turbines.ppt

Figure 4.13:
Offshore wind farms

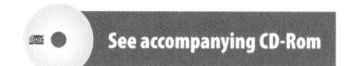

See accompanying CD-Rom

Wind farms.ppt

Figure 4.14:
Wind farm zones around the UK

See accompanying CD-Rom

Wind farms.ppt

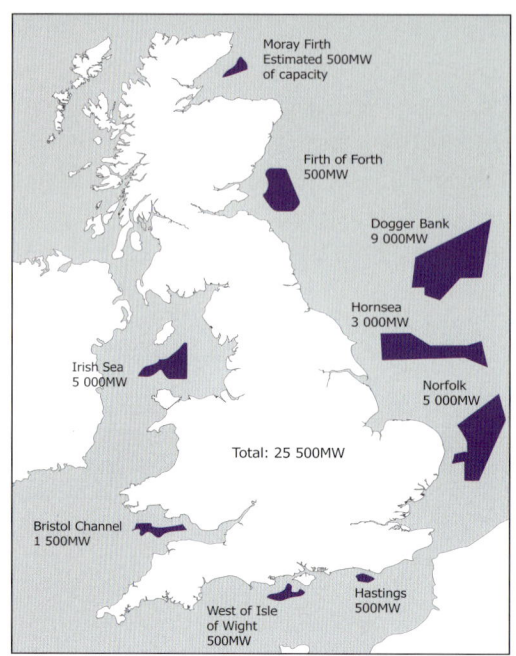

Moray Firth Estimated 500MW of capacity
Firth of Forth 500MW
Dogger Bank 9 000MW
Hornsea 3 000MW
Irish Sea 5 000MW
Norfolk 5 000MW
Total: 25 500MW
Bristol Channel 1 500MW
West of Isle of Wight 500MW
Hastings 500MW

Source: adapted from *The Guardian*, 9 January 2010.
Drawn by Ann Chapman.

Contemporary Approaches to Geography Volume 3: Environmental Geography — Chris Kington Publishing

> **Teaching idea 4.6**
>
> Ask students to investigate a wind farm in their region, either offshore or onshore, why was the particular location chosen, what issues have surrounded its development? (For information on the world's biggest windfarm, the London Array off Kent, see www.londonarray.com).

Solar power

Solar power is the second-fastest growing renewable energy source. Between 2004 and 2008, new investment in the sector grew from just US$600 million to US$33.5 billion (compared with US$51.8 billion for wind). Solar energy falls into two main categories: thermal, which converts solar energy into heat; and photovoltaic (PV), by far the most commonly used, where solar cells are used to convert energy directly into electricity. Some 70% of the world's total solar water heating capacity is in developing countries.

In some countries, such as Spain, government subsidies have been effective in significantly increasing levels of solar power (Spain is now second in the world behind Germany in its production). As with wind power, when the wind isn't blowing, the potential of solar will depend on how well the energy source can be balanced when the sun is not shining. The introduction of 'feed-in tariffs' in the UK in April 2010 means that households and businesses with solar panels and wind turbines are paid for the electricity they generate, even if they use it all themselves; it is intended that this will encourage a shift towards low carbon living.

Biofuels

Biomass, in the form of wood and charcoal, has been a fuel since the beginnings of civilisation. In carbon terms, unlike fossil fuels, it is broadly carbon neutral, merely returning to the atmosphere the carbon that was taken in during the growing of the plant (whereas fossil fuels release carbon that has been stored underground for millennia).

Brazil is the second-biggest producer of biofuels after the USA (see figure 4.15 on p100). The country launched Pró-Alcool, its ethanol programme, in 1975 in response to falling world prices in sugar and the increasing cost of oil. With higher oil prices, ethanol became a cost-effective substitute for oil. The programme helped to reduce dependency on imported oil, and saved about US$52 billion between 1975 and 2002 in foreign exchange, while creating 900,000 relatively well-paid jobs. It also resulted in reductions in local air pollution in cities, and cut greenhouse gas emissions (UNEP, 2007). Brazil has plans to expand rapidly its sugar cane-based ethanol industry, producing 25 billion litres in 2008/09, approximately 30% of the world's total.

Today, most cars in Brazil can run on both ethanol and gasoline, a necessary response, given that sugar cane producers switched back to sugar production during the 1980s when oil prices fell. There are currently limits to the amount of ethanol that most cars can run on (in the US, blended fuel is not allowed more than 10% ethanol), and just 3% of cars on US roads are designed to run on higher ethanol blends. However, expansion of biofuel production needs to be carefully planned. Brazil expects to double the production of ethanol in the next two decades. As a result, the cultivated area is increasing rapidly in order to produce enough crops to reach these production

**Figure 4.15:
Ethanol and biodiesel output, 1995-2015**

See accompanying CD-Rom

Biodiesel.ppt

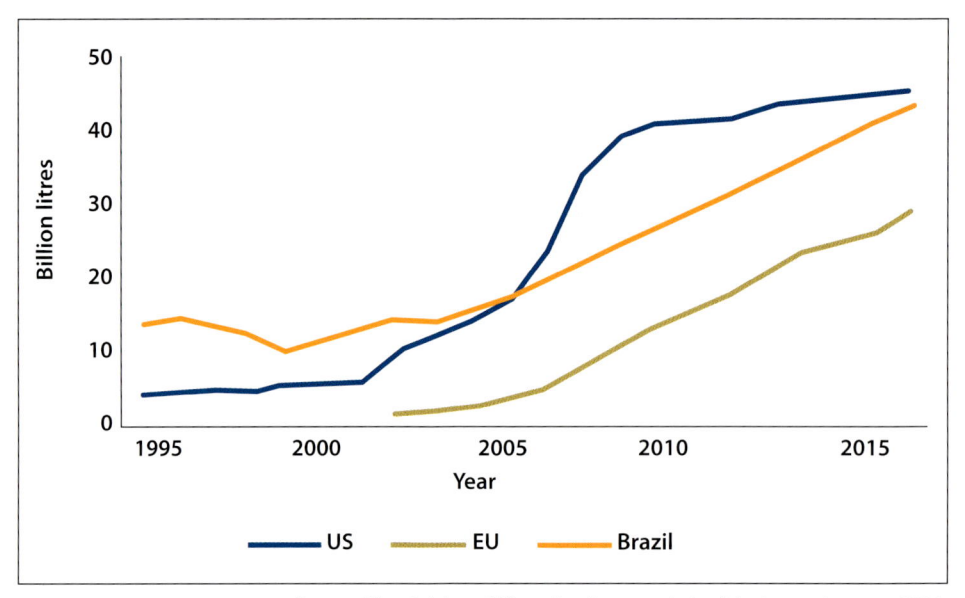

Source: The Cabinet Office, *Food: an analysis of the issues*, January 2008.

See ch 1, Ecosystems (p15).

See ch 5, Food supply.

targets. As a result, the cultivated area is increasing rapidly. The growth of this form of farming jeopardizes entire ecoregions, like the Cerrado, one of the world's biodiversity hot spots (UNEP, 2007).

Ethanol is termed a 'first generation' biofuel. As such it is derived from products that might otherwise be used for food. Indeed, it is estimated that one-quarter of all maize and other grain crops grown in the USA now end up as biofuel rather than as food. While this may or may not have resulted in problems relating to food supply, the increased demand for grain products has resulted in significant increases in prices as a result of growing demand for the crops.

Teaching idea 4.7

'There is a direct link between biofuels and food prices. The needs of the hungry must come before the needs of cars' (Meredith Alexander, biofuels campaigner at Action Aid – *The Guardian*, 23 January 2010). Ask students to investigate this issue, to what extent do they agree with Alexander? See *www.actionaid.org.uk* for more information on the position of Action Aid.

New technologies are currently being developed for second and third generation fuels. Such technologies include using enzymes and bacteria (see figure 4.16 on p101) to break down the starch in plant waste such as straw; growing oil-producing algae; and converting wood chip to gas and then ethanol. There are still major technological issues with these developments, but they all have the advantage of not competing directly with food production because they do not require agricultural land or fresh water.

The production of biogas from food waste and other organic sources is a related development in attempting to produce carbon neutral energy. Biogas is generated in anaerobic digesters where microbes break down the materials and release methane and carbon dioxide. The biogases can be used to make electricity or be injected into the national gas network (see *www.ecotricity.co.uk* for details of a recent scheme to develop biogas from food waste).

Figure 4.16:
Biofuels from waste

Biofuels from waste.doc

TMO Renewables (*www.tmo-group.com*) has developed a unique biological process for converting woody biomass – including domestic waste and leftovers from agriculture, forestry and industry – into ethanol. Costs are kept down, greenhouse gas emissions are reduced, and our cars no longer have to compete for food with hungry people.

A humble bacterium called *geobacillus*, normally at home in compost heaps, feeding off a wide range of carbohydrates, including complex sugars and cellulose, and producing lactic acid and a small amount of ethanol, has had its DNA slightly modified to increase the proportions of ethanol it produces. As a result, 400kg of ethanol are now produced for every tonne of complex carbohydrate in the feedstock. This cellulose-based ethanol produces almost four times the energy used to make it.

TMOR's technology has now digested 25 different feedstocks over more than a year's continuous operation at its demonstration plant in Surrey. In the next five years it plans to roll out commercial production across the EU, the US, China and Brazil, converting a range of waste materials into green ethanol, including distiller's grain, corn fibre, wheat straw and sorghum and bagasse.

Every year the UK produces 7 million tonnes of surplus wheat straw – convert that into ethanol using TMOR's process and you've met 10% of the UK's current petrol demand. At an estimated 13p to 18p per litre, it is projected to be cheaper than food-based ethanol – but even more important, it won't cost the Earth.

Source: adapted from *The Guardian*, 19 December 2009. Note: bagasse is the fibrous residue remaining after sugarcane or sorghum stalks are crushed to extract their juice.

Teaching idea 4.8

The article in figure 4.16 discusses one of the companies that received a Carbon Trust Innovation Award in 2009. Ask groups of students to investigate the other award winners before presenting their findings to the whole group. Such a series of presentations will demonstrate the range of strategies being attempted to reduce carbon emissions (see *www.carbontrust.co.uk* for more information).

The emissions-reduction performance of biofuels has been mixed, and in some instances the overall effect may well have been negative. There may be serious environmental consequences from growing crops such as palm oils for biofuels where this results in the destruction of rainforests. For instance, there is evidence of significant environmental damage in South-east Asia, where deforestation has occurred to make way for oil palm plantations. While electricity produced by biomass could be used to reduce overall levels of carbon emissions, the growth of such crops is highly dependent on the relative price of food. Farmers will grow the most profitable crop, and when food prices rise, acreages of biofuels are cut back unless there are external factors such as government subsidies.

Biofuels such as miscanthus and willow (see figure 4.17 on p102) are now being grown in areas of arable England. However, it is estimated that to produce 1 gigawatt of electricity, it would be necessary to increase the acreage of miscanthus 80-fold, thereby covering approximately 6.5% of the total agricultural land in England. Such figures clearly illustrate some of the issues facing the widespread adoption of biofuels. The multiple pressures on land in the UK to provide food, other commodities, wildlife, recreation, beautiful landscapes and ecosystems are a major policy challenge for any future energy provision based on biofuels (Wildlife and Countryside Link), although it should be stated that cultivation of miscanthus enhances the biodiversity in arable areas, creating habitats for a range of wildlife including reed-nesting birds.

Figure 4.17: Biofuels in Lincolnshire

See accompanying CD-Rom

Biofuels.ppt

Willow

Miscanthus

The future for biofuel production would appear to be on low-grade land or as a by-product of the food industry. The Drax power station in Yorkshire now burns peanut husks, sunflower husks, straw pellets and olive cake, a by-product of the olive oil industry. Drax is planning to build one to three pure biomass plants, each with a 300 megawatt capacity – that would make them among the biggest in the world.

Tidal and wave power

Tidal barrage systems work by creating different levels of water on either side of a barrage, then running turbines off the fast flow of water when gates are opened between the two sides of the barrage. The largest commercial operation is La Rance barrage in northern France with a capacity of 240 megawatts. Plans for a barrage across the River Severn are under active consideration at the time of writing (early 2010), while South Korea is also considering expanding a small tidal barrage off Jindo Island. However, barrages are expensive as a result of the huge engineering works involved, and can have a negative impact on the environment, both in terms of effects on marine life and sediment levels.

> **Teaching idea 4.9**
>
> Ask students to investigate the debate around the possible construction of the Severn tidal project (a Google search should provide a range of source material). Having evaluated the evidence, do they think the project should go ahead?

The need to replace the existing bridge over the Firth of Forth has triggered debate in Scotland about whether to build another bridge, a tunnel or a barrage with a road on top. Such a barrage would enable the harnessing of the river for tidal energy, as well as helping reduce the impact of future storms and floods. On the negative side, concerns about the impact on the marine environment, along with discussions of the very high cost involved, mean that this debate is likely to continue for some time to come.

Geothermal

Geothermal energy is, literally, heat from the Earth. At present, only about 10 gigawatts of geothermal electricity is generated around the world, less than ten medium-sized coal-fired power stations. The geothermal electricity generator at Larderello in Italy provides power for 1 million homes and accounts for about one-tenth of the world's thermal power generation. In Iceland, with five geothermal power plants, geothermal power is used for electricity and heating.

In areas of the world with significant seismic activity, the prospects of maximising the potential of geothermal energy have led to a range of developments. Improvements in drilling technology now enable engineers to reach more than 10 kilometres into the Earth's crust, and costs have fallen as techniques have improved. However, there are also potential drawbacks, in that the use of geothermal energy also releases gases, including carbon dioxide and sulphates, thus reducing the effectiveness of the energy source in terms of greenhouse gas emissions.

In Japan, there are plans for substantial investment in geothermal energy. It is envisaged that a new generation of power plants will tap into Japan's vast supply of heated water and steam found deep below ground. Japan is a country with 108 active volcanoes. However, there are conflicts, as with the small spa town of Kusatsu, which depends for its living on the tourist trade brought in by the heated waters. Currently, the hot springs are kept at a constant 54°C by the volcano Mount Shirane. The water gushes out of the ground naturally, and is also used to heat schools, homes and roads during the town's bitterly cold winter. Plans for a nearby geothermal plant could well disrupt this system and the centuries old tradition of hot-water bathing. On the other hand, critics say that the current system wastes energy.

> **Teaching idea 4.10**
>
> Ask students to investigate the Japanese spa town of Kusatsu and its culture and to consider whether more effective use of geothermal energy should take precedence over historic traditions and the demands of the tourist industry (for more information see: *www.kusatsu-onsen.ne.jp/foreign*).

The localisation of energy

Greater self-sufficiency in energy production is seen as both attainable and desirable by many nations. On the one hand, this means developing conventional local supplies as effectively and efficiently as possible, but it also means an increasing focus on micro-generation through schemes such as local heat and power. Solar power, which does not have any real economies of scale, is likely to benefit from this approach (unlike, for instance, wind power, where larger turbines are more efficient). Such an approach will be particularly effective if producers are able to put unused energy back into the grid, enabling them to benefit financially (as with the 'feed-in tariff' scheme discussed on p99). At a more general level, an integrated approach to the construction of new buildings is likely to ensure that they are much more energy-efficient in the future (see figure 4.18 on p104-105).

Chapter 4: Energy

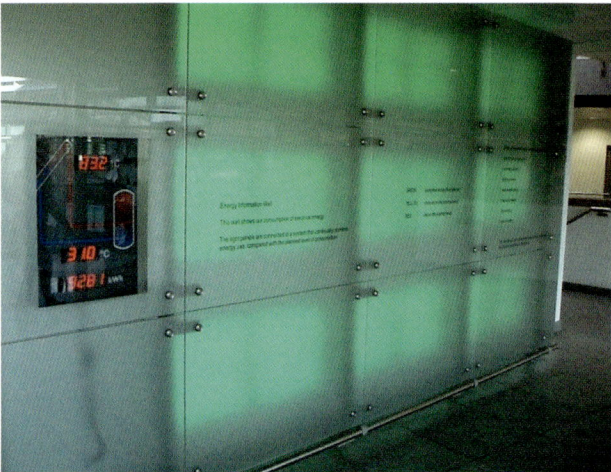

**Figure 4.18a:
The Faculty of Health building, Edge Hill University**

See accompanying CD-Rom

Faculty of Health.ppt

Teaching idea 4.11

Ask students to list the range of features that have been incorporated into the Faculty of Health building at Edge Hill University (see figures 4.18a and 4.18b). How many of these features do they have in their own homes? How many of these features are incorporated into the design of their school? Could any of them be easily and economically incorporated into their own school/home? If so, which ones and why?

104   Contemporary Approaches to Geography Volume 3: Environmental Geography   Chris Kington Publishing

The Faculty of Health building, Edge Hill University, Ormskirk, Lancashire

The building was opened in December 2007. Sustainability was intrinsic to the design and construction of the largest project the University had ever undertaken. In this context, sustainability was defined as low energy consumption and producing a building with minimal long-term demands on the environment. The building was designed to reduce energy requirements and CO_2 emissions.

This was achieved through a variety of measures:

- Ground source heat pump (GSHP) technology (using geothermal energy). A ground source heat pump, installed with a 50% grant from the Carbon Trust, draws water from an underground aquifer and provides heating and additional cooling. This has, in turn, been extended to a nearby building, resulting in an immediate 27% reduction in this building's carbon footprint. The GSHP system has also been engineered to make maximum use of the university's cheap off-peak electricity by pre-heating the building during the off-peak electric tariff (12am to 7am). Any energy used at this cheaper rate reduces the amount of higher rate electricity required during the day.

- Orientation of the building and the distribution of accommodation. The building has a generally shallow plan to minimise the need for mechanical systems such as lifts, and external glazing to maximise natural light. The glazing is limited on the south-facing elevation to avoid unwanted solar heat. The areas producing high internal heat loads (*see Footnote*) are the teaching rooms; these are located on the north-east side of the building away from afternoon sun. The facades to these rooms allow for high levels of natural light and extensive natural ventilation while controlling insulation. Smaller rooms with low internal heat loads, such as offices, are located on the west side of the building.

- Passive measures, maximising daylight and natural ventilation, use of materials, etc. The building has been designed with fully glazed curtain walling and roof lights to increase the amount of natural daylight into the north of the building, thus reducing the amount of lighting required while managing solar heat build-up. The central space is naturally lit and ventilated.

- Solar thermal energy. Roof-mounted solar thermal panels currently provide over 50% of the building's hot water demand.

- The 'Passiv haus' concept has been employed, limiting air leakage, increasing insulation levels and building to much higher standards than normal building codes. Engineering controls such as high-efficiency lighting and high-performance insulation are saving an estimated 65 tonnes of CO_2 annually. The classrooms have occupancy sensors, which, when empty, ensure the lights turn off to reduce energy consumption by the building. LED lights are used in the central spaces to provide lighting with low cost and low energy consumption. More energy efficient computing facilities (Sun Ray thin client) have been provided. A standard PC and monitor uses 105 watts of power, the Sun Ray solution uses 41 watts, a 61% saving in energy consumption. This has proved to be so successful that a further 200 machines have already been deployed elsewhere on the university campus, doubling the numbers within the first six months and saving over 19 tonnes of carbon dioxide annually.

As a result of the success of the building, within six months the cooling and heating ground source system was linked to a second building, and the University had totally revised its purchasing policy for personal computers and monitors.

Footnote

The main internal heat sources are the people themselves, the electric lights they need and the electric equipment they use. Buildings that have high levels of use may generate so much internal heat that they need cooling in any season. Lower internal heat loads mean that rooms can remain with natural cooling, or use air-conditioning less frequently.

Figure 4.18b:
The Faculty of Health building, Edge Hill University

Faculty of Health.doc

Chapter 4: Energy

Teaching idea 4.12

Figure 4.19 shows the Pendle Vale Campus in Lancashire, which opened in September 2008 as part of the Building Schools for the Future programme, and incorporates a range of environmentally friendly features. If your school is part of the same programme, ask students to identify aspects of the building that have been designed to minimise environmental impacts (see 'Useful websites' at the end of the chapter).

Figure 4.19: Pendle Vale Campus

See accompanying CD-Rom

Pendle Vale.ppt

Energy and development

Access to energy for heating, cooking, transport and electricity is considered a basic human right. Various studies have investigated the consequences of meeting the minimum standards set out in the Millennium Development Goals [☞], and found that the total amount of primary energy required to meet the standards is negligible on the global scale. Electricity for lighting (in homes, schools and rural health facilities), liquefied petroleum gas (LPG) for cooking fuel (for 1.7 billion urban and rural dwellers), and diesel used in cars and buses for transport (for 1.5 million rural communities) would require less than 1% of total annual global energy demand, and would generate less than 1% of current annual global CO_2 emissions. Energy services could be provided to meet the Millennium Development Goals without significantly increasing the environmental impacts of the global energy sector (UNEP, 2007).

See Volume 1: Human Geography, ch 7, Development geographies, figure 7.9.

Energy futures

Attempting to write a section headed 'energy futures' is full of pitfalls. As we have seen, there have been dramatic changes in energy production, preferences and policies in recent years. However, it seems likely that the current thrust of intended policy towards reducing emissions in order to minimise climate change effects seems certain to continue. In the developed world in particular, large power plants are facing increasingly tight environmental standards, while cleaner energy options have proliferated over the past 20 years. More uncertainty remains about the effectiveness of these policies in achieving their intended goals, given the accompanying requirement to at least maintain living standards, and preferably to boost economic growth at the same time.

In terms of energy futures, there are a range of scientific options that are being considered, which may (or may not) result in significant changes to future generations. Energy efficiency improvements and energy conservation have a high priority in the energy development strategies of many countries, including developing countries, while high energy efficiency and clean technology are seen as crucial to achieving a lower emission future. For instance, carbon capture and storage are considered viable propositions with the possibility of pumping CO_2 back to the ocean and storing it under the North Sea, possibly in old oil and gas fields.

In the longer term, British marine geologists have been looking at the North Atlantic Ridge as a potential source of energy in the future. The ridge is very hot, and so there is a possibility that it could be utilised as an energy source, perhaps turning it into electricity and transmitting it back to Europe. However, it might be useful to conclude this chapter by referring back to the note of caution expressed in the 1970s textbook about the difficulties of predicting energy futures, beyond reaffirming that the issue of energy is set to be a major concern on global political agendas for the foreseeable future.

Summary

This chapter has demonstrated the fundamental importance of energy supply to the global economy and, at the same time, has demonstrated the potential threat that an over-reliance on fossil fuels poses to the global environment. While it is dangerous to make firm predictions about future energy usage and provision, it is clear that provision of adequate, more environmentally benign energy supplies will remain at the top of the political agenda for the foreseeable future.

Useful websites

www.carbontrust.co.uk – an independent body set up by the UK government to provide support for businesses in developing low carbon technology.

The Commission for Architecture and the Built Environment (CABE) produces a range of teaching materials looking at the built environment. CABE has produced a teacher's toolkit ideal for use when a school (or part of it) is being refurbished, aimed at optimising the opportunities for involvement by pupils. Aspects of the toolkit could be applicable to all schools – www.cabe.org.uk/files/our-school-building-matters.pdf

www.energy.gov – the US Department of Energy website contains a useful section for educators.

www.decc.gov.uk – the UK Department of Energy and Climate Change website.

Further reading

Financial Times, 'The future of energy', supplement, 2 November 2009.

Garcier, R, 'The nuclear "renaissance" and the geography of the uranium fuel cycle.' *Geography*. 94,3, Autumn 2009 pp198-206.

Wlidlife and Countryside Link, *Bioenergy in the UK: turning green promises into environmental reality*. Available at: *http://wcl.org.uk/Bioenergy%20in%20the%20UK.htm*

Food supply

Charles Rawding

Introduction

Food, like many other global commodities today, is the product of highly industrialised systems of production, which include not only farming but also the production of a wide range of chemical and biotechnological inputs, and the processing, distribution and retailing of food products to the consumer (figure 5.1) [☞]. As such, when considering the topic of food supply, we need to take into account a range of industries such as the production of fertilisers, pesticides and seed (including genetically modified varieties), food-processing industries and sophisticated transportation systems such as 'cool chain' delivery (see p119), as well as the marketing and branding industries that present the finished product to prospective consumers (Clark et al, 2008: 370).

The complexities shown in figure 5.1 help illustrate why growers receive a relatively small proportion of the final price of food products, something which is particularly noticeable in less economically developed countries (LEDCs) producing export crops for the markets of the wealthy nations (see figure 5.2 on p110). Allied industries are generally more profitable than farming itself, partly at least as a result of the unequal conditions of trade faced by many farmers.

See Volume 1: Human Geography, ch 5, Rural geographies.

**Figure 5.1:
The components in the mainstream food supply chain**

The components in the mainstream food supply chain.ppt

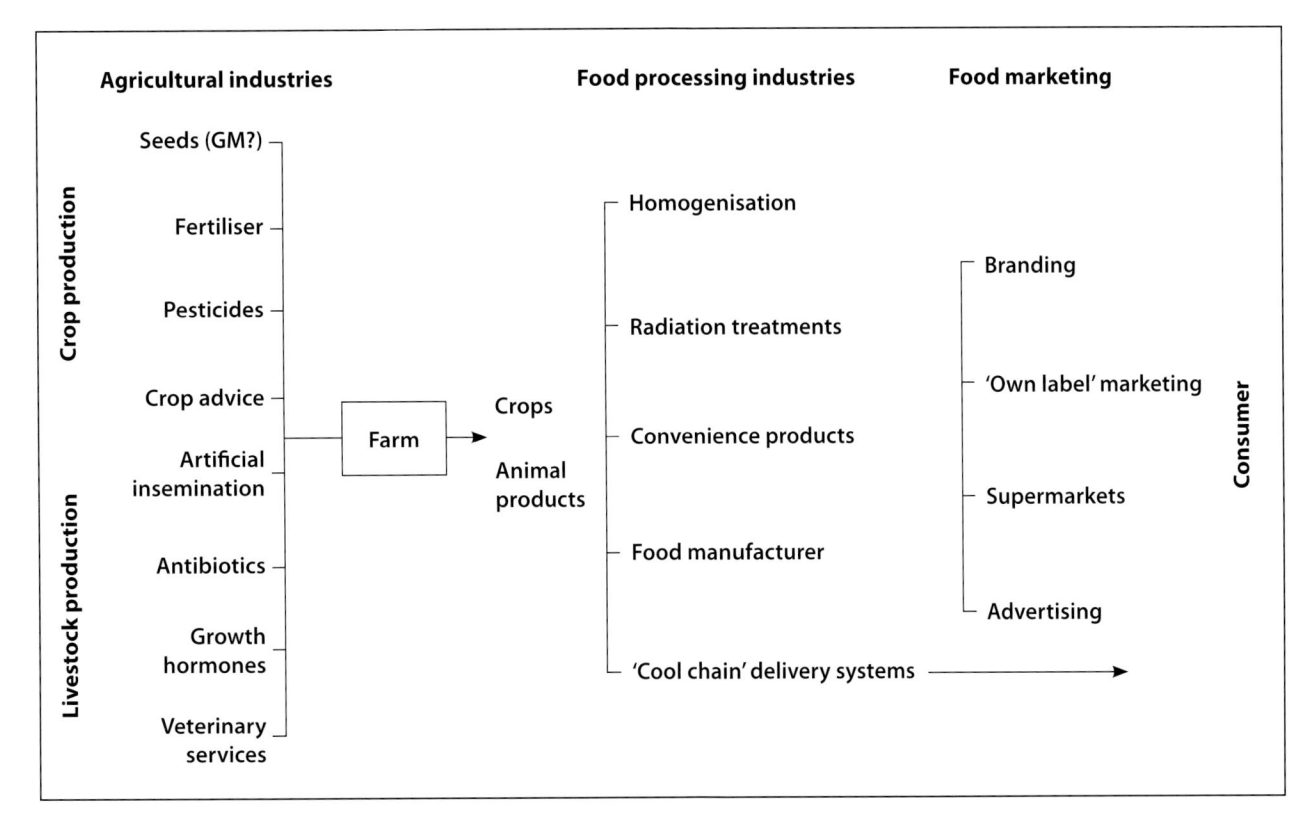

Agricultural industries

Crop production:
- Seeds (GM?)
- Fertiliser
- Pesticides
- Crop advice

Livestock production:
- Artificial insemination
- Antibiotics
- Growth hormones
- Veterinary services

→ Farm → Crops / Animal products

Food processing industries
- Homogenisation
- Radiation treatments
- Convenience products
- Food manufacturer
- 'Cool chain' delivery systems →

Food marketing
- Branding
- 'Own label' marketing
- Supermarkets
- Advertising

→ Consumer

**Figure 5.2:
Who gets what – tea and bananas**

Who gets what.ppt. and Who gets what.xl

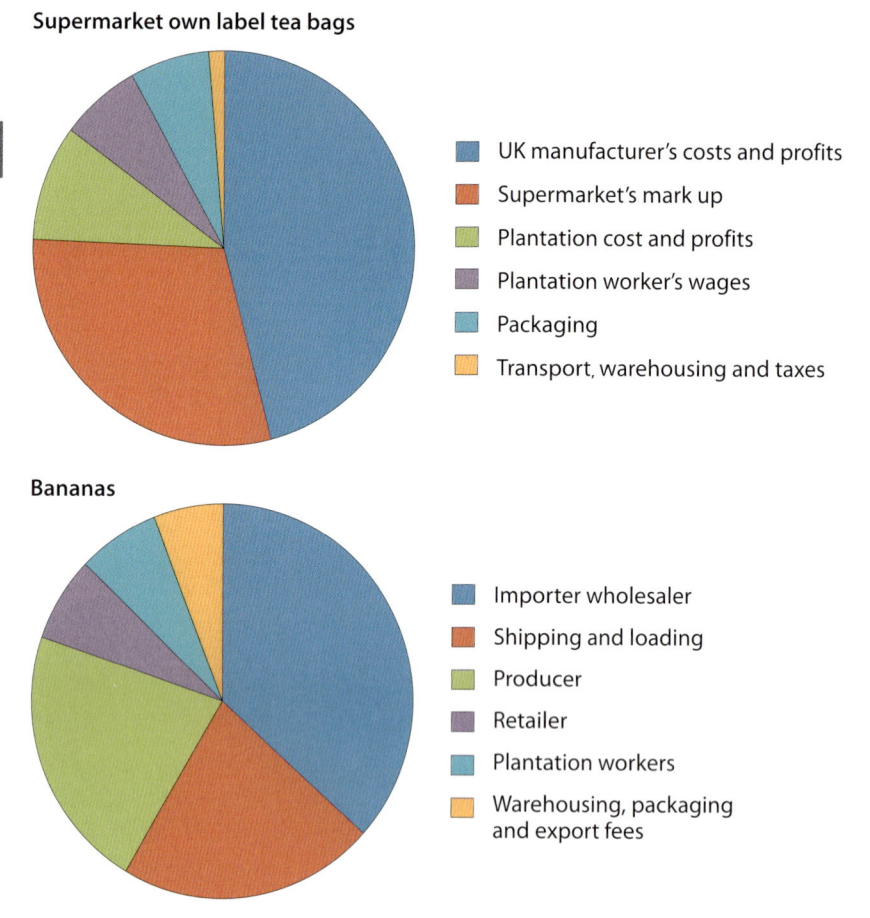

Supermarket own label tea bags

- UK manufacturer's costs and profits
- Supermarket's mark up
- Plantation cost and profits
- Plantation worker's wages
- Packaging
- Transport, warehousing and taxes

Bananas

- Importer wholesaler
- Shipping and loading
- Producer
- Retailer
- Plantation workers
- Warehousing, packaging and export fees

The involvement of government

Unlike most industrial products, government involvement in all aspects of the food chain is very significant in many countries of the world. Government policies in relation to agricultural production can be broadly divided into two categories: financial support in the form of subsidies for food production and tariffs to protect domestic farmers from competition from foreign producers. A third category relating to environmental considerations might be added where this has an impact on levels of production.

If we take the example of the United Kingdom, the food and drink supply chain is a major part of the UK economy, accounting for 7% of GDP and employing 3.7 million people in everything from food retailing to restaurants and canteens to farming and fishing. Food manufacture is the UK's single largest manufacturing sector, accounting for 15% of UK manufacturing output (Cabinet Office, 2008b). Attitudes to food production and supply in the country have changed dramatically during the past 70 years. The very real threat of starvation during the Second World War (after a period between the wars when much of UK farming experienced severe depression) meant that government policies from 1939 until the late 1980s were geared to maximising production (what has been termed the 'productivist'[1] period). By the end of the 1980s, these policies had been so successful that 'wine lakes', 'butter mountains' and the mounting costs of the Common Agricultural Policy ensured radical reform of agricultural policies. As a result of these changes, the UK is now far more dependent on imported foodstuffs than at any time since before the Second World War. Indeed,

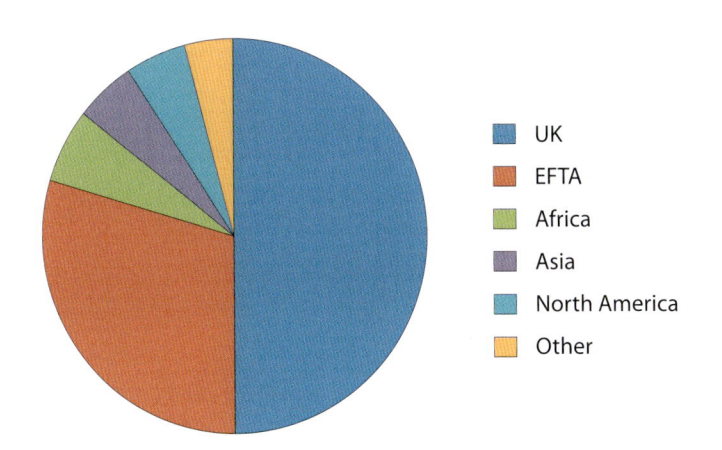

Figure 5.3:
Origin of food in the UK

See accompanying CD-Rom

Origin of food.ppt and Origin of food.xl

Source: Cabinet Office, 2008a: 59.

the UK's self-sufficiency is now 27% lower than it was in 1990, and has dropped by 7% since 2002 (Smith, 2009). Only around half of the food we eat today comes from the UK, a third comes from elsewhere in Europe and the rest from Africa, Asia and the Americas (figure 5.3). However, this measure does not take account of food produced for export. In value terms, overall food production (including exports) amounted to around 60% of domestic consumption in 2007 (Cabinet Office, 2008b: 50). Nevertheless, it would be a mistake to suggest that all these changes are recent. For instance, the export of dairy produce and meat from New Zealand was facilitated by the advent of refrigeration in 1882 (Butlin, 2009: 75).

Food supply and diet

Food supply and diet have been transformed in recent years. The increasing availability of produce from all over the world has resulted in a breadth of provision unimaginable 50 years ago. From the 1980s onwards, there has been a steady growth in the value of world trade in high-value foods. A range of factors have influenced these developments, including changes in diet in the wealthier countries, with foods being produced [☞] to satisfy the tastes and lifestyles of particular groups of consumers. Many of these changes have been made possible as a result of improvements in transportation and food handling and the role of supermarkets in developing reliable worldwide supply chains.

See Volume 1: Human Geography, ch 5, figure 5.8.

Today, more people enjoy more food from more places than ever before, while a larger portion of producers serve distant consumers. This is particularly the case with high-value foods, which have become increasingly global in their distribution and consumption, leading to seasonal products being displaced from supermarket shelves by 'permanent global summertime' (Dicken, 2007: 348). Fresh horticultural goods now make up approximately 5% of global commodity trade (a level equivalent to the trade in crude petroleum) and the principal exporters of such produce are located widely through the developing world (Elliott, 2006: 151). UK spending on food has increased five-fold in the past 30 years while national disposable income has increased 12-fold; however, the poor allocate a higher share of total household expenditure to food than the rich (Cabinet Office, 2008a: 24).

> **Teaching idea 5.1**
>
> Ask students to look at the origins of the food in their kitchen – to what extent do they have a 'global' diet? Alternatively, what food do they purchase that is local in origin? Ask students to identify the country of origin of vegetables in their local supermarket. Carry this activity out in different seasons of the year to identify variations in sources according (or not) to seasonality. What evidence can they find of 'permanent global summertime'?

Most agricultural production today is based on high chemical inputs, global trade and centralised processing and distribution networks, designed to provide the cheapest possible food. However, our food systems are dependent on external inputs such as natural gas for fertiliser and diesel for farm machinery and subsequent transportation and distribution. It has been calculated that we are currently using ten calories of energy to produce each calorie of food. This level of dependence on external inputs has resulted in discussion of the prospects of a food security crisis (see p128) triggered by rising fuel prices and rising demand from economies such as China and India, leading to increasing food prices and food scarcity (figure 5.4).

Figure 5.4:
An alternative food plan?

See accompanying CD-Rom

An alternative food plan.doc

> 'All it takes is a tornado/terrorism incident/conflict in the Middle East/lorry drivers' strike (take your pick) and the grid could go down due to fuel scarcity. In that scenario how long could I keep farming? The answer is less than 12 hours! My farm is, to quote George Bush, seriously addicted to oil, along with other power derived from fossil fuels. My tractors, the milking machine, the water heaters – all these and more need external energy and, as with most farmers in Britain, I have no alternative supply.
>
> This personal revelation – of total dependence and vulnerability – has had a strangely galvanising effect. Far from precipitating depression, it sparked a determination to develop a farm-based renewable-energy system. Our plans include wind turbines to power electric tractors and pumps, solar water heaters, ground-source heat pumps and more.'
>
>   Patrick Holden, Director of the Soil Association and organic dairy farmer in west Wales.

Source: *National Trust Magazine*, Spring 2009, p15.

> **Teaching idea 5.2**
>
> Ask students to study figure 5.4. To what extent do they think the strategies identified by Patrick Holden will succeed in achieving his objectives? What else could the farmer introduce to reduce his reliance on oil?

Population and food supply

The ideas of Thomas Malthus (1766-1834) have enjoyed an unwarranted longevity in school geography. Malthus argued, in 1798, that an ever-increasing population would place intolerable stresses on food supply with catastrophic consequences. In fact, although the world's population has increased from about 2.5 billion in 1950 to approaching 7 billion today, catastrophic consequences for food supply are far from obvious. Indeed, world food supply outstripped population growth between the years 1960 and 2000 (see figure 5.5 on p113). According to the World Health Organization (WHO), daily per capita availability of calories increased globally by 450 kilocalories per capita per day and by over 600 kilocalories per capita per day

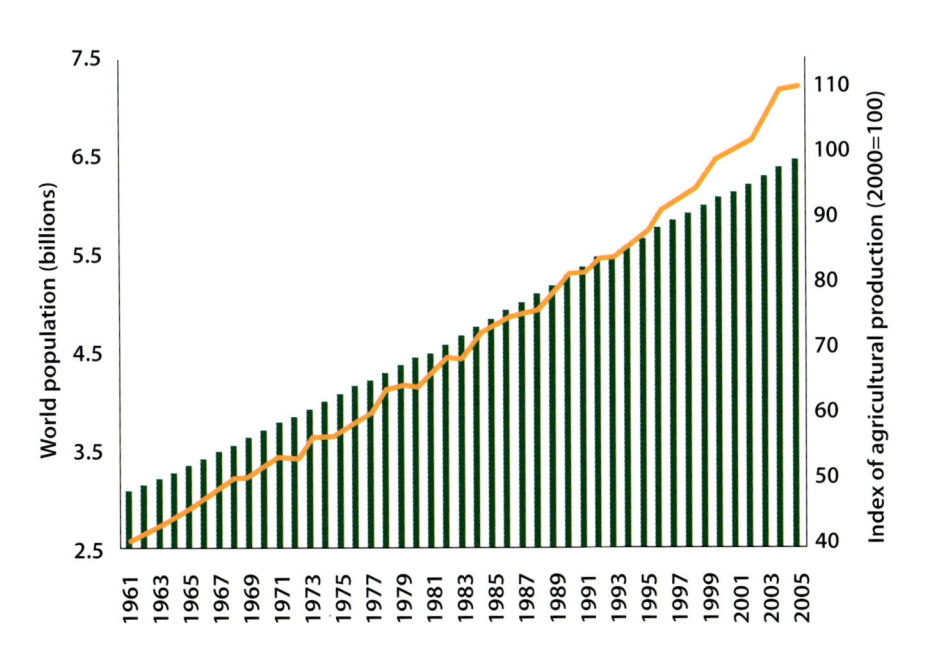

Figure 5.5:
World population and agricultural production, 1961-2005

Population and agricultural production.ppt

Source: Defra, 2006: 32.

in developing countries between the mid-1960s and the late 1990s (Collins, 2009: 49). These figures far outstrip the basic food energy requirements of about 2,100 kilocalories per capita. However, the change has not been equal across regions. Some 850 million people in the world are undernourished but 2 billion are overweight [☞] (Cabinet Office, 2008a: 64). Meanwhile, calorie supply has remained almost stagnant in sub-Saharan Africa. By contrast, per capita supply of food energy has been rising dramatically in East Asia.

See Volume 1: Human Geography, ch 9, Geographies of health and environment (p183-185).

The principal reasons for the overall lack of correlation between population increase and food supply problems during the second half of the 20th century were that new technologies and methods addressed overall food needs (Collins, 2009: 49-50). Land is now used much more intensively. In the 1980s, on average a hectare of cropland produced 1.8 tonnes; today it produces 2.5 tonnes. At the same time, large areas of land have been converted to cropland. More land was converted between 1950 and 1980 than in the 150 years between 1700 and 1850. Cereal yields have increased by 17% in North America, 25% in Asia, 37% in West Asia, and by 40% in Latin America and the Caribbean. Only in Africa have yields remained static and low (UNEP: 2007).

Agriculture is the most important sector in lower income countries, usually being responsible for between a quarter and a half of their gross domestic product (GDP). Growth in agricultural output can be directly correlated with personal wellbeing, notably in terms of the incomes and livelihoods of farmers. For every dollar earned by farmers in low-income countries, there is a US$2.60 increment in incomes in the economy as a whole. Therefore, an increase in crop yields has a significant impact on the upward mobility of the poorest members of rural society. The World Bank estimates that a 1% increase in crop yields reduces the number of people living under US$1/day by 6.25 million (UNEP, 2007).

There is plenty of evidence that where rural populations grow, the natural consequence is an intensification of farming practices to increase productivity. With increased population and land intensification, plot boundaries generally become more clearly defined, often with fences, trees or bushes to demarcate one household's land from another. As fallow periods become shorter, fertility can no longer be maintained without additions to the soil, which usually takes the form of animal manure or compost made from kitchen waste and other organic material. Another response to increasing population pressure is to cultivate hitherto unused land, perhaps by constructing terraces or irrigation systems (Potter et al, 2008).

However, population growth has outpaced the rate of increase of food production in many less economically developed countries (LEDCs), which has resulted in imports becoming necessary to maintain food consumption levels. At the same time, countries such as Brazil and Kenya have expanded their agricultural exports while neglecting domestic production of food staples. This has been necessary to earn foreign exchange to repay debts acquired to fund development [🔗] programmes. At the same time, incomes have risen in some LEDCs, resulting in the import of higher-value food products by the wealthier sections of their population (Daniels et al, 2005: 169-70). From this discussion, it becomes clear that the relationship between food supply, population levels and economic development is an extremely complex one.

See Volume 1: Human Geographies, ch 7, Development geographies (p142-144).

Globalisation and food

Food production is fundamentally different from other industries, being literally fixed in a locality. Food production remains a local process. Yet at the same time, it can be argued that the first forms of globalisation related to the trade of food. The desire to extend diets and provide new foods led to European merchants seeking ways to reach Asia in search of spices during the early modern period, resulting in, among other things, the quintessentially British cup of tea, now a central element of British identity [🔗]. From the beginning of the 19th century, increasing agricultural outputs and specialisation led to the creation of world markets for food.

See Volume 1: Human Geographies, ch 3, Population geographies (p65).

The development of the European colonial [🔗] empires during the late 19th and early 20th centuries marked the beginnings of the plantation system of farming, where large-scale estates were developed specialising in one crop, such as tea, coffee or sugar. Many former plantations, often run by agribusiness transnational corporations (TNCs), have applied intensive and industrialised systems of farming, including the employment of wage labour and the application of capital and advanced technology to their production activities. The classic export commodities of the plantation system have now been complemented by high-value foods such as fruits, vegetables, poultry and shellfish.

See Volume 1: Human Geographies, ch 10, Globalisation (p197-200).

Producing food for a global market requires huge capital investment. Global food production and distribution create significant environmental disturbances in terms of the exploitation of natural ecosystems, the application of chemical fertilisers and pest-controlling agents, and attempts to genetically modify seeds, plants and animals. Transnational corporations such as Monsanto (USA) and Bayer Aventis (Germany) have taken a lead role in agro-industrial expansion; indeed, ten corporations now supply 33% of the global seed market compared to thousands of companies 20 years ago (Elliott, 2006: 153).

Trends towards increased size of operations can be seen across the agricultural sector. For instance, changes in the nature of UK egg production over the past half-century illustrate clearly trends towards more industrialised forms of farming. In 1950, just 5% of laying hens were kept in flocks of more than 1,000 birds; by 1995, this was 95%. Today, three-quarters of the UK's eggs come from fewer than 300 units, each with more than 20,000 layers. The largest unit has more than 500,000 birds (Whatmore and Clarke, 2008: 392).

At the same time as significant elements of the agro-food industry have developed transnational and global dimensions, the largest UK supermarkets and other food retailers have come to dominate the trade in imported produce. For instance, the major retailers control 70 to 90% of fresh produce imports from Africa (see Kenya p119). Interestingly, as supermarkets have required higher standards, there has been a shift in emphasis from those activities that lower production costs, to those that add value. This includes investing in post-harvest facilities such as cold storage, bar-coding products packed in trays to differentiate varieties, countries and suppliers; moving into high-value-added items such as ready-prepared vegetables and salads and developing logistics in order to reduce the time between harvesting, packing and delivery. Pushing back these functions in Africa can reduce costs for UK supermarkets, because African labour is relatively cheap, but can also increase competitiveness for African producers and increase the proportion of value retained in Africa (Lechner and Boli, 2008: 182). Indeed, the big food manufacturers, such as Nestlé, form one side of a sometimes tense relationship with the largest retail operations, such as Wal-Mart and Tesco, as these retailers have become increasingly transnational and powerful in recent times.

Point for consideration

How do we best investigate conflicting interest groups and issues when discussing food production and consumption?

In some cases, increases in awareness of a locally specific crop can have significant development implications. Binns (2009: 101) discusses the growth in popularity of red bush tea and subsequent economic growth in the remote areas of South Africa's Western Cape Province. By 2006, some 170 farmers were producing over 100 tonnes of red bush tea, which was exported to Europe through the Fairtrade network (see p120).[2]

Over the past few decades, there have been major changes in the food production and supply chain in the UK. The globalisation of the food industry has resulted in an increase in both the import and export of food, and a wider sourcing of food consumed within the UK, especially imports of fresh fruit and vegetables from areas such as Africa, the Far East and New Zealand. At the same time, food supply has become concentrated into fewer, larger companies capable of providing an all-year-round supply of uniform produce. This concentration can be linked to the success of the major supermarket chains in coming to dominate the food market (see figure 5.6 on p116). Two-thirds of food bought from retailers is sold through supermarkets. Linked to this market domination has been the development of regional distribution centres by supermarkets and a trend towards the use of larger heavy goods vehicles (HGVs) to deliver produce.

Figure 5.6:
Consolidation over time in the UK grocery market, 1900-2010

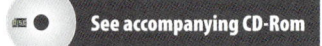

See accompanying CD-Rom

Supermarkets.ppt

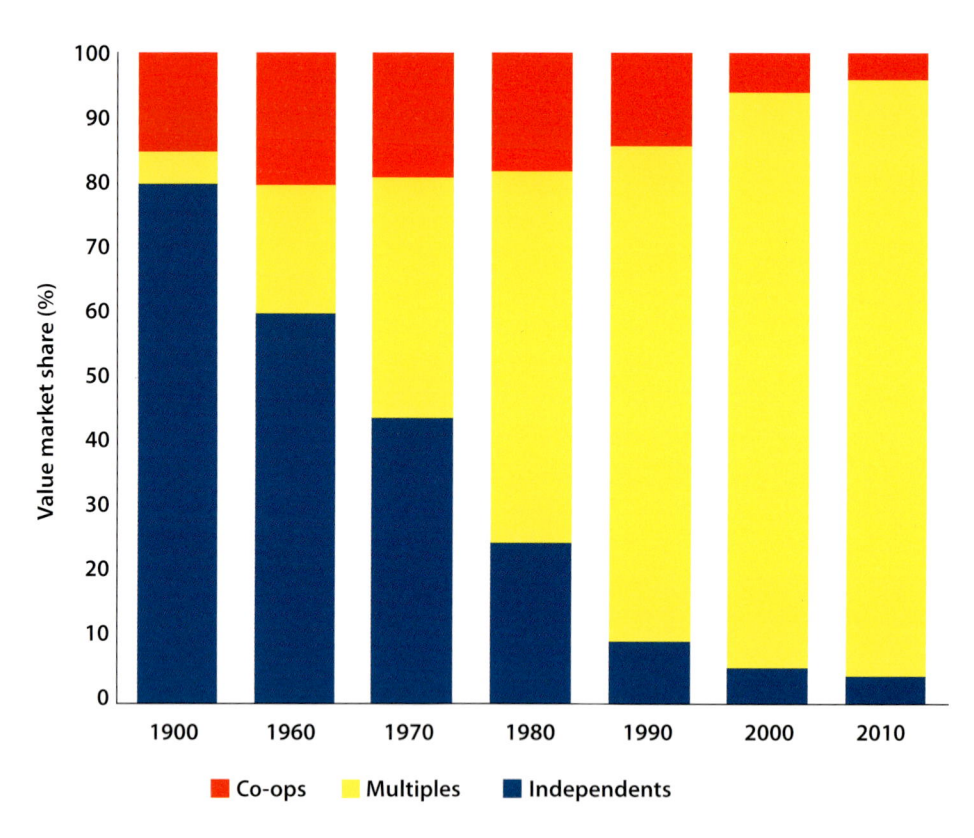

Source: Defra, 2006: 59.

Food miles

These trends have led to a large increase in the distance food travels from the farm to consumer, known as 'food miles'.[3] Food miles are simply the distances travelled by foodstuffs from farm gate to consumer. They are generally measured as tonne-kilometres, ie the distance travelled in kilometres multiplied by the weight in tonnes for each foodstuff. However, to measure the environmental impact of food miles, it is necessary to convert them into vehicle kilometres, ie the sum of the distances travelled by each vehicle carrying food (figure 5.7).

Figure 5.7:
Food miles?

See accompanying CD-Rom

Supermarkets.ppt

Asda delivery van, Broughton in Furness, Cumbria

HGV delivering to Aldi, Port Sunlight, Wirral

Since 1978, the annual amount of food moved in the UK by HGVs has increased by 23%, and the average distance for each trip has increased by more than 50%. The rise in food miles has led to increases in the environmental, social and economic costs associated with transport, including carbon dioxide emissions, air pollution, congestion, accidents and noise. Growing concern over these impacts has led to a debate over whether to try to measure and reduce food miles (figure 5.8). Transport is the largest single user of energy in the UK food chain (see figure 5.9 on p118).

**Figure 5.8:
How supermarket influence on supply chains affects food miles**

See accompanying CD-Rom

Food miles.doc

> Over the past 30 years there has been a huge increase in the influence of supermarkets over the food supply chain. While expanding their share of the retail market, they have also been assuming greater responsibility for food distribution from the factory and farm.
>
> They initially created their own regional distribution centres (RDCs), consolidating deliveries to shops. This centralisation of distribution was closely associated with the centralisation of purchasing. Shop managers ceased to have any responsibility for buying, with all purchasing negotiations confined to the retailer's head office. Any links that had previously existed between shop managers and local suppliers were severed, and managers were unable to exert much influence on the product range available in their stores. There are currently around 70 RDCs in the UK. As the RDCs are much more centralised and serve wider hinterlands, the last link in the chain from warehouse to shop has lengthened, and increased food tonne-kilometres, although the consolidation of retailer-controlled deliveries in much larger vehicles may well have reduced total vehicle-kilometres. Prior to the development of retailers' distribution systems, small suppliers lacked the means of distributing their products to all the shops in a retail chain. This either prevented them from securing a contract with the retailer, or confined their sales to branch stores in a particular region. By channelling their products through retailers' RDCs, smaller producers can gain access to national chains of shops, substantially expanding their market areas.
>
> The market dominance and centralised distribution systems of UK supermarket chains also make it easier for foreign food producers to penetrate the UK market. Bulk deliveries to a relatively small number of RDCs can give them wide exposure across major supermarket chains. In other countries with much more fragmented retail and wholesale sectors, importers face much greater logistical constraints.
>
> Over the past 30 years, supermarket chains have greatly increased the proportion of supplies channelled through their RDCs, leaving only a few lines of 'morning goods' (eg milk, bread and eggs) to be delivered directly to the shop by suppliers. Companies' replenishment systems are based on centralised ordering and receipt of goods at the RDCs where they are checked and sorted for onward distribution. This can create logistical anomalies. A sandwich company in Derbyshire, for example, supplies its products to a major supermarket chain and has a plant within a few hundred metres of one of its shops. The sandwiches arriving on this shop's shelves, however, have to be routed through one of the retailer's RDCs on a round-trip of approximately 160 kilometres.

Source: adapted from *https://statistics.defra.gov.uk/esg/reports/foodmiles/final.pdf* p24.

Figure 5.9:
Energy use in the UK food chain, excluding packaging, catering and domestic cooking

See accompanying CD-Rom

Energy use.ppt and Energy use.xl

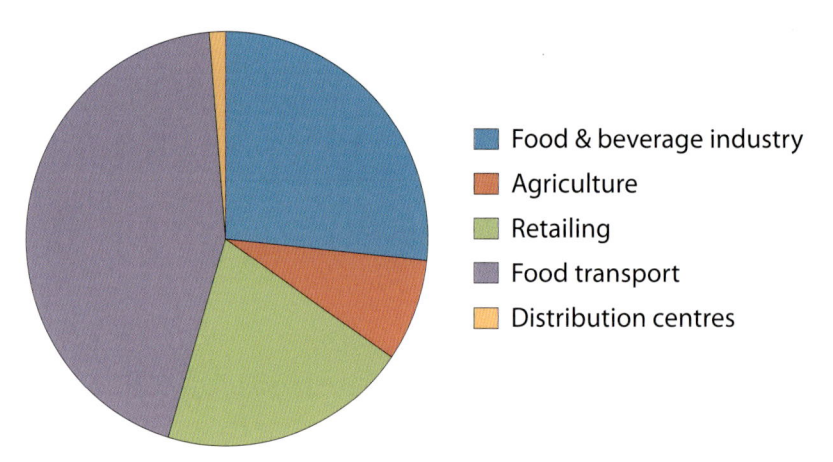

- Food & beverage industry
- Agriculture
- Retailing
- Food transport
- Distribution centres

Source: Cabinet Office, 2008a.

The focus on 'food' miles, as opposed to any other type of product miles, can partly be related back to notions of rurality and the feeling that food ought to be more local (unlike perhaps a German car which might actively market its origins in order to trade in on perceptions of reliability and build quality). But the environmental case for 'local' is less clear (figure 5.10).

Figure 5.10:
The environmental impact of food products

See accompanying CD-Rom

Food miles.doc

'Food miles' are a poor indicator of the environmental impact of food products and small-scale production is not necessarily resource efficient or low impact. Evidence suggests that at some times during the year, transporting produce from other countries may have a lower environmental impact than heating or refrigerating produce grown in Britain. For consumers, driving six and a half miles to a shop to buy food emits more carbon than flying a pack of green beans from Kenya to the UK. And there are social equity arguments for imports as well as more local food – UK demand for fresh produce grown in Africa supports over 700,000 workers and their dependants.

Source: Cabinet Office, 2008b: 33.

Teaching idea 5.3

Ask students to consider the two documents (figures 5.8 and 5.10) contained in Food miles.doc. Ask them to identify the advantages and disadvantages of:
- centralised distribution systems
- local produce as opposed to fresh produce brought in from significant distances.

For an example of food miles from a particular perspective see http://seeinggreen.typepad.com/my_weblog/images/2008/04/01/tesco.jpg which recounts the tale of Tesco's long-haul birds.

Teaching idea 5.4

Figure 5.11 on p119 provides details of the principal ports through which food supplies are imported. Provide students with a blank UK map and ask them to annotate it using the information provided *or* ask students to investigate in more detail the nature of food produce coming into a port of their choosing. Where have the goods come from? Are they already processed? Where do they go to from the port?

- Grimsby together with its sister port of Immingham is the UK's largest port complex and handles 10% of the UK's entire seaborne trade. Grimsby has become well known as the UK's premier centre for the frozen food industry and plays a pivotal role in the UK fishing industry.
- Immingham is the largest dry bulk-handling port in the country, as well as being the UK's second-busiest ro-ro (roll-on, roll-off) port. It is handling ever increasing volumes of fresh fruit and vegetables with current imports mainly from the Mediterranean, with potatoes and citrus fruits from Israel. Large volumes of fish are also handled.
- Hull is a leading cocoa import centre, providing dedicated storage facilities for major producers such as Nestlé and Cadbury's. It is also a major contributor to the UK fishing and fish-processing industries.
- Southampton is home to the second-largest container operation in the UK and is the sole UK port for all Canary Islands fresh produce, such as tomatoes, peppers, cucumbers and avocados. It is also a growing force in the import of dry bulk cargoes sector.
- Liverpool is the UK's leading import port for grain and animal feed, while cocoa is also imported from West Africa.
- Sheerness claims to be the leading port when it comes to handling fresh produce including apples, pears, grapes, citrus fruit, bananas, melons, mangoes, avocados and potatoes. Nearly 900,000 tonnes of fresh produce were imported in 2003.
- Ipswich handles over 1 million tonnes of agribulk cargoes every year, including cereals, animal feed and pulses.
- Portsmouth handled almost 700,000 tonnes of fruit on 305 ships during 2005, including all of Morocco's 45,000 citrus fruits, and 70% of the UK's consumption of bananas, along with other exotic fruits from South and Central America, the Caribbean, Jamaica and the Windward Islands.
- Tilbury specialises in refrigerated cargoes such as Australian and New Zealand meat. The terminal also handles frozen and chilled goods, butter, cheese, fruit, edible oils including sunflower, rapeseed, palm, coconut and olive oils, and further upriver raw sugar is imported from African, Pacific and Caribbean countries at Silvertown. Tilbury grain terminal is one of the largest grain facilities in the UK, handling imports of wheat, maize and soya beans.

Source: Defra, 2006: 75.

Figure 5.11: UK ports and their role in food imports and distribution

See accompanying CD-Rom

UK ports.doc

Figure 5.12: UK food handling ports

See accompanying CD-Rom

UK ports.ppt

The example of Kenya

Over the past 20 years, Kenya has dramatically increased its exports of horticultural products, and huge investments have been made to expand production of cut flowers and pre-packed vegetables, mainly to attract and maintain lucrative contracts with British supermarket chains. The export of cut flowers, especially roses and carnations, has been increasing at about 20% per annum since the early 1990s. High-value fruit, vegetables and cut flowers require speed in harvesting and packaging as well as in transportation. In many cases, this requires a 'cool chain', that is to say, temperature-controlled handling and packaging to ensure delicate products arrive at their destination in top quality condition. The chain mainly comprises large-scale commercial growers able to make the necessary investments. Indeed, the three largest producers/exporters of horticultural produce in Kenya have set up their own export and freight companies and proudly claim that within 48 hours of being harvested, produce can be on supermarket shelves in Britain. It is quite clear that the supermarkets are the most powerful actors in this process. They determine quality and payment and their requirements for documentation about sourcing and traceability mean that horticultural exports from Kenya are increasingly becoming concentrated in the hands of large, highly capitalised producers, while small-scale local producers are becoming marginalised. The paradox of this whole system is that the introduction of 'productivist' methods has been to satisfy the demands of consumers in the developed world rather than domestic demands for staple foods (Daniels et al, 2005: 175-7).

> **Teaching idea 5.5**
>
> Ask students to consider the pros and cons of food production for export, compared with food production for domestic consumption, in less developed countries.

Alternative food networks (AFNs)

Alternative food networks (AFNs) are designed to promote more just and sustainable forms of food production while appealing to consumers who wish to spend more 'ethically' rather than solely according to prevailing market forces. Perhaps the best known example of an AFN is the Fairtrade movement (see below), while other examples include the RSPCA's Freedom Food label (*www.rspca.org.uk/freedomfood*) guaranteeing animal welfare on farms, Cafédirect, organic production (*www.soilassociation.org*) and local farmers' cooperatives [✍]. Effectively, AFNs provide the organisation and infrastructure to enable individual consumers to behave in a more ethical fashion, while enabling producers to have access to markets that would otherwise be extremely difficult to penetrate.

See Volume 1: Human Geography, ch 5, Rural geographies (p113).

The success of an AFN depends on two principal strategies: firstly, ensuring the traceability of a product – for instance, organic foods require meticulous record keeping to ensure that methods of production can be ascertained; secondly, AFNs make the ethical credentials of their products reliable, thereby developing consumer trust (Whatmore and Clarke, 2008).

Fairtrade [✍]

See Volume 1: Human Geography, ch 7, Development geographies (p146) and ch 1, Geographies of consumption, Teaching idea 1.3 (p13).

During the final quarter of the 20th century, the price of many primary products, including jute, rubber, cocoa, coffee, sugar, bananas, tea and cotton, fell significantly, with serious consequences for producers, most of whom were located in LEDCs. To provide just one example, cotton prices in Mali fell by 24% during 2005/6. Such instability makes it all but impossible for farmers to operate effectively. These price reductions had dire consequences for many producers in LEDCs, who saw their already small incomes significantly reduced or their livelihoods wiped out by forces beyond their control.

One consequence of the collapse in commodity prices was the establishment of the Fairtrade Foundation in 1992 by a group of charities including Christian Aid, Oxfam and Traidcraft (see *www.fairtrade.org.uk*). The organisation has its origins as a Christian movement (although it is now ecumenical), with the first product being Green & Black's Maya Gold chocolate bar. The aim of the organisation is to work with disadvantaged farmers in the developing world, providing them with an agreed and stable price for their produce, while developing longer-term trading relationships that enable producers to develop their businesses and plan ahead. At the same time, producers receive an investment premium to be spent on locally agreed improvements, such as better health care, clean water supplies or schooling. Emphasis is placed on more sustainable farming methods, although there is no insistence on organic production.

In the case of cocoa producers in Belize, a fair trade agreement meant that in 2009 they received a price of around US$3,500 per metric tonne, compared with a market price closer to US$2,000. At the same time, the Fairtrade organisation encourages producers to undertake the next stages of processing in order to add value to their product and to diversify. The organisation provides the link between the consumer in the UK and the producer in LEDCs.

> **Teaching resources**
>
> The Lorna Young Foundation (www.lyf.org.uk) provides details of projects it is assisting in Africa to enable producers 'who've taken the first step in evolving from subsistence farming to commercial sustainability'. This includes a coffee project between an Oromo Ethiopian community now settled in Manchester [☞] and small coffee producers in Ethiopia, cutting out the middleman.

> **Point for consideration**
>
> To what extent do notions of fair trade undermine campaigns to eat local produce? Can we justify the food miles involved in purchasing fair trade produce if it impacts on locally produced items which have a much smaller carbon footprint? An enthusiastic endorsement of fair trade goods sits uneasily alongside condemnation of long-distance transport, as does encouragement to students to consume healthy fruit juices made from imported tropical fruits.

Organic farming

Organic farming places a strong emphasis on the protection of wildlife and the environment. In organic farming, pesticides are severely restricted, with organic farmers required to develop nutrient-rich soils to grow strong healthy crops and encourage wildlife to help control pests and disease. Artificial chemical fertilisers are prohibited. Farmers are required to develop fertile soils by growing and rotating a mixture of crops using clover to fix nitrogen from the atmosphere. Animal cruelty is prohibited and a free-range life for farm animals is guaranteed. The routine use of drugs, such as antibiotics and wormers, is disallowed. The farmer is expected to use preventative methods, like moving animals to fresh pasture and keeping smaller herd sizes. The production and use of genetically modified products in animal feed is banned. (*www.soilassociation.org*; *www.organicfarmers.org.uk*)

See Volume 1: Human Geography, ch 3, Population geographies (p66).

In order for a farm in the UK to be considered organic, it must have been clear of artificial additives for two years, and the farm is inspected annually to ensure organic standards are maintained. It should be stressed, however, that there are no recognised international standards for organic production.

Organic producers argue that organic production is good for the consumer, the planet and is better for animals and wildlife. The absence of chemical fertilisers significantly reduces the carbon footprint of organic farmers (see p124). At the same time, organic food avoids pesticides and controversial additives including aspartame, tartrazine, monosodium glutamate and hydrogenated fats. UK government research suggests that plant, insect and bird life is up to 50% greater on organic farms. Organic farming relies on wildlife to help control natural pests, so wide field edges are left uncultivated for bugs, birds and bees to flourish. In addition, these edges are not sprayed away by the fertilisers, chemicals and pesticides routinely used on non-organic farms.

Clough Bottom Farm, Lancashire

Clough Bottom Farm[4] (*www.cloughbottom.co.uk*) is an organic beef farm of 360 acres in the Ribble Valley in Lancashire. The farm also raises organic chickens and produces a range of trees and shrubs along with fodder crops for the animals and some vegetables, which are used by the on-farm catering facilities which have been developed as part of the farm's policy of diversification. The farm has deliberately developed its farming operations in as sustainable and self-sufficient a manner as possible, including the processing of biodiesels and the planned development of small-scale hydroelectricity. In common with many smaller farm units, Clough Bottom has diversified into a range of other activities, including holiday cottages and a corporate management training centre (see figure 5.14 on p123).

See Volume 1: Human Geography, ch 5, Rural geography (p110).

Figure 5.13: Clough Bottom Farm

See accompanying CD-Rom

Clough Bottom.ppt

> **Clough Bottom organic beef**
>
> **A model for conservation**
>
> 'A contented, healthy cow is a very succulent steak'
>
> It's nice to know where your food comes from; that it's had a pleasant and peaceful life, well cared for in a natural environment.
>
> We don't name our Limousin and Aberdeen Angus cows, but we treat them with dignity and ensure that they want for nothing – after all, a contented, healthy cow is a very succulent steak!
>
> We raise organic beef following natural farming methods and adding clover and herb mixtures to the grass to enrich the land naturally. No artificial fertilisers or additives are used. In addition, our fields are bordered by conservation shelterbelts, which provide a natural haven for wildlife.
>
> **Why buy organic?**
>
> You know that the welfare and humane treatment of our cows is of paramount importance to us. In fact, our cattle are allowed to mature gradually, with the cows and calves living together until they naturally part and outgrow each other – but how does this benefit you?
>
> You get delicious, very high quality food – the organic beef is hung for a minimum of 28 days before it is sold to the butcher. This process increases the flavour in the meat.
>
> When you purchase organic beef it is a darker red colour (showing that it has been hung for longer) and has improved marbling (traces of white fat) through the meat, which makes it more tender.
>
> We sell our organic beef 'on the hoof' (a technical term!) and it can be found in major regional supermarkets and retailers – look out for it in the organic section!

Source: www.cloughbottom.co.uk/organic-beef.html

Figure 5.14: Clough Bottom organic beef

See accompanying CD-Rom

Clough Bottom.doc

> **Teaching idea 5.6**
>
> Ask students to identify the elements from the website statement in figure 15.4 that distinguish organic production from conventional production. Do they have a preference between the two? If so, why?

The ethics of food supply

There has been an increasing awareness in recent years of ethical issues surrounding farming, for instance relating to food safety, the ethics of genetic modification and particularly in terms of the treatment of livestock both on the farm and during transportation. The arrival of bovine spongiform encephalopathy (BSE), commonly known as 'mad-cow disease', in the UK in the 1990s put the spotlight on animal feedstuffs, the export of live veal calves from the UK was a highly controversial issue during the mid 1990s, while the outbreak of foot and mouth in 2001 vividly illustrated how animals were routinely moved over long distances around the country. Of equally high profile have been animal welfare campaigns on issues such as the conditions for raising battery hens and the whole process of 'factory farming'. Without doubt, the agro-food industry has become a battleground on several fronts, between producers and producers, between producers and consumers, between producers and governments and between governments (Dicken, 2007: 348).

> **Teaching idea 5.7**
>
> Ask students to investigate one of the issues discussed in the paragraph above. What opinions do they hold on these practices? Are their views informed by their own food preferences? How do they think ethical issues should be addressed in farming? A Wikipedia search will provide the historical context and, on the one hand, charities such as Compassion in World Farming and the RSPCA provide information on these issues, while from an alternative perspective, the National Farmers Union provides the views of the farming industry – see 'Useful websites' at the end of the chapter for weblinks.

However, ethical issues are not always as straightforward as they might appear. For instance, the spread of bovine tuberculosis across Wales and the west of England has been attributed to the growth in badger populations, in itself a consequence of one environmental policy that is now having significant implications for livestock farmers.

Food supply and carbon footprints

See ch 4, Energy (p93).

While the discussion earlier in the chapter highlighted the issue of food miles both in terms of socio-economic and environmental impacts, the largest emitter of greenhouse gas emissions in food production relates to agriculture, and in particular to livestock. Animals require a large amount of vegetable protein to produce a relatively small amount of meat. In LEDCs, extensive deforestation is occurring to produce feed for cattle to meet the growing global demand for beef. Methane emissions from cows also count as food-related emissions, as do emissions relating to processing, packaging, and, to a lesser extent, transport and waste. Over 20% of the UK's greenhouse gas emissions come from food and farming. Indeed, 3% of the world's energy is used in the manufacture of fertilisers.

The Carbon Trust has been involved in working with several large food companies, such as Walkers and Cadbury, to reduce their carbon footprint, while supermarkets, such as Tesco, have begun to label the carbon footprint on their produce (see figure 5.15 on p125). Figure 5.16 on p125 shows the carbon footprint for a packet of Walkers crisps. In this context, if the world wishes to reduce carbon footprints, then food supply will need to shift away from meat, dairy and processed food towards an increasing intake of seasonal fresh and local fruit and vegetable produce. A further area for effective reduction would be to eliminate the 30% of food that is currently wasted in the UK, a figure that includes 370,000 tonnes being thrown away each year after passing its 'best before' date.

Chapter 5: Food supply

Figure 5.15: Tesco becomes UK's first retailer to display carbon footprint on milk

Supermarket giant Tesco has become the first UK retailer to display the full carbon footprint of milk – one of the top-selling products in its stores.

From today, all Tesco own-label, full fat, semi-skimmed and skimmed milk ranges will display the carbon footprint label as part of an ongoing drive to help shoppers make 'green' purchasing decisions. It has pledged to 'footprint' 500 products by the end of the year. The new labelling will not apply to organic milk, where greenhouse gas emissions are generally much lower than for conventional milk.

The move comes alongside new research which found that 50% of customers surveyed now understand the correct meaning of the term 'carbon footprint', compared with only 32% of people surveyed in 2008. The research also revealed that customers increasingly want to be green. Over half said that they would seek lower carbon footprint products as part of their weekly shop, compared with only 35% last year.

Tesco said that with milk it is the agricultural stage that accounts for by far the biggest portion of the carbon footprint – in this case the most significant factor being methane emissions from the cows themselves. Dairy cows account for 40% of all UK livestock emissions and 75% of the carbon footprint of milk production. A spokesman said: 'We are currently embarking on a number of research projects to reduce the carbon emissions from milk production. For example, we're working on using different feeds that might help reduce methane emissions from cows, and encouraging the use of renewable energy on farms.'

Source: adapted from *The Guardian*, 17 August 2009. For the full article see www.guardian.co.uk/environment/2009/aug/17/tesco-milk-carbon-footprint

Tesco carbon footprint.doc

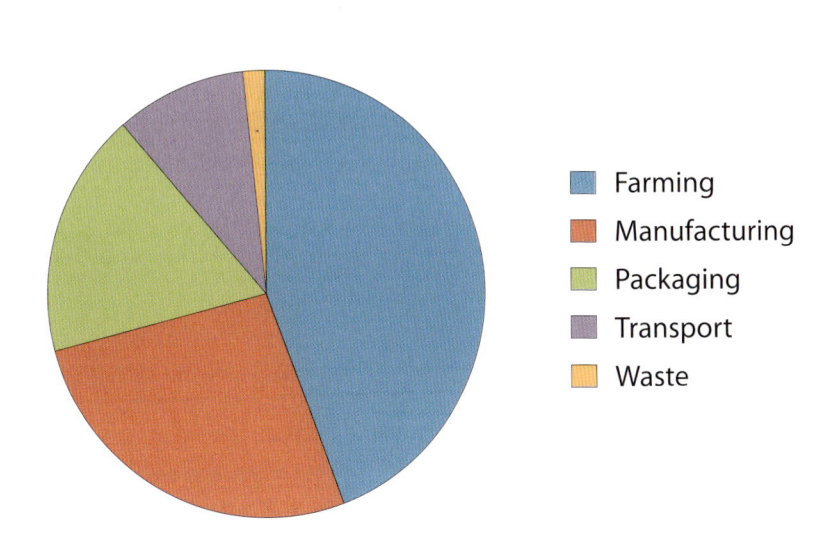

Figure 5.16: Carbon footprint proportions of a packet of Walkers crisps

- Farming
- Manufacturing
- Packaging
- Transport
- Waste

Walkers crisps.ppt and Walkers crisps.xl

Note: waste includes disposal of empty packets.
Source: www.walkerscarbonfootprint.co.uk/walkers_carbon_trust.html

See ch 7, Environmental management (p179).

> **Teaching idea 5.8**
>
> Using the information contained in figures 5.15 and 5.16 on p125, ask students to identify the carbon footprint on food products they have purchased. Can they think of ways in which this carbon footprint might be reduced?

Local cropping practices in less economically developed countries (LEDCs)

Industrial agriculture, as practised in more economically developed countries (MEDCs), depends on a relatively restricted number of commercial varieties. Similar practices have been developing in export-oriented farming in LEDCs. By contrast, cropping practices for locally grown produce in the less developed world are far more varied and represent significant sources of biodiversity [🔗]. This diversity may apply equally to livestock. Indeed, diversity is one of the key features of rural livelihood systems. For example, in the savannah lands of Nigeria, the Hausa and Fulani societies secure their sustenance in close proximity but through very different agricultural systems, based on permanent cultivation and semi-nomadic pastoralism respectively. The Turkana in Kenya have mixed herds, with camels, which browse resources that are available even in the dry season, and cattle, which are more productive in the wet season but have to move out of the plains into the hills during the drier months. Such systems offer a relatively low output, but are very sound environmentally in maintaining a steady livelihood for the pastoralists involved.

See ch 1, Ecosystems (p15).

> **Point for consideration**
>
> Students in Britain are likely to be familiar with one system of farming (if they are familiar with farming at all!) which usually focuses on single crops in fields based on crop rotation, or on grassland cultivation with animals. Photographs and discussion of farming practices in LEDCs may result in significant misconceptions if the reasons for a given farming practice are not fully explored, and may produce dangerous stereotyping and over-simplistic solutions.

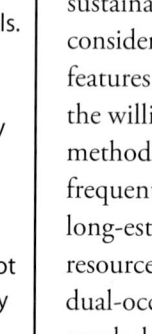

In many ways these forms of crop cultivation and livestock rearing are much more sustainable methods of agriculture than those found in MEDCs (see 'Point for consideration', left). The insecurity of rural livelihoods and the need to minimise risk are features of many small-scale food production systems and can be key factors affecting the willingness of farmers to innovate. Innovations such as new crops and production methods, like irrigation and the application of fertilisers and pesticides [🔗], are frequently costly, unavailable or unreliable, and require significant change from long-established methods. Farmers with low-level technology and limited financial resources cannot afford to take such risks. It is also not uncommon for farmers to be dual-occupationalists. For instance, in many parts of South-east Asia, farmers are also regularly industrial workers (Potter et al, 2008; Elliott, 2006).

Figure 5.17 on p127 itemises some aspects of cropping practices that are designed to ensure the sustainability of local farming systems.

See ch 7, Environmental management (p160).

However, it would be a mistake to imply that the actions of indigenous peoples are always imbued with environmental wisdom, since it is clear that local communities have been equally capable of wreaking environmental chaos through unsuitable and unsustainable over-exploitation of environments. For instance, some 2 billion people depend on drylands, 90% of them in developing countries, yet 6 million square kilometres of drylands bear a legacy of land degradation (UNEP, 2007).

Intercropping	The growing of two or more crops simultaneously on the same piece of land. Benefits arise because crops exploit different resources, or interact with one another. If one crop is a legume it may provide nutrients for the other. The interactions may also serve to control pests and weeds.
Rotations	The growing of two or more crops in sequence on the same piece of land. The benefits are similar to those arising from intercropping.
Agro-forestry	A form of intercropping in which annual herbaceous crops are grown interspersed with perennial trees or shrubs. The deeper rooted trees can often exploit water and nutrients not available to the herbs. The trees may also provide shade and mulch, while the ground cover of the herbs reduces weeds and prevents erosion.
Sylvo-pasture	Similar to agro-forestry but combining trees with grassland and other fodder species on which livestock graze. The mixture of oats, grasses and herbs often supports mixed livestock.
Green manuring	The growing of legumes and other plants in order to fix nitrogen and then incorporating them in the soil for the following crop.
Conservation tillage	Systems of minimum tillage or no tillage, in which the seed is placed directly in the soil with little or no preparatory cultivation. This reduces the amount of soil disturbance and so lessens run-off and loss of sediments and nutrients.
Biological control	The use of natural enemies, parasites or predators, to control pests. If the pest is exotic, these enemies may be imported from the country of origin of the pest; if indigenous, various techniques are used to augment the numbers of the existing natural enemies.
Integrated pest management	The use of appropriate techniques for controlling pests in an integrated manner that enhances rather than destroys natural controls. If pesticides are part of the programme, they are used sparingly and selectively so as not to interfere with natural enemies.

Source: Elliott, 2006: 166.

Figure 5.17: Agricultural technologies with high potential sustainability

Agricultural technologies.doc

See ch 2, Ecosystems (p22) and ch 7, Environmental management (p166).

See ch 4, Energy (p92).

Forestry

Discussions relating to forestry within the school curriculum have tended to be focused on issues such as deforestation and its impacts both on local communities and on global issues such as climate change. Clearly these are major issues, and the countries of the developing world are, on average, losing their forest resources at a rate of 1.1% per annum. However, trees, woodland and forests are multi-purpose resources that provide a range of functions in rural society. Approximately 60% of the world's 'closed forests', conventionally defined as where tree crowns cover more than 20% of the land area, are in the humid tropics. All tropical regions have examples of where farmers incorporate trees into their production as part of traditional systems of shifting cultivation.

There is a wide variety of ways in which woodland has been incorporated into farming systems in less developed countries. Where woodland forms a significant part of the system, this has been termed agro-forestry and might include such elements as: hedgerow intercropping; combining crops with plantation crops; creating shelter belts and windbreaks; using large numbers of herbaceous and wood plants, and apiculture with bees (Potter et al, 2008). Agro-forestry has the potential both to generate livelihoods and preserve environmental quality. Successful examples include palm oil production in semi-natural rainforests, and gum arabic production in drylands.

For many rural people in the less developed world generally, it is the resources of open woodland and scrub vegetation that play a particularly significant role in farming systems and livelihoods. There is a generally high dependency on biomass for energy, while woodlands provide a whole host of products: 'building timber, wood for kraal fences, tools, transport and construction (boats, scotchcarts, sledges, etc); edible leaves, pods, nuts and fruits; honey; natural fibres; medicines; utensils; and a whole range of other items.' (Munslow cited in Potter et al, 2008).

Figure 5.18:
Aspects of food security

See accompanying CD-Rom

Food security.doc

Aspect	Interpretation
Availability	Volume and reliability, provenance and diversity of supplies
Access	Affordability, physical accessibility
Affordability	Household food poverty and insecurity
Safety	Many recent crises relate to food safety; in the UK people are more likely to die of food poisoning than starvation
Resilience	Ability of the supply chain to withstand shocks and disruption
Confidence	Public confidence in the availability, safety and quality of food

Source: Cabinet Office, 2008a: 73.

Food security and food shortages

While the earlier discussion has suggested that food production has kept pace with population growth and, indeed, that (most) people are eating more food with a wider variety of products in their diet than ever before, food security remains a major issue that poses a significant threat globally. National food security is of greater urgency for developing countries than for the richer countries of the developed world. However, food security remains an issue for all countries. To illustrate this point, the severe Australian drought of 2008 devastated the wheat harvest. Largely as a consequence, wheat prices across the globe more than doubled and shopping bills rose by 15% in the UK. The interconnectedness of food supply is reinforced when one considers that British farmers now produce between eight and ten tonnes of wheat per hectare, double the output of 50 years ago, yet British shopping costs still rose as British harvests were purchased on the global market. Food security is a wide-ranging term (see figures 5.18 to 5.21 on p128-130), which can at times complicate discussions; however, ensuring food security is essentially a matter of identifying, assessing and managing the risks to food supply.

Figure 5.19:
Potential threats to food security

See accompanying CD-Rom

Food security.doc

	Political	Technical	Demographic and economic	Natural
Food supply reductions	• Wars	• Radioactive fallouts		• Floods • Droughts • Plants/animal disease
Decline in productive capacity		• Decline in non-renewable energy		• Water scarcities • Desertification • Soil erosion • Climate change
Global demand			• World population growth • Incomes growth	
Crises of affordability			• Poverty • Currency devaluations • Economic crises	
Disruption to trade and distribution	• Strikes • Wars • Trade embargoes • Export restrictions	• IT corruption	• Absenteeism due to pandemic flu	• Earthquakes

Source: Defra, 2006: 70.

	Situation	Issues	Scope for government involvement
Availability	• Wide range of products • Wide diversity of supply sources, including overseas • UK has about 60% market share	• Dependence on fuel and energy • Global food security • Food security of developing countries • European productive potential	• Promoting energy security • Focus on global availability/research • Strengthening trading system • Mitigating climate change
Access	• Competitive retail structure • Sophisticated distribution system • 80 to 90% of food consumption through retail sector; remainder through food services sector	• Dependence on lorry and car transport for distribution and purchasing • Excessive retailer concentration at local/regional level	• Promoting energy security • Ensuring key sectors are supplied in crisis • Competition policy • Contingency planning for severe disruptions
Affordability	• UK has very high per capita incomes • Real price of food has declined over time • Food a declining share of household budgets	• Low income groups • Possible 'food deserts'	• Tackling poverty directly • Inclusive and integrated transport • Reducing import tariffs (through WTO) • Competition policy
Nutrition and quality	• UK suffers from calorie excess, not deficient nutrition • Widespread assurance schemes	• Related to affordability – poor nutrition linked with low income • Excess calorie intake; obesity	• Promoting healthy diets
Safety	• Food Standards Agency • EU and international laws and codes • Occasional food scares • Private assurance and traceability	• Cross-border contamination • Food terrorism	• Food Standards Agency • EU safety laws
Confidence	• Consumers have confidence in retailers but have high expectations of food supply • Occasional panic-buying of essentials	• Confidence issues linked to provenance and assurance rather than actual quantity of food	• Importance of communication with industry particularly when crises arise

Source: Defra, 2006: 94.

Figure 5.20: Summarising UK food security

Food security.doc

Teaching idea 5.9

Figures 5.18 to 5.20 discuss food security from a UK government perspective. Ask students to identify one or more elements within the table and to investigate more fully how such issues may cause problems, and what might be the best future scenarios to prepare for potential food security shortfalls.

Figure 5.21 on p130 discusses the same issues from the perspective of the rural communities of less developed countries. Ask students to contrast the two perspectives relating to food security.

Issue	Processes influencing food security	Intervention options
Distribution/inequitable supply and access	• Terms of trade • Globalisation	• Trade negotiations • Fair trade • Debt adjustment
Fresh water supply	• Environmental change • Climate change • Conflict	• Sustainable development • Conservation • Conflict resolution over water access
Techno-agriculture	• Large-scale intensive farming • Increased use of GM crops and pesticides	• Avoid mono-cultivation • GM interventions based on ethical, cultural, social or economic rationale
Land tenure	• Changing rights of access to productive land	• Respecting the rights of local communities
Ecosystem resilience	• Ecological changes	• Lower input sustainable agriculture • Use of local methods and appropriate technology

Source: adapted from Collins, 2009: 155.

Figure 5.21:
Food security – issues and options

Food security.doc

Drought has already been mentioned as a major trigger for food shortages. Crop diseases have also had widespread impacts on food supply across the world. This is particularly the case in areas where agricultural systems are heavily dependent on a small range of crops. In such situations, producers are much more vulnerable to the threat of diseases and pests. Genetically modified crops may provide resistance to some plant diseases, but may also require more nutrients from the soil, resulting in any benefits of production being cancelled out. Similarly, the development of disease-resistant strains is essential to reduce damage to crops. For instance, a new variety of the wheat disease black stem rust (Ug99) in 1999 in Uganda led to widespread damage to crops, and the disease has spread through Africa and into Asia. However, a recently discovered strain of wheat, known as Sharon goat grass, is resistant to Ug99, raising hopes that the disease can be contained. The use of pesticides has increased dramatically around the world, as attempts are made to increase output by controlling pests and diseases. Yet, where these substances are also hazardous, there may also be consequences for human health (Collins, 2009: 128).

Food shortages are a major issue for vulnerable areas in the world. In the developing world, urban areas are more likely to experience difficulties with food shortage than rural areas, with the urban poor in the developing world spending up to 65% of their income on food (figure 5.22). Nevertheless, experience suggests that, in many instances, the issue relates more to failure of the food market to function effectively than to actual harvest failures. A range of indicators can be deployed to identify the likelihood of food shortage and to make arrangements to minimise impacts (see figure 5.23 on p131).

Figure 5.22:
Food price inflation in urbanising developing countries, 2007-2008

Food price inflation.doc

- 'Tortilla riots' in Mexico were triggered by large increases in the cost of the maize flour that is the staple food
- Pork price hikes in China caused by growing demand, higher feed prices and the impact of pig disease on supply pushed up inflation and prompted the government to impose price controls
- India imposed a ban on wheat exports to protect domestic food supplies.

There is potential for unrest in the developed world too:
- In Italy there were protests against the increased price of pasta, as the high price of wheat was passed on to consumers by manufacturers.

Source: Cabinet Office, 2008a: 71.

> - Rains late or failed
> - Crop failure
> - Deteriorating economic situation
> - Increased grain prices
> - Unseasonable disappearance of foods
> - Low levels of household stores
>
> **Stress indicators**
> - Increased dependence on wild foods
> - Increased dependence on food aid
> - Decreased number of meals
>
> **Outcome indicators**
> - Increased malnutrition
> - Increased mortality
> - Outmigration

Figure 5.23: Early indicators of food shortage

See accompanying CD-Rom
Early indicators.doc

Source: Collins, 2009: 209.

Media images of starvation in Africa have heavily influenced thinking in MEDCs about farming practices and population levels in less developed countries. Coverage of the two Sahel famines of the 1970s and 1980s, for instance, were widely interpreted in a neo-Malthusian context – that is to say, that a decline in food production had resulted in insufficient food for the existing population. These ideas were graphically portrayed on our televisions and culminated in the Live Aid concert of 1986. However, it is now accepted that famine is a phenomenon with complex causes and that many of these causes are economic and political. In the case of the Sudan famine of 1984, for instance, famine was a result of drought and market failure. Severe reductions in rainfall in 1984 triggered widespread speculation in food which pushed prices beyond the reach of ordinary rural people. Nationally there was sufficient food, but poor distribution allowed the famine to develop (Adams, 2009: 220-225).

A further factor likely to have major impacts on food supply is climate change [☞]. Climate change will dramatically alter the growing seasons for many crops and have a range of impacts on production at a variety of scales. Changes in rainfall patterns (such as the Australian drought mentioned on p128) and rising temperatures will present major challenges for farmers (figure 5.24). More than 90% of climate model simulations predict lower rainfall in sub-tropical regions, with sub-Saharan Africa and South Asia likely to face the biggest food security challenges.

See ch 3, Climate change.

> In 2003, Europe experienced a summer with temperatures up to 6°C above long-term norms, and rainfall deficits of up to 300mm. There were marked impacts on agriculture:
>
> - In the Po Valley, Italy, maize yields dropped 30%
> - In France, maize yields fell 25% compared to the previous year and fruit harvests fell 25%
> - Forage production fell on average by 30% in France.
>
> The (uninsured) economic losses for the EU agriculture sector were estimated at €13 billion; losses in France alone measured at €4 billion.

Figure 5.24: Impacts of the 2003 heatwave on agriculture in Europe

See accompanying CD-Rom
2003 heatwave.doc

Source: Cabinet Office, 2008a: 80.

At a slightly more benign level, temperatures in most Australian wine growing regions are projected to rise by between 0.3°C and 1.7°C by 2030. This could lead to a deterioration in grape quality, with varieties such as pinot noir and sauvignon blanc, which require cooler climates, disappearing from the mainland and being produced on the island of Tasmania. Decisions to alter cropping patterns may be relatively painless when compared with other scenarios relating to pests and diseases. The spread of bluetongue, a virus carried by midges that affects cattle, sheep, deer and goats, to north-west Europe in 2006 has been attributed to warmer temperatures in the region. However, the major threats may come not from exotic pests but from reinvigorated local ones. Aphids cause about £100 million of damage annually in the UK to cereal crops, but as the weather warms, aphids are arriving in the fields earlier than previously when crops are younger and the damage inflicted is greater. One solution to this problem has been to plant nettles around wheat fields so that parasitic wasps arrive to feed off the aphids found in the nettles and remain to deal with the aphid infestation as the wheat grows. Such biological controls would appear to be one part of the solution in a lower-carbon future where pesticide use is reduced.

Summary

Food supply is an essential element in our existence. Whenever we consume goods such as coffee or tea, we use an agricultural product that has been grown, harvested, processed, packaged, shipped and marketed. If we choose to purchase our coffee or tea through the fair trade movement, then we are engaging in similar transactions within an alternative network of relationships.

Over the past half century, the developed world has experienced huge improvements in the quality and quantity of food available as a result of changes in agriculture, industry, retailing, technology and transportation. However, these benefits have not always been felt in less developed areas of the world, and a major challenge for the next generation is to ensure security of food supply against a backdrop of changing climate and growing populations. More food will be required from less land, using less water and fertiliser, while producing fewer greenhouse gas emissions.

For the teacher, the essential advantage of teaching about food supply is that all students have to engage with the process merely to survive, therefore building on the known world of the student provides a clear way in to developing student consciousness of the complexities of the issues involved.

Endnotes

1. 'Productivist' farming refers to systems of farming that aim to maximise outputs, often by providing a very capital-intensive form of farming with large-scale inputs. The period of maximised EU production that resulted in wine lakes, butter mountains and so on in the 1980s' has subsequently been replaced by what has been termed 'post-productivist' agriculture, where a range of factors other than simply maximising outputs are taken into account as part of the farming system.

2. The Redbush Tea Company provides 'a percentage of the profits' from the sale of its tea to 'benefit the indigenous peoples of the Kalahari.' See *www.kalaharipeoples.org*

3. For a detailed discussion of government approaches to food miles see: *https://statistics.defra.gov.uk/esg/reports/foodmiles/final.pdf*

4. This farm has been deliberately chosen as a case study because of its close proximity to the examples used in chapter 5 of Volume 1: Human Geography – Bashall Barn,

See Volume 1: Human Geography, ch 5, Rural geographies (p110).

Backridge and Bowland Fresh. Together, the case studies provide a range of examples of the complexities of 'the new rural' in the English countryside.

Useful websites

www.bgci.org/ The Botanical Gardens Conservation International website contains a range of reports on the impacts of climate change and provides educational resources.

www.face-online.org.uk/ Farming and Countryside Education provides a range of educational resources on farming issues.

Oxfam has a range of information on food security including an interactive map with images and videos at *www.oxfam.org.uk/oxfam_in_action/issues/food_crisis/map.html*

www.compassioninworldfarming.org is a farm animal welfare charity that provides a range of educational materials.

www.rspca.org.uk similarly provides a range of information on animal welfare issues.

www.cla.org.uk/ is the website of the Country Landowners Association and provides a perspective on farming from the point of view of the larger landowners and farmers.

www.nfuonline.com/ is the website of the National Farmers Union, providing an industry perspective on farming issues.

www.soilassociation.org/ is the website of the Soil Association, which campaigns for 'planet-friendly organic food and farming'.

www.carbontrust.co.uk/ is an independent body set up by the UK government to provide support for businesses in developing low carbon technology.

http://europa.eu/index_en.htm is the official website of the European Union – includes sections on agriculture, the environment and regional policy.

www.defra.gov.uk/ is the UK government department responsible for the environment, for food and farming, and for rural matters.

www.fao.org/ The United Nations Food and Agriculture Organization – includes an extensive range of statistics on food production and trade.

Sustainability

Vanessa Holden

Introduction – what is 'sustainability'?

The concept of sustainability [☞] – the ability to achieve economic growth and social development while maintaining environmental systems – is one that very few people can disagree with. It is a concept that, if it could be achieved, would please all of the people, all of the time. Because of this, the word (if not the concept) has been adopted globally by industrialists, politicians and environmentalists as something to aim for, something to commit to and publicly support. In reality, it is a very difficult, some may say almost impossible, ideal, but one that is nevertheless essential in order to try to 'manage' the development of human society without cost to poorer societies or the natural environment.

See Volume 1: Human Geography, ch 7, Development geographies (p147).

Interestingly, when the word 'sustain' is entered into a commonly used electronic thesaurus, the three alternative words that are given are 'maintain', 'nourish', and 'suffer'. These three words can indeed form the basis of a good understanding of the concept of sustainability. The ideal is to maintain current economic, social and environmental systems, without the situation in any of the three becoming worse. Optimists would say that sustainability will allow nourishment, both of natural systems and of human society – that by appreciating the cost of development on a global scale, humans will ultimately develop a less materialistic and better quality of life. Pessimists, however, could argue that by reducing human exploitation of natural resources and potentially limiting growth, both current and future generations, particularly in developing societies, could suffer.

Sustainability is not a new idea. The United Nations Conference on the Human Environment in 1972 was an early example of the recognition that economic growth should be possible without environmentally damaging outcomes. The first widely adopted definition, and the one that has subsequently been used globally to describe the concept, appeared in the 1987 Brundtland Report [☞] *Our Common Future* (Gro Harlem Brundtland was the chairperson of the Assembly, and later became the prime minister of Norway), which was published by the World Commission on the Environment and Development (WCED). The report stated that sustainable development was 'development that meets the needs of the present without compromising the ability of future generations to meet their own needs'. This somewhat indistinct definition has been widely quoted and, arguably, its fuzziness is one of the reasons why it has been so broadly adopted by so many different people. The report, however, was one of the first to acknowledge that environmental protection and human development and growth could not be separated, and that growth will always have an environmental impact to some degree. Similarly, the health of the environment will often determine the sustainability of growth.

See ch 8, Globalisation (p183).

As a direct result of the Brundtland Report, the UN acknowledged the global necessity for furthering the advancement of sustainable development, and subsequently held the United Nations Conference on Environment and Development (commonly called the 'Rio Conference') in 1992. Its successor in 2002 was the World Summit on Sustainable Development in Johannesburg.

Indeed, this basic definition of sustainable development is still applicable 20 years after the publication of *Our Common Future*, with the UK government Sustainable Development Strategy of 2005 aiming to 'enable all people throughout the world to satisfy their basic needs and enjoy a better quality of life without compromising the quality of life of future generations' (HM Government, 2005: 7). In many cases, the exact definition used by an organisation or individual will depend greatly upon their particular 'cause'. For example, environmentalists will be concerned largely with the exploitation of natural resources and ecosystems, while a politician may consider the ability of transport systems to meet increasing demands to be more important. It is the concept of sustainable development that aims to bring all issues into the same arena. In order to achieve true sustainability, social development, economic growth, human use of natural resources, and continuation and health of ecosystems cannot, and should not, be considered in isolation from any one of the other issues (figure 6.1). This chapter is therefore structured around each of those issues; however, it should be remembered that these individual issues should not be considered in isolation. They are dealt with separately purely for ease of reading and to try to give some structure to the fuzzy concept of sustainability.

Figure 6.1:
Sustainable development

See accompanying CD-Rom

Sustainable development.ppt

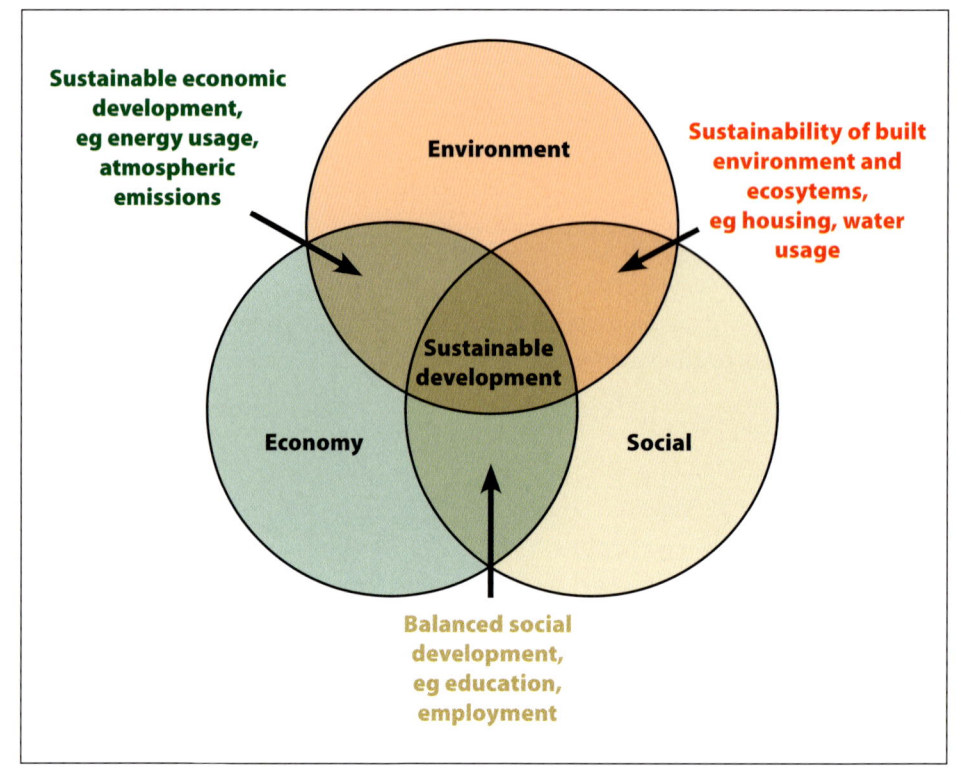

> **Teaching idea 6.1**
>
> Ask students to reflect on their own priorities for sustainable development. How would they rank: protecting the environment, economic growth, and a better quality of life for people in communities? Then ask them to consider how different groups in society might have different views about the relative importance of the elements of sustainable development. Contrasting examples might include affluent urban dwellers in developed cities and farming communities living in rural villages in the less developed world.

Social development and sustainability

Social development refers to the process of changes that occur within a particular society. This can sometimes be referred to as the 'evolution' of a society. In terms of sustainability, social development is related to the changing standards of living of communities, and the subsequent impacts (or otherwise) on the environment, and associated economic change. Traditionally, positive social development has been associated with improvements in standards of living and the quality of life of people. It has often been considered in relation to increasing monetary wealth, and increased access to technologies, particularly in the more economically developed countries (MEDCs). However, more recently, in addition to the 'material' aspects of development, issues such as the improved rights of minority groups and social integration, particularly in less economically developed countries (LEDCs), have risen up the political agenda. Although many of the issues are relevant across all societies, the degree to which there is potential for development varies greatly around the world. Issues such as access to education, employment, and reducing poverty are seen as basic rights in MEDCs, and as such 'development' is regarded as improvements to established systems. However, in certain LEDCs these issues are very much in their early stages of development, with access to an education all too often being viewed as a privilege rather than a basic right. In addition, LEDCs often have distinct issues associated with indigenous populations (see *www.un.org/esa/socdev*).

Social development and sustainability need to be considered in terms of the ever increasing population of the world. Since 1950 the global population [☞] has doubled, from around 3 billion (3 thousand million) to almost 7 billion in 2010 (see figure 6.2 on p138). Although the rate of growth is thought to be slowing, there is still projected to be a population of around 9 billion by 2050. This growth, due to a number of factors, such as reduced mortality as a result of medical advances, is making the issue of sustainability of much greater relevance, as more stress is being placed on the limited natural resources currently used by people, at the same time as greater impacts on the environment are occurring per person, and more and more people require basic requirements such as access to enough food, water and space to live.

See Volume 1: Human Geography, ch 3, Population geographies (p55).

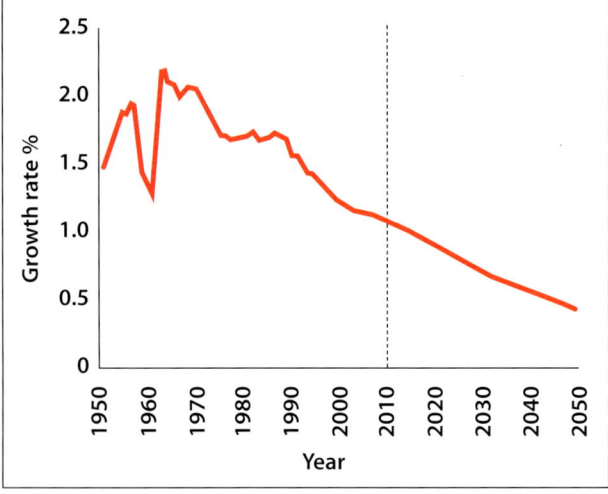

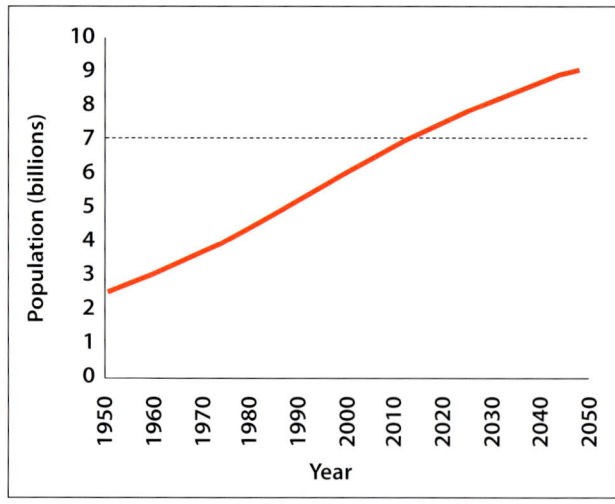

Chapter 6: Sustainability

Figure 6.2:
(left) Growth Rates in World Population, 1950-2050
(right) World population, 1950-2050

Source: adapted from US Census Bureau International Data Base. December 2009 update.

See accompanying CD-Rom

World population.ppt

Teaching idea 6.2

Provide students with population data for a set of countries at contrasting levels of development (see *http://data.worldbank.org/data-catalog* for data on more than 200 countries for any year from 1950 to 2050), along with selected socio-economic data such as GDP, rates of urbanisation, etc. A wide range of such data can be downloaded as a spreadsheet from *www.imf.org/external/pubs/ft/weo/2009/01/weodata/weoselgr.aspx*, where data such as GDP and employment is available at country level worldwide. Ask students to evaluate the possible impacts of changes in population on the future sustainability of environments in those countries and to consider which countries are most likely to be experiencing pressures in the future.

Social development in LEDCs

We have already seen how social development has a range of meanings according to different perspectives. Nowhere is this more obvious than in the perception of issues in the less developed world when viewed from the perspective of the wealthier nations. For instance, if we approach the topic of tropical rainforests from the perspective of the social development of the indigenous peoples, then a rather different narrative develops compared with conventional discussions of rainforest destruction (see figure 6.3 on p139). It is often too easy for wealthier nations to condemn the destruction of rainforests [🔗] because of their role in providing extremely important habitats for wildlife and for counteracting carbon emissions produced (often in the developed countries). However, people local to such environments are often struggling to survive, living in poverty, with minimal (if any) health care and education provision, and may be faced with no alternative but to work for companies that are logging the forests. Ultimately, the corporations that are responsible for the deforestation are all too often owned by shareholders in developed countries.

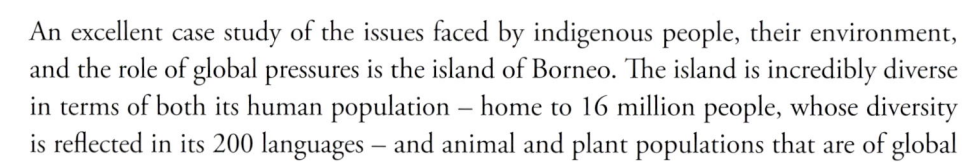

See ch 7, Environment management (p166).

An excellent case study of the issues faced by indigenous people, their environment, and the role of global pressures is the island of Borneo. The island is incredibly diverse in terms of both its human population – home to 16 million people, whose diversity is reflected in its 200 languages – and animal and plant populations that are of global

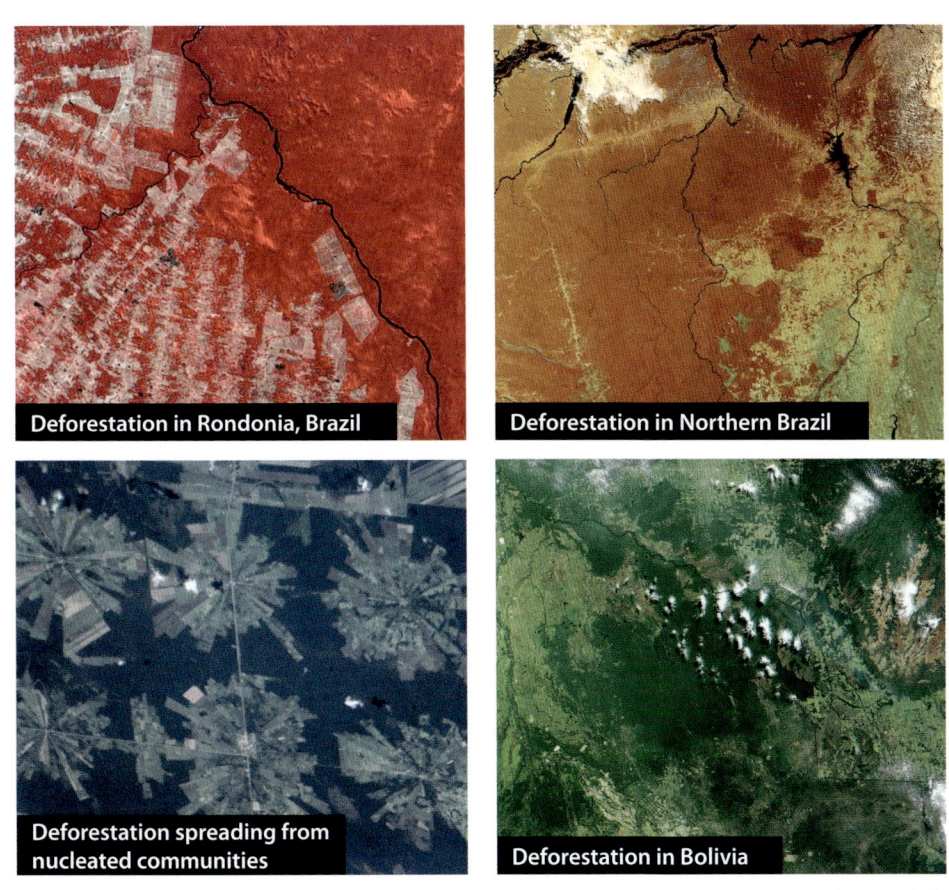

Figure 6.3: Deforestation in the tropical rainforests of Brazil and Bolivia

See accompanying CD-Rom

Deforestation.ppt

Deforestation in Rondonia, Brazil

Deforestation in Northern Brazil

Deforestation spreading from nucleated communities

Deforestation in Bolivia

Source: (top left) NASA/GSFC/METI/ERSDAC/JAROS and US/Japan ASTER Science Team; (bottom left) Earth Sciences and Image Analysis Laboratory at Johnson Space Center; (right) Jacques Descloitres, MODIS Land Rapid Response Team, NASA/GSFC. *www.visibleearth.nasa.gov*

significance in terms of both diversity and rarity. The forests of the island continue to support a large number of people that are dependent upon its natural resources for survival. However, increasingly, the forests are being destroyed to clear land to allow massive single crop plantations of palm oil. The palm oil is ultimately transported to industrialised nations to be used in food, biofuels, cleaning products, and for industrial applications. The impacts of palm oil plantations on Borneo are an extremely emotive issue for many people, not only because of the plight of the indigenous people, but also of key animal species such as orang-utans. As such, there are constantly updated reports and news articles available via the internet covering the range of arguments in this case. For example, the environmental campaigning organisation Friends of the Earth has produced a number of summary documents available on their website (*www.foe.co.uk*). Conservation charities, from their own distinctive perspective, produce large amounts of information – for example, the Borneo Orangutan Survival Foundation, which promotes itself as working with local people to develop higher sustainable incomes by non-destructive means (*www.savetheorangutan.info*), and the UK-based conservation charity Orangutan Appeal UK (*www.organutan-appeal.org.uk*). With the issues surrounding Borneo focused around palm oil export, many UK (and multinational) companies are now covering sourcing of such products in their corporate and social responsibility reports (for example, see Sainsbury's supermarket CSR 2009 report at: *www.j-sainsburys.co.uk/cr/files/pdf/cr2009_report.pdf*).

Social development in MEDCs

It is often the issues facing developing countries that are at the forefront of debate relating to notions of sustainability; however, there are equally significant issues within developed countries, such as the UK, that have major impacts on the communities and society that live there. Relatively affluent societies, such as the UK, may be in the fortunate position of being able to take steps towards achieving environmental sustainability, although the extent to which these steps can be considered successful is variable.

The subject of sustainability is a vast topic. It can easily fill an entire book, not just a chapter. Although the issue of moving towards sustainability is a global requirement, for the purposes of this chapter it is impractical to try to discuss the huge global issues, along with the 'local' or national issues faced in the UK. Therefore, although consideration is given to global issues to provide clarity, by virtue of necessity the issues considered in the chapter will pertain predominantly to those facing the UK, with specific reference being made to UK government strategies and policy. Similarly, the following sections are aimed at giving a broad overview of some of the main issues rather than an impossibly comprehensive overload of facts and figures.

The next section will look at attempts within the UK to achieve greater sustainability in relation to its housing stock. The UK has an expanding and ageing population and at the same time is experiencing significant change in terms of household structure. All these changes are creating pressures on the housing stock and this requires an effective government response if future housing needs are to be addressed in a sustainable manner. Over the next few decades, more houses will be required in the UK. A UK government green paper of 2007 outlined a strategy to deliver 3 million additional homes by 2020 (Department for Communities and Local Government, 2007). However, in an attempt to offset the environmental impacts of this new construction, various steps are beginning to be implemented.

See ch 4, Energy (p104-105).

Figure 6.4:
The Code for Sustainable Homes

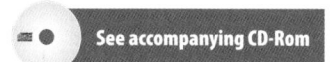

See accompanying CD-Rom

Sustainability.doc

Since April 2007, building developers in England and Wales have been able to choose to have their buildings assessed under the 'Code for Sustainable Homes' (figure 6.4; see 'Useful websites' on p155). This is a national standard to encourage sustainable design and building in new homes. From May 2008, all new homes have had to be rated against this standard before they can be sold. The standard has been developed to assist in achieving the goal of the UK government to reduce carbon emissions by 80% by 2050.

Category	Exemplification
Energy usage and CO$_2$ emissions	Lighting; low carbon technologies.
Waste management	Construction waste; storage of recyclable and non-recyclable household waste.
Water	Water usage internally and externally.
Material usage	Environmental impact of materials; sourcing of materials.
Surface water run-off	Control of surface water run-off from new developments.
Ecology	Change in ecological value of site.
Pollution	Emissions of nitrous oxides; environmental impact of insulants.
Health and wellbeing	Sound insulation; daylight provision.
Management	Construction site impacts; security.

Source: adapted from Department for Communities and Local Government, 2008.

Currently, housing is estimated to be responsible for 27% of the UK's carbon emissions. With reference to the standard, each home is assessed on a set of nine issues, including its energy efficiency, water efficiency, and the use of materials in its construction. A further government target is that all new homes will have zero carbon emissions from 2016.

> **Teaching idea 6.3**
>
> Do any of your students live in a recently built house? If so, what characteristics can they identify that make it more sustainable than older housing? Ask students who live in older houses to identify aspects of the property that could be modified to improve its overall sustainability. (The Commission for Architecture and the Built Environment provides a wide range of related teaching resources on its website: **www.cabe.org.uk**) [☞]

See ch 4, Energy, Teaching idea 4.12 (p106).

Economic growth and sustainability

Economic growth can be defined as an increase in the services and/or goods that are produced by a specific area. Traditionally, such growth has been focused around accompanying technological development, or stimulated by the availability of natural or human resources. As such, it is often viewed as being in conflict with the requirements of natural ecosystems. But with growing awareness of the concept of sustainable development, increasingly the principles of sustainability are being included in definitions of economic growth.

Economic growth in LEDCs

Areas with the greatest perceived need for economic growth, ie the less developed regions of the world, are usually the areas where conflicts of interest in terms of sustainability are most marked. A cynic might suggest that this is because those areas that have already been developed have already passed through stages of environmental degradation relating to economic growth and are now seeking to prevent underdeveloped regions from following a similar course of development [☞]. There is a particular conflict of interest where development of land for economic improvement, for instance by introducing agricultural techniques from the wealthier nations, may reduce biodiversity, and can result in water pollution or increased soil erosion. On the other hand, the failure to adopt such developments may well exacerbate issues such as rural poverty, and hinder social development and attempts to improve the health of the population. Similarly, efforts to conserve habitat and biodiversity by strictly managing land use, such as in national parks and designated protected areas, need to be made in a way that does not restrict the ability of indigenous communities to develop economically and socially.

See ch 4, Energy, Point for consideration (p86).

Such tensions do not mean that the problems are intractable. Solutions are beginning to be developed, for example through schemes that allow local communities to be involved in the management and the development of wildlife tourism (see figures 6.5 and 6.6 on p142-143) within a protected area, hence enhancing economic developments (Adams, 2009). However, there are situations where the rapid increase in tourism is leading to large influxes of people seeking employment in tourism industries, greatly (and sometimes unsustainably) increasing local populations.

Chapter 6: Sustainability

Figure 6.5:
Wildlife tourism in the Galapagos Islands

Galapagos Islands.ppt

Note: people are attracted by the unique landscape and wildlife. Due to the only relatively recent influx of humans, much of the wildlife has not yet developed a fear of humans.

Chapter 6: Sustainability

**Figure 6.6:
Wildlife tourism in Ecuador and the Amazon Rainforest**

Ecuador and Amazon.ppt

See accompanying CD-Rom

Chris Kington Publishing   Contemporary Approaches to Geography Volume 3: Environmental Geography   143

Figure 6.7:
Wildlife tourism

See accompanying CD-Rom

Wildlife tourism.doc

> Wildlife tourism can be broadly defined as trips to destinations with the main purpose of the visit being to observe the local fauna. The global market size of wildlife tourism is estimated as being 12 million trips each year. Africa accounts for around one-half of all these trips, with South Africa, Kenya, Tanzania and Botswana being the top destinations. Some destinations rely heavily on wildlife tourism, (wildlife tourism contributes roughly US$500 million to the Kenyan economy, or 14% of GDP). On the other hand, places such as the Galapagos Islands rely almost exclusively on wildlife tourists (wildlife tourism contributes £60 million to the local economy). Other destinations are enjoying increased influxes of visitors due to strong interest in certain mammals. For example there has been considerable growth in whale watching at Kaikoura in New Zealand and Puerto Piraminde in Argentine Patagonia.
>
> There is still considerable potential for growth within this market, and it is expected to expand by between 8% and 10% per annum over the next decade. The age group that will most influence this growth will be the increasingly wealthy, healthy and active 55+ age group.
>
> Tour operators from the UK include: Wildlife Worldwide (*www.wildlifeworldwide.com*) and Naturetrek (*www.naturetrek.co.uk*).

Source: www.onecaribbean.org

Teaching idea 6.4

Ask students to investigate one of the UK tour operators cited in figure 6.7. What evidence can they find of sustainable practices being developed for the tourist packages they are selling? Alternatively, ask students to investigate a specific example of sustainable rural development, for instance community-based natural resource management in Namibia where rural communities form a 'conservancy', which is legally registered to manage its own wildlife in a sustainable way. This includes rights to management for tourism (*www.irdnc.org.na* or *www.wwf.org.uk/what_we_do/ safeguarding_the_natural_world/wildlife/namibia2*)

Economic growth in MEDCs

Similar conflicts of interest may be identified within wealthier nations, although in many cases such nations have developed structures, such as planning regulations, to ensure that conflicts are handled according to the prevailing guidelines at the time. This, of course, does not mean that conflict is absent. For example, in an urbanised area that is at risk of coastal flooding due to rising sea levels, there may well be calls for expenditure on improved sea defences to protect economically valuable land, often through solutions based on hard engineering [📖]. However, this will often be at the expense of coastal habitats, which may be home to rare and at-risk species. There are therefore difficult decisions to be made regarding the protection of economically valuable buildings and land, and the safeguarding of rare species of both plants and animals and their specialised habitats.

See Volume 2: Physical Geography, ch 3, Coasts (p83).

Large corporations are now likely to have specific policies relating to environmental and social responsibility, developed perhaps largely as a consequence of negative publicity generated by environmental and social pressure groups during the 1980s and 1990s. These policies have the potential to influence societies and individuals positively, through activities such as sponsorship and 'endorsement'. At the same time, they can have significant sway in political situations, compelling policy decisions, and raising awareness. The extent to which these policies are simply 'green-washing' is open to debate, and many transnational businesses are often viewed as those that are most likely to be operating against the principles of sustainable development. Criticisms may be voiced about them exploiting developing communities [☞], being major polluters, and utilising vast quantities of natural resources, through energy demand, packaging, transport, and so on.

See ch 8, Globalisation (p194).

> **Teaching idea 6.5**
>
> Ask students to investigate the environmental policies of a major transnational corporation that operates in their local area, or manufactures products commonly used by students (such as a food producer). How does the company claim to support sustainability? What claims does it make in relation to environmental awareness? To what extent do they consider that the policy documents reflect the reality of their local experiences? (For a range of possible websites see Weblinks.doc [☞])

Weblinks.doc

While much of the focus of pressure groups has been on 'big' business, small and medium-sized companies in fact constitute the majority of economic activity in the UK. Many of these companies view sustainability as something that will 'detract' from their everyday business, or will be something thrust upon them that will ultimately cost them money. Much of this view is based on notions of increased taxation and rising costs, either as an attempt to reduce (for example) energy usage, or through a reflection of real increased costs due to scarcity of materials or increased costs elsewhere in the supply chain. However, there are businesses that view sustainability in a more proactive sense. For these more forward-looking companies, there are programmes and accreditation schemes aimed at highlighting a company's commitment to environmental improvement. These include schemes [☞] such as the ISO 14000 series standards of environmental management, to which a company can operate in areas such as Life Cycle Assessment and Eco Labelling. Environmental Management Systems (EMS) can be accredited, for example to British Standard ISO 14001, or through the European Eco-Management and Audit Scheme (EMAS). Participating companies can then use their commitment to such schemes to promote their business as having an environmental awareness of its operations.

Weblinks.doc

It should be stressed here that not all schemes that are presented in terms of their friendliness towards the environment or their contribution to sustainability are as effective as their supporters claim them to be. In the UK, the recent 'car scrappage scheme' (operating throughout 2009) was a joint financial incentive by the government and motor manufacturers to encourage owners of older vehicles to trade them in for brand new cars. Although the scheme boosted manufacture of new cars, with the economic benefits that brings to the communities involved in both car production and car retailing, the environmental impact may not be as positive. Although many new cars are more 'environmentally friendly' to run, with improved fuel consumption and lower exhaust emissions, the complete life cycle of the vehicles did not appear to be fully acknowledged by the scheme. A significant amount of the energy use during the life of a car relates to the initial manufacture of the vehicle, therefore a scheme that encourages the premature replacement of ageing vehicles raises issues concerning the

See ch 7, Environmental management (p179).

overall energy efficiency savings incorporated into the scheme. At the same time, the scrappage of older vehicles leads to a greater level of disposal and consequent demands upon waste management [].

Transport and sustainability

One of the key elements of modern society has been the dramatic increase in mobility; both personal mobility and the movement of goods and produce around the world. Increases in mobility are inextricably linked to economic growth. Manufactured goods are increasingly transported by sea, air and road. The large growth in disposable incomes experienced across much of the world over the past 50 years has resulted in more people purchasing more goods than ever before. Most international trade [] is carried out by sea-borne vessels, which have at best a patchy environmental record. Although transport by sea allows vast quantities of goods to be moved en masse, the huge engines driving the vessels require immense amounts of fuel from non-renewable fossil fuel sources. Although thankfully rare, because of the scale of the movement of goods by this manner, when things go wrong they do so on a massive scale. Environmental disasters involving oil spills from damaged ships have led to significant ecological problems in a number of coastal and marine areas.

See Volume 1: Human Geography, ch 10, Geographies of globalisation (p206).

The traffic of goods by air is projected to be three times higher in 2025 than it was in 2005 (International Transport Forum, 2008). 'Food miles' and issues relating to the transport of fresh produce around the globe are discussed in more detail elsewhere []; suffice it to say here that issues relating to the desirability of consuming local produce may well be in conflict with the possible implications of a reduction in the trade of food produced in developing countries, with potentially severe consequences for those economies. Examples such as this illustrate the problems of an over-simplified conception of sustainability.

See ch 5, Food supply (p116).

Leaving aside issues of trade, travel [] by car is considered by many to be an essential element of modern life as well as an indicator of affluence and wealth, with ownership worldwide expected to treble by 2050. Road transport as a whole accounts for around 20% of the total man-made emissions of CO_2, with cars accounting for around half of CO_2 transport emissions (International Transport Forum, 2008). During the past decade, there has been a significant reduction in emissions from vehicles, largely due to improvements in vehicle performance, and awareness by drivers. However, for the environmental impacts of transport to be further reduced, it is clear that a range of cultural changes are required. According to the International Transport Forum (2008), many people choose to travel by car because alternative forms of transport, such as public transport, are viewed as unreliable, costly or inconvenient. There is therefore an obvious dilemma: should money be invested in improving the infrastructure of the public transport network to entice people away from cars, or should money be put into improving the current road networks to reduce congestion and the increased emissions related to congestion? Attempts have been made to encourage road users to drive less-polluting cars by introducing taxation classes based upon the CO_2 emissions of a car. A fairer system for non-commercial drivers may be taxation based upon mileage travelled rather than emissions, although such schemes have been viewed with hostility in rural areas where distances travelled may well be greater, irrespective of income.

See Volume 1: Human Geography, ch 4, Urban geographies (p83).

> **Teaching idea 6.6**
>
> Provide students with a range of personal scenarios and ask them to identify which cars would be their best purchase in terms of environmental impacts, taking account of size requirements, income and other relevant information. If they were in such a situation would they buy a car using environmental criteria?
>
> Scenarios might include: a young family with two children on a middle income where one parent has a significant commute to work; a young single person on a high income living near their work in the centre of a city; a retired couple with a reasonable pension with family scattered around the country, etc.

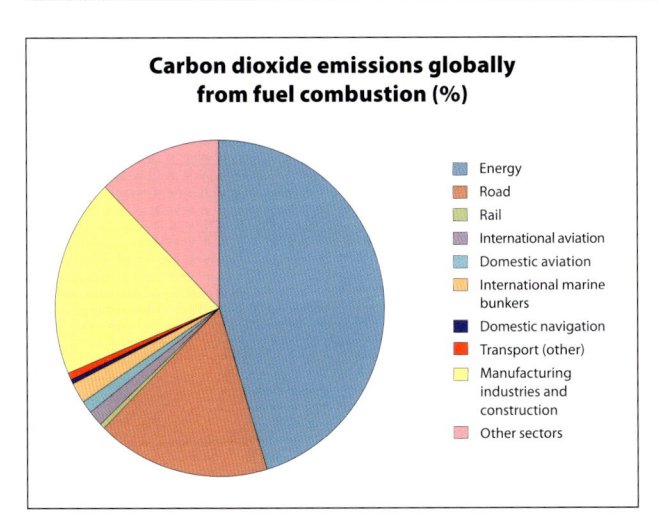

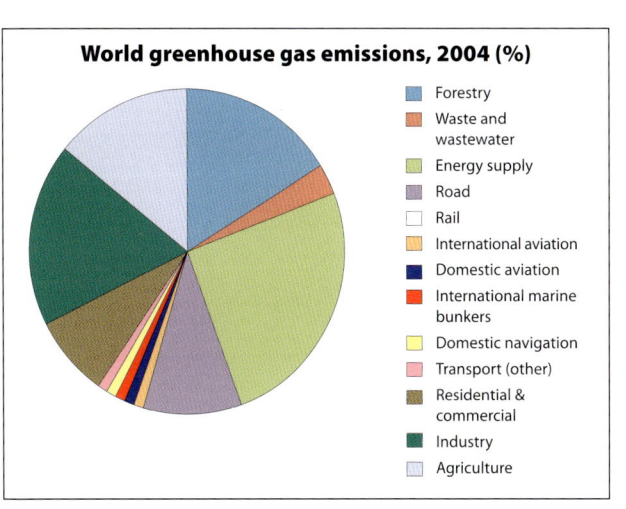

Carbon dioxide emissions globally from fuel combustion (%)
- Energy
- Road
- Rail
- International aviation
- Domestic aviation
- International marine bunkers
- Domestic navigation
- Transport (other)
- Manufacturing industries and construction
- Other sectors

World greenhouse gas emissions, 2004 (%)
- Forestry
- Waste and wastewater
- Energy supply
- Road
- Rail
- International aviation
- Domestic aviation
- International marine bunkers
- Domestic navigation
- Transport (other)
- Residential & commercial
- Industry
- Agriculture

Source: adapted from data presented in International Transport Forum, 2008.

Figure 6.8: Relative CO_2 and greenhouse gas emissions from transport

See accompanying CD-Rom

CO_2 emissions from transport.ppt

Debate also surrounds the effectiveness of supposedly more environmentally friendly technologies such as the relatively new 'hybrid' cars and the next generation of electric vehicles, such as the Nissan Leaf, which is to be built in Sunderland with production planned for 2013. Although such products have a greatly reduced direct demand for fossil fuels, they are still reliant upon a source of electricity, which may ultimately be provided from fossil fuel combustion. The emerging technologies are also currently extremely resource-hungry – for example, in the production of the batteries and composite materials that are required, as opposed to the well-established technologies of 'traditional' combustion engines. Nevertheless, pressures on the automotive industry to reduce emissions are resulting in an ever-developing range of alternatives to the internal combustion engine, be it in the form of hydrogen, electric or other forms of fuel.

In 2009, the UK government launched a range of policies aiming at 'decarbonising' the economy. A series of documents were produced: *The UK Low Carbon Transition Plan*; *The UK Renewable Energy Strategy*; *The Carbon Reduction Strategy for Transport* and *The UK Low Carbon Industrial Strategy* (see 'Useful websites' on p155). The latter involves £405 million being invested to support low carbon industries and 'advanced green manufacturing'. These industries include the development of wind and tidal power, renewable construction materials and ultra-low carbon vehicles (Department for Business, Innovation and Skills, 2009). Although containing some controversial technologies, such as nuclear power, policy documents such as these do at least acknowledge the social and economic benefits of embracing more environmentally friendly technologies.

Natural ecosystems and sustainability

With the increasing global population, so more and more land is required to be cultivated for agriculture to produce increasing quantities of food. Intensive agricultural practices, as are commonly employed for mass food production, require water for irrigation, which is particularly an issue in arid and semi-arid climates, where climate change appears to be exacerbating existing problems. In addition, the use of chemical fertilisers and pesticides further alter the natural ecosystems of the environment. The food produced ultimately requires transportation, often thousands of miles around the globe.

In the highlands of Papua New Guinea, indigenous communities have lived entirely self-sufficient lives for thousands of years. Pioneering research by Worsley (see original work in Oldfield et al, 1985) has shown that by using a system of raised 'gardens' and tools derived from local resources to cultivate all their crops, their methods of 'farming' were wholly sustainable, with absolutely no detrimental effects, such as soil erosion, arising from their activities (figure 6.9). This was the situation for thousands of years. However, from the 1950s, with the introduction of 'modern' tools, such as metal implements, and involvement from Westernised people, more intensive agricultural practices are now resulting in signs of environmental degradation, such as soil erosion.

Figure 6.9: Indigenous farming in Papua New Guinea

See accompanying CD-Rom

Indigenous farming.ppt

Note: owing to the age of these photographs some of the detail is not clear - for a fuller explanation of what can be seen in them see the notes in the PowerPoint *Indigenous farming.ppt* on the accompanying CD-Rom.

Mixed land use in Papua New Guinea

PHOTOS: ANN WORSLEY

The marine environment is critical in the influencing of the global climate and weather systems. Approximately 10% (around 600 million people) of the global population live in coastal regions, where their homes and livelihoods are at risk from rising sea levels. This applies across both the LEDCs and MEDCs. Historically, the sea has not been treated in a sustainable way, particularly in terms of its use as a waste depository. Until relatively recently, the dumping of rubbish at sea was regarded as acceptable, due to the perceived ability of the sea to 'dilute and disperse' human waste. For instance, it was only as a result of the linking of diseases such as polio and cholera with the pollution of coastal waters that improved practices over the treatment of sewage were introduced. However, it is now accepted that regulation of marine pollution is essential, and many countries now regulate to prevent polluting activities.

The fishing industry is one of the industries high on the media agenda for issues around sustainability (figure 6.10). It is accepted that fish stocks are not infinitely renewable, with overfishing [☞] leading to the depletion of many fish stocks. However, many of the regulations put in place to try to ensure sustainability within the global industry have led to major inequalities within the communities employed in fishing. For generations, many fishermen themselves have acknowledged the concept of sustainability to be able to continue fishing in their known fishing grounds. On a global scale, the Marine Stewardship Council (MSC) is the largest certification and eco-labelling scheme for the seafood industry. This scheme encourages and promotes sustainable practice within the seafood industry globally, and provides a means for those within the industry who operate in a sustainable manner to promote their activities through the increasingly recognised MSC eco-label.

See ch 7, Environmental management (p171).

Figure 6.10: Fishing industry

See accompanying CD-Rom

Fisheries.ppt

Source: NOAA (US National Oceanic and Atmospheric Administration). Photos right and centre left Allen M. Shimada. *www.photolib.noaa.gov*

> **Teaching idea 6.7**
>
> Ask students to investigate examples of sustainable fisheries around the UK or globally (www.msc.org/track-a-fishery). How are these fisheries attempting to ensure that they are able to fish economically while preserving marine ecosystems?

See Volume 1: Human Geography, ch 9, Geographies of health and environment (p185-187).

Pollutants in the air, particularly oxides of nitrogen and sulphur, react with water vapour forming nitric and sulphuric acid. This then makes the rain, snow, sleet, etc that precipitate out of the atmosphere more acidic. This acidity is sufficient to pose a major threat to the environment by acidifying lakes and rivers and, particularly, by acidifying the soil, leading to the death of many plant species. As the pollutants are held in the atmosphere, acid rain is a global problem, as the sources of the pollutants usually originate in a completely different country or even continent to where the effects are felt. A well-publicised example of this is the damage to many Scandinavian environments caused by pollution originating in the UK. In addition, air pollution is directly linked to increasingly poor human health [👁], particularly respiratory diseases.

Sustainability and biodiversity

See ch 1, Ecosystems (p14).

It is well documented how the number of species of plants and animals becoming extinct is increasing at a rate greater than ever before [👁]. With the progressive evolution of nature, some species will become extinct for 'natural' reasons. However, the rate of extinctions is now so great that it is being declared by some as being at 'catastrophic' levels (*www.guardian.co.uk/science/2006/may/02/biodiversity.conservationandendangeredspecies*) and is estimated to be approaching a similar level to that which was responsible for the extinction of the dinosaurs. With the evolution of 'new' species unable to keep pace with the loss of species, so the number of species is declining, hence a reduction in biodiversity. The plight of species near extinction often makes us think of tropical rainforests and other distinctive environments, where species are being lost due to destruction of their highly specialised habitat. However, increasingly, there is growing concern for loss of species in the temperate climate of the developed world. For example, the numbers of many 'garden' birds in the UK are drastically reducing, leading to fears over the ability of many species to survive in the future if measures are not put in place to protect them (see RSPB in 'Useful websites' on p155). Much of this reduction in numbers is due to habitat destruction (either complete loss or fragmentation) as a result of human activities. Some species are threatened due to a reduction in their food source. For example, some species of moth are declining in numbers due to changes in agriculture practices or climate change (whereby more hardy species of moth can 'take over' the feeding grounds of other species, 'out-competing' them). Moths are not only important plant pollinators, they are vital sources of food for many small birds; if the moth numbers decline, so do the birds.

In terms of sustainability, there are a number of threats to biodiversity, each of which varies in its severity depending upon the specific location, and the management protocols that may (or may not) be in place. Firstly, loss of habitat or the fragmentation of habitat that stops animals and plants from moving to other suitable areas is a major cause of loss of biodiversity in an area. All too often, this loss is due to human activities, such as wetlands being drained to provide land for agriculture. A second cause is increasing human populations: people need more space, more food, and more 'resources' to live and these requirements are often met at the expense of habitats for other species. In particular, the unsustainable use of natural resources where species are either exploited by humans to near or total extinction, or their habitat or environment is destroyed, is a serious biodiversity threat. A third factor is climate change, either directly, with the climate becoming too hot or cold in certain areas for certain species, or indirectly, due to increasing extreme weather, such as storms, and rising sea levels flooding coastal areas, leading to loss of specialised coastal habitat.

Fourthly, pollution of the air, water and land can result in a loss of biodiversity, as it can either kill animals and plants directly, or it can make their habitat unsuitable for them to live in. (Such pollution is often also a threat to human health.) A further threat is from the introduction of non-native species of plants and animals, whether intentionally by humans or through species being forced to migrate due to climate change. This results in native species being 'out-competed' for food and resources, or it can allow the introduction of disease to which the native species have no resistance.

Teaching idea 6.8

If your school is in an urban area, ask students to identify a habitat, perhaps in the school grounds or nearby, such as a pond, that could be very important for wildlife. Does this habitat have any form of environmental protection? How many and what species are there? How many species live there permanently (eg waterborne insects)? How many species visit it for food or shelter (eg frogs)? What would species do if the habitat was threatened, could they migrate somewhere else? What would be the knock-on effects for other species (eg birds)?

A key agreement made during the 1992 Rio Earth Summit was the Convention on Biological Diversity. The three main goals of the Convention are: (i) to conserve diversity; (ii) the sustainable use of its components; and (iii) the sharing of benefits from its genetic resources (CBD, 2000). Following this, in 1994, the UK government launched 'Biodiversity: the UK Action Plan'. Alongside national targets, there are also over 180 Local Biodiversity Action Plans (LBAP) in the UK (*www.ukbap.org.uk*). In 2007, the updated framework for conserving biodiversity document was published (UK Biodiversity Partnership, 2007).

Teaching idea 6.9

Ask students to investigate their local biodiversity action plan (*www.ukbap.org.uk*). What specific elements are being put into place with regards to their local area to encourage biodiversity and sustainability?

Biodiversity is an essential element in sustainability. It is vital to the natural systems of the Earth, with various species all contributing to the functioning of the planet. It is crucial for humans to be able to produce all the food and many of the medicines [☞] that may be required for future generations. Over 7,000 plant species are cultivated globally, but only around 30 crop species provide the mainstay of global agriculture (IPGRI, 2002). Therefore, if species are lost we could be losing the potential to provide more

See ch 8, Globalisation (p196).

effective food supplies in the future. Many insects that live in the soil are vital to the 'health' of the soil to help the decomposition of dead leaves, which in turn adds nutrients to the soil, making it better able to support the next generation of plants. The burrowing action of these insects also improves the structure of the soil. For humans, this is of vital importance for agriculture and the growing of food crops. Insects also play a vital part in the food chain of larger animals. At the same time, plants absorb carbon dioxide and release oxygen, while bacteria remove pollutants from water. Many of the functions that are carried out by plants and animals cannot be replicated by humans alone. Humanity needs animals and plants to survive. Every species of animal or plant that is lost through extinction potentially makes it harder for the Earth to adapt to the changes that humans are causing (Convention on Biological Diversity, 2000). The United Nations has declared 2010 to be the International Year of Biodiversity. The main aim of this global initiative is to raise awareness of the impacts of loss of biodiversity among national governments and, particularly, the public and communities, and to promote solutions to the biodiversity crisis.

Human use of natural resources

Since the beginnings of human life on the Earth, we have been using and modifying the resources around us. Whereas many thousands of years ago this may have meant chopping down a single tree to provide shelter and heat, we are now capable of removing an entire forest for commercial timber, housing, industry or simply to access the land underneath to grow crops or excavate minerals. Our advances in technology have meant that not only are we capable of doing more, but we need more in order to maintain lifestyles that have been progressively developed, and become steadily more resource-intensive over the centuries.

See ch 9, Environmental management (p166-168) and ch 1, Ecosystems (p22-23).

The extent of forested areas is gradually increasing in temperate regions [✎], but is decreasing in tropical areas. Forests are important for biodiversity, soil conservation, fuel, medicine, evapotranspiration and carbon storage (although this last factor is at risk if there is a rise of 2.5°C, due to the increasing stress to trees). Deforestation, particularly in tropical areas, is a well-publicised environmental and social issue. Measures designed to improve sustainability are being taken to control the trade in tropical timber, for example through the adoption in many countries of the Forestry Stewardship Council (*www.fsc-uk.org*).

No trade in tropical timber can currently be considered to be truly sustainable. Even where timber is felled and replanted, if the new trees that are planted are single species plantations they can in no way compare to the incredibly diverse forests that naturally occur. Many species of tree found in tropical forests can easily take in excess of 100 years to reach maturity and be suitable for felling. This kind of timescale is obviously not conducive to the business operations of the logging companies, and is generally beyond the timescales of the majority of regulations and political conditions. In addition, to achieve truly sustainable operations, other aspects of the forest system need to be maintained, such as the hydrology and soil properties of the area.

Attitudes towards the exploitation of natural resources by humans vary dramatically. At one extreme is the view that humans have the right to use or take whatever resources they can find to further develop as individuals or as a society, with little or no regard either for future generations, or for the implications for other species. At the other end of the spectrum is the view that humans must undergo a complete cultural shift and endeavour to maintain the integrity and diversity of other species regardless of costs (either financial or social) to current populations. To maintain currently developed societies, and to allow developing societies to continue to grow, requires the continued use of natural resources. However, the challenge is to try to control the exploitation of resources that are not only approaching the point of exhaustion, but also have, under current scientific understanding, the most impact upon natural systems. In this latter category would be the burning of fossil fuels.

Energy and sustainability

Modern society is effectively underpinned by the use of energy derived from a range of sources [☞]. Economic growth and a rise in general prosperity have been accompanied by large-scale rises in energy production and consumption. However, if society is to achieve any recognisable level of sustainability, then human use of fossil fuel has to be reduced dramatically. On the one hand, these non-renewable resources will become exhausted relatively quickly, while on the other their contribution to greenhouse gas emissions threatens the sustainability of the planet. To achieve a more sustainable energy future it therefore becomes imperative to develop alternatives to non-renewable sources of energy.

See ch 4, Energy (p86).

Sustainability and political processes: the role of Agenda 21

Throughout the previous discussion of sustainability, there has been frequent reference to a range of local, national and international government policies that have clear implications for future sustainability. In many ways, the umbrella document for all such initiatives is Agenda 21. Agenda 21 was a major output of the 1992 Rio Conference. Each country that pledged to support Agenda 21 is challenged with enabling the development of societies by focusing on the preservation of the value of its natural resources within the environment. The document highlights that a nation's 'wealth' should not be viewed from a purely monetary point of view, but also from the value of its resources (such as tropical forests). The aim of this approach is to encourage actions at a local level. Agenda 21 is a 40-chapter document outlining the ideals of sustainable development, covering the social, environmental and economic aspects of such development, issues relevant to it, and how effective sustainability might be realised (*www.un.org/esa/dsd/agenda21/res_agenda21_00.shtml*).

The four areas of the agenda are:

- Social and economic dimensions
- Conservation and management of resources
- Strengthening the role of major groups
- Means of implementation.

Included in the 'major groups' were local authorities, hence the now commonly adopted acronym of LA21 – Local Agenda 21, whereby councils set out their plans for promoting, encouraging and implementing the sustainable development agenda.

> **Teaching idea 6.10**
>
> Ask students to investigate Local Agenda 21 with reference to their local council. Information will be held on the specific local council's website. What aspects of sustainability are council policies focused on? Can they suggest additional aspects that might be considered for their local area?

Increasingly, there is recognition among governments that there is a need to consider the global aspects of developments, both negative and positive. This is reflected, in the case of the United Kingdom, with the publication in 2005 by the Department for Environment, Food and Rural Affairs (Defra) of the *One Future – Different Paths* document (*www.defra.gov.uk/sustainable/government/documents/SDFramework.pdf*). This outlined a 'shared framework for sustainable development' across the UK. In 1999, the UK government, along with the devolved administrations of Scotland, Wales and Northern Ireland, had identified their own priorities and goals, and strategies for achieving them, while the more recent document committed the various administrations to a shared approach to common goals.

In order to monitor progress towards goals set out in the strategy for sustainable development, the UK government has formulated a set of indicators (figure 6.11), which it reports on (along with the Scottish Executive and the Welsh Assembly Government) annually.

Figure 6.11: UK government Sustainable Development Framework indicators

See accompanying CD-Rom

Sustainability.doc

Greenhouse gas emissions	River quality	Pensioner poverty
Resource use	Economic output	Education
Waste	Active community participation	Health inequality
Bird populations	Crime	Mobility
Fish stocks	Employment	Social justice
Ecological impacts of air pollution	Workless households	Environmental equality
	Childhood poverty	Wellbeing

Note: an annual review of the indicators is published by the UK government, www.defra.gov.uk/sustainable/government/progress/data-resources/sdiyp.htm and is available as a PowerPoint presentation.

> **Teaching idea 6.11**
>
> Ask students to select a couple of the indicators that they think are most important if we are to achieve a sustainable future, from those listed in figure 6.11. Secondly, ask them to identify what a sustainability agenda means in relation to these indicators for their own local plan.

Political recognition of the increasingly globalised aspects of sustainability is largely in response to countries' increasing dependence on one another, particularly, for example, in the trade of manufactured goods and fuel. This globalisation can be seen both economically and environmentally: the UK would struggle to function socially without the import of manufactured goods that are no longer made in sufficient quantities in the UK (for example, televisions), while it has been reported for many years that atmospheric pollution produced within the UK (and all other developed countries) crosses many continental boundaries, often having deleterious impacts many thousands of miles away from its source (for example, acid rain).

Summary

The concept of sustainability is a huge, all encompassing, rather fuzzy means of addressing the issues facing the contemporary world. The subjects that need to be considered under the concept range from the global, such as atmospheric pollution that crosses transnational boundaries, and the depletion of the ozone layer that affects the global population, through all national and regional scales, down to individual and local site-specific issues, such as loss of habitat from a local pond, or what brand of frozen fish to buy from a supermarket.

The term can be applied to every environment – land, sea and air. There is therefore no place or process that does not have relevance to sustainability. As such, the concept of sustainability could be used as a means to bring all geographical issues together, both human and physical, under a single cohesive banner. It can be used as a means to educate about previous environmental and social problems, and to inform about improved, long-term means of enhancing and developing societies, their economy and the environment. The emphasis on the long term and future generations is key to the concept of sustainability, raising awareness that actions now have implications in the long term. It is crucial that there is an acknowledgement of the importance of sustainable development, not just by policy makers and scientists, but by anyone who lives and travels in the modern world. Having said this, as educators, we still need to demonstrate a healthy scepticism towards claims of sustainable development and sustainability, depending on the source of such claims. The concept of sustainable development represents both an opportunity and a challenge.

Useful websites

UK government policies
On additional homes in the UK – Department for Communities and Local Government, 2007: *www.communities.gov.uk/documents/housing/pdf/439986.pdf*

On sustainable homes: *www.communities.gov.uk/planningandbuilding/ buildingregulations/legislation/codesustainable/* and the downloadable leaflet at *http://bit.ly/GreenerHomes*

UK government strategies to reduce carbon emissions can be found at: *www.berr.gov.uk/whatwedo/sectors/lowcarbon/index.html*. Policy documents are available at: *www.decc.gov.uk/en/content/cms/publications/lc_trans_plan/lc_trans_plan.aspx*

The RSPB
There are many surveys that rely on volunteers and sometimes web-based information gathering to monitor various animal species, details of which can be found at: *www.rspb. org.uk/thingstodo/surveys/other.asp*

In addition, the RSPB provides a number of teaching resources under different areas of the curriculum, available to download at: *www.rspb.org.uk/ourwork/teaching/resources*

Each year in January, the RSPB coordinates the UK Birdwatch, where people in the UK are asked to record all the birds they see in one location (eg their garden) for one hour. The results then form part of the huge national survey of bird populations. The link for the 2010 survey can be found at: *www.rspb.org.uk/birdwatch/about*

Further to this, the RSPB organises a schools birdwatch throughout January each year. Further information can be found at: *www.rspb.org.uk/schoolswatch/about/index.aspx*

Fisheries

The Marine Stewardship Council (*www.msc.org*) has teaching resources for primary schools on its website *www.fishandkids.org* and is currently developing resources for secondary education.

The organisation 'Seafish' is a public body that works across the seafood industry. Further information can be found at: *www.seafish.org*. There are a large number of downloadable files on the website, including a readily accessible guide to the seafood industry and sustainability at: *www.seafish.org/upload/file/about_us/SeafishGuidetoSustainability_200905.pdf*

Biodiversity

The Darwin Foundation is an international not-for-profit organisation providing research and assistance in the preservation of the Galapagos Islands: *www.darwinfoundation.org/english/pages/index.php*

7

Environmental management

Charles Rawding

Introduction

It goes without saying that the environment is an essential element in human life and therefore that effective management of that environment is crucial in sustaining livelihoods and human wellbeing.[1] At the global scale, over 1.3 billion people depend directly on the environment for employment. Nearly half of all employment depends on fisheries, forestry or agriculture. Such employment is skewed towards certain regions of the world. For instance, in Asia and the Pacific, small-scale fisheries contribute 25% to the total fisheries production of Malaysia, the Philippines and Thailand, while small-scale agriculture accounts for more than 90% of Africa's agricultural production. In Africa, more than seven in ten people live in rural areas, with most engaged in resource-dependent activities. In locations such as these, when environmental resources become degraded, the livelihoods of small-scale producers are placed at risk. Other regions of the world, such as the urbanised areas of Western Europe and North America, may appear to have a less direct dependency on the environment, yet, as this chapter will demonstrate, the effective management of environmental change is an essential element in all societies.

It can be argued that economic growth has led to improvement of the environment in many ways. Wealthier countries are better able to introduce stronger legislation, encouraging investment in better and cleaner technologies, often to ameliorate environmental conditions that were created during earlier periods of industrialisation and economic growth. On the other hand, many global trends remain strongly negative, and much of what is currently regarded as development is unsustainable. Increasingly, global attention has focused on national strategies designed to promote sustainable development [☞] and increase the awareness of the importance of environmental management.

See ch 6, Sustainability (p135).

Environmental change is a major challenge facing the world today. While much of this change may be attributable to natural factors, there is clear evidence that anthropogenic factors are having far greater impact than at any time in the past. The growth of environmentalism [☞] from the 1960s and 1970s has been seen as a response to a perceived global environmental crisis. This crisis has been felt particularly in poorer areas of the world and where people are living in fragile environments that can be easily degraded.

See ch 8, Globalisation (p183).

Issues in environmental management

Land degradation

See ch 1, Ecosystems (p15).

Land degradation is a long-term loss of ecosystem function and services, caused by disturbances from which the system cannot recover unaided (figure 7.1). It blights a significant proportion of the surface of the globe, and as much as one-third of the world's population. Land degradation in the form of soil erosion, nutrient depletion, water scarcity, salinity and disruption of biological cycles is a fundamental and persistent problem. Land degradation diminishes the productivity, biodiversity and other ecosystem services of an area, and contributes to climate change. It is a global development issue. Land degradation hits the poor disproportionately, as they are far more likely to be directly dependent on the land than wealthier sections of the community. This is particularly the case in the rural areas of less developed countries. The damage caused can be arrested, or even reversed in some circumstances, but this is only possible where long-term decisions are taken and investment is forthcoming from government and individual land users. As yet, examples of such strategies are relatively rare (see discussion of the Dust Bowl on p159).

Figure 7.1: Land use change and potential negative environmental impacts

See accompanying CD-Rom

Environmental management.doc

Change in land use		Environmental impact
Cropland expansion and intensification		Loss of habitat and biodiversity; soil water retention and regulation; disturbance of biological cycle; increase of soil erosion, nutrient depletion, salinity and eutrophication.
Loss of forest, grassland and wetlands		Loss of habitat, biodiversity, stored carbon, soil water retention and regulation, disturbance of biological cycles and food webs.
Urban expansion		Disruption of hydrological and biological cycles; loss of habitat and biodiversity; concentration of pollutants, solid and organic wastes; urban heat islands.
Land degradation	Soil erosion	Loss of soil, nutrients, habitat and property; siltation of reservoirs.
	Chemical contamination	Polluted soils and water.
	Water scarcity	Diminished stream flow and groundwater recharge.
	Salinity	Unproductive soils, unusable water resources, loss of freshwater habitat.
Nutrient cycles		Eutrophication of inland and coastal waters, contaminated groundwater; depletion of phosphate resources; nutrient depletion, impoverished soils.
Desertification		Loss of habitat and biodiversity, reduced groundwater recharge, water quality and soil fertility, increased soil erosion, dust storms and sand encroachment.
Acidifying cycles		Acid depositions and drainage damaging land and water ecosystems; acidification of ocean and freshwaters.

Source: adapted from UNEP, 2007: 87-88.

Agricultural practices

Soil erosion

Erosion is the natural process of removal of soil by water or wind. As such it is an essential element in the development of soil profiles and in the sustenance of natural systems. It is estimated that, globally, 20,000 to 50,000 square kilometres of top soil are lost annually through land degradation, chiefly soil erosion. Losses are between two and six times higher in Africa, Latin America and Asia than in North America and Europe. The most important factor determining actual erosion is the quality of land management.

Soil erosion only becomes a problem when the natural process is accelerated by inappropriate land management. Removal of topsoil means loss of soil organic matter, nutrients, water-holding capacity and biodiversity, leading to a reduction of soil fertility and output. Eroded soil is often deposited where it is not wanted, resulting in costs such as damage to infrastructure, sedimentation of reservoirs, streams and estuaries, and loss of hydropower generation. These costs may be much greater than the losses in farm production where the soil erosion occurs. Examples of problematic land management include: inappropriate tillage and overgrazing; and the clearance of forest and grasslands, which is then followed by agricultural practices that provide inadequate ground cover, leading to subsequent erosion of exposed top soils. Soil erosion may also result from activities such as mining, the development of infrastructure including transport networks, and from urban development. In such instances, however, well-designed and well-maintained conservation measures may prevent erosion.

Soil erosion can be clearly identified where barren ground is found rather than vegetated surfaces; this may take the form of landslips of varying sizes, from small terracettes to major landslides [☞] that result in multiple fatalities. Alternatively, rills and gullies may form on slopes, resulting in the development of new drainage networks and further erosion of surfaces. The removal of topsoil may also occur as sheet erosion over a wide area.

See Volume 2: Physical Geography, ch 6 (p162).

The principal elements of soil erosion may vary from region to region, dependent on land use, climate and surface geology. For instance, wind erosion is the major problem in West Asia, with as much as 1.45 million square kilometres, one-third of the region, affected. In extreme cases, mobile dunes encroach upon farmland and settlements. Soil erosion by water is the main form of land degradation in Latin America, where it has been a major problem, leading to the abandonment of farmland, for example, in north-west Argentina. Over the past 25 years, the large-scale adoption of conservation tillage, which increases infiltration of rain into the soil, compared to conventional ploughing, has improved the situation in some areas. The area under conservation tillage in Latin America increased from almost zero in the 1980s, to 250,000 square kilometres in 2000. Such practices have been concentrated on large, mechanised farms in Argentina and Brazil, while the adoption rate by smaller farms is lower.

Soil erosion: the Dust Bowl of the United States

Attempts to tackle soil erosion around the world have met with mixed success. One of the most successful large-scale programmes followed the Dust Bowl in the United

States in the 1930s. In the late 1920s, good crop yields and high prices for wheat encouraged a rapid increase in the area under crops. When prolonged drought hit in the following decade, there was severe soil erosion. Millions of people lost their living and were forced to migrate. By 1940, 2.5 million people had left the Great Plains. Soil erosion and dust storms in the American Midwest and the experience of dust over the east coast generated huge public concern in the USA.

> **Teaching idea 7.1**
>
> *The Dust Bowl Ballads* album by Woody Guthrie was produced in 1940 and is considered to be the first concept album. Ask students to listen to one of the songs, such as 'Talkin' Dust Bowl Blues' or 'The Great Dust Storm' – what impressions do they get from the songs of the conditions in the Midwest at that time?

A package of measures was developed by the United States government that lasted over a long timescale and was effectively enforced. The US government provided both short-term relief and longer-term agricultural research and development. The Emergency Farm Mortgage Act was designed to prevent farm closures by helping farmers who could not pay their mortgages, while the Farm Bankruptcy Act restricted banks from dispossessing farmers in times of crisis, and the Farm Credit Act enabled local banks to provide credit. At the same time, the Works Progress Administration provided employment for 8.5 million people.

Alongside the measures designed to minimise the economic impacts on farmers, a range of environmental measures were introduced, in order to ensure there was no repetition of the crisis. The Administration bought land that could be set aside from agriculture and provided training and work for struggling families. The Department of Agriculture set up the Soil Conservation Service in 1935, which developed and implemented new soil conservation programmes as a consequence of the Soil Conservation Act of 1935. An ongoing implementation of the latest technologies has ensured that the impact of subsequent droughts has been much less severe, and the American Midwest has remained a prime agricultural region.

Chemical contamination

See ch 5, Food supply (p128).

Modern farming practices [📖] have come to depend increasingly on a range of chemical inputs designed to raise productivity. In environmental terms, the use of pesticides and inorganic fertilisers has been the most contentious development. 'Pesticides' is the generic term covering insecticides, herbicides, fungicides and other biocidal agents. The extensive use of pesticides has been extremely effective in reducing a range of diseases, both plant and animal, and thereby increasing yields from agriculture, as well as improving human health. However, the massive increase in the scale of their use since the Second World War has also resulted in chemical pollution. For instance, aerial dusting with DDT in central Africa, designed to reduce incidences of sleeping sickness by eradicating the tsetse fly, left a potentially lethal chemical cocktail on the land. Fortunately, much more targeted techniques using traps coated with pesticides and baited with chemicals attractive to tsetse are now in use. These are cheaper, more effective and less risky.

Crop losses through pest attack are a major problem in the developing world, particularly for those farmers unable to afford appropriate pesticides. At the same time, the crops at the forefront of the Green Revolution (designed to improve crop yields in order to raise living standards in LEDCs) are heavily dependent on a range of pesticides, fertilisers and irrigation methods. Thus, one of the principal criticisms of the Green Revolution has been the way in which poorer farmers have been excluded from the potential benefits of the new cropping techniques.

The long-term effectiveness of continued pesticide use has also been questioned. For instance, the onchocerciasis control programme for river blindness began spraying an insecticide to control the fly that carried the disease in 1974. By 1980, resistance to the insecticide was being identified, with the result that the programme was forced to switch to another organophosphorus compound. Yet again, resistance to the chemical appeared, and the compound had to be withdrawn.

It is very difficult to calculate the relative costs and benefits of pesticide use in environmental management. While the benefits in terms of increased crop yields are evident, the longer-term persistence of chemicals such as DDT in the environment, for instance, in terms of contaminated drinking water, means that the full implications and costs for human health are not yet known. Similarly, impacts on the wider environment are not always clear. In the case of DDT, which was used in Britain in the 1950s and 1960s, it became clear that the chemical did not metabolise but became stored in fatty tissue, which led to the poisoning of farmland birds and a concentration of the chemical at the top end of the food chain. Equally, the accumulation of DDT in soils led to changes in soil organisms with a range of consequences for soil fertility. Pesticide residues may also be found in the food they are designed to protect.

A final area of concern relates to the health of farm workers applying the pesticides. Accidental poisoning by pesticides is still a major problem, particularly in the less developed world where health and safety regulations may be wholly inadequate (Adams, 2009: 351-359).

Water scarcity

It is estimated that by 2025, about 1.8 billion people will be living in countries or regions with absolute water scarcity [☞], while two-thirds of the world population could be under conditions of water stress – that is to say, where societies are experiencing pressures to meet the water requirements for agriculture, industry, energy and the home. People now use between 40% and 50% of all available freshwater running off the land, and water withdrawals have doubled over the past 40 years. It is estimated that 50 countries are currently facing moderate or severe water stress, and the number of people suffering from year-round or seasonal water shortages is expected to increase as a result of climate change.

See ch 3, Climate change (p79).

Water scarcity does not merely equate to use of water for personal purposes. Industrial processes are major consumers of water. Global pressure on freshwater resources is increasing, as a result of growing demand for water-intensive products such as meat, dairy products, sugar and cotton. For example, meat, milk, leather and other livestock products account for 23% of global water use in agriculture, equivalent to more than

Zone	Water-related risks	Ecosystem	Rain-fed farming system	Risk management strategies
Hyper-arid	Aridity	Desert	None	None
Arid	Aridity	Desert – desert scrub	Pastoral, nomadic or transhumance	Nomadic society, water harvesting
Semi-arid	Drought one year in two, dry spells every year, intense rainstorms	Grassland	Pastoral and agro-pastoral: rangeland, barley, millet, cow-pea	Transhumance, water harvesting, soil and water conservation, irrigation
Dry sub-humid	Drought, dry spells, intense rainstorms, floods	Grassland and woodland	Mixed farming: maize, beans, groundnut, or wheat, barley and peas	Water harvesting, soil and water conservation, supplementary irrigation
Moist sub-humid	Floods, waterlogging	Woodland and forest	Multiple cropping, mostly annuals	Soil conservation, supplementary irrigation
Humid	Floods, waterlogging	Forest	Multiple cropping, perennials and annuals	Soil conservation, drainage

Source: adapted from UNEP, 2007: 98.

Figure 7.2: Ecosystem and farming system responses to water scarcity

Environmental management.doc

1,150 litres of water per person per day, while 3.7% of the global water use in crop production goes to produce cotton, the equivalent of 120 litres of water per person per day (WWF, 2008).

Issues of water supply and scarcity are not solely the preserve of less wealthy, or even 'drier', countries. For instance, the UK is commonly perceived as being a wet country, although rainfall varies significantly, with the north and west being wetter than the south and east. However, population densities are high, particularly in the south and east. This means that there is relatively little water available, especially in the south-east of England and some of the major urban areas. Hosepipe bans, and the threat of standpipes in the streets during drier periods, highlight the sometimes precarious nature of water supply in some areas of England and Wales. Figure 7.3 shows the availability of water supply across England and Wales.

Figure 7.3: Availability of water supply, England and Wales

Water supply.ppt

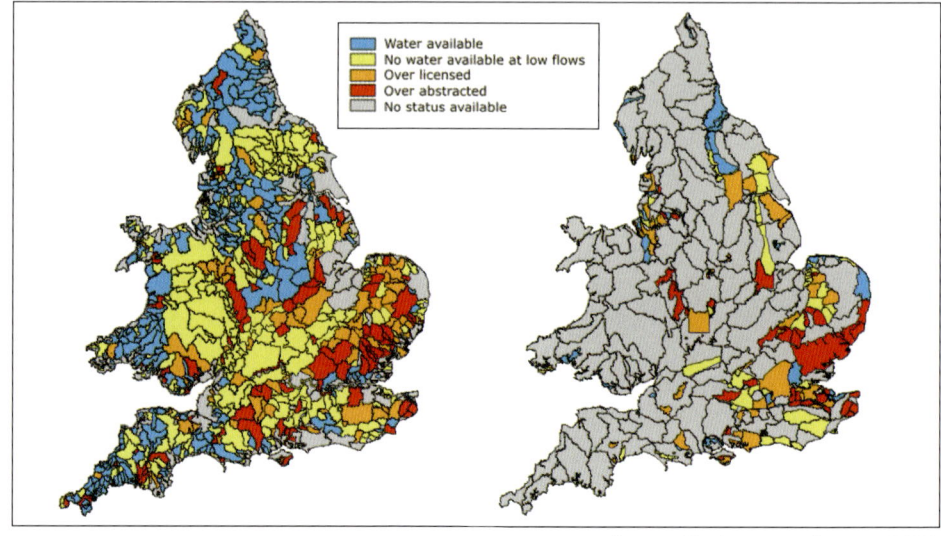

Source: Environment Agency, 2008.

Salinity

In reality, salinity is salt in the wrong place. It is where levels of salt are higher than desired for the preferred land use option. This is the case with farmland, and drinking and irrigation water, and in freshwater habitats. Soils, streams and groundwater in arid and semi-arid areas naturally contain significant amounts of salt. Salt inhibits the absorption of water by plants and animals, breaks up roads and buildings, and corrodes metal. However, a build-up of salinity is usually triggered by inappropriate forms of land use and management. Most irrigation systems apply much more water than either rainfall or natural flooding and, nearly always, more than can be used by the crops the system is designed to help. This additional water itself contains salt. Leakage from irrigation canals, ponding because of poor land levelling, and inadequate drainage all contribute to a raising of the water table. As a consequence, water is drawn to the surface by evaporation, further concentrating the salt, which may eventually create a salt crust on the soil surface. If there is inadequate drainage to carry the salt out of the soil, then irrigation will increase the likelihood of salinity.

Salinity is a threat to livelihoods and food security in dry areas, where most farm production is from irrigation, and farmers use whatever water is available. In the long run, this renders the land unproductive. Salinity will increase unless the irrigation networks are efficient at removing surplus water. Worldwide, some 20% of irrigated land (450,000 square kilometres) is salt-affected. On the other hand, dryland salinity is caused by the replacement of natural vegetation with crops and pastures that use less water, so that more water infiltrates into the ground than before. Where this salt is then drawn to the surface, more salt enters streams and this forms salt crusts.

In the case of West Asia, saline soils cover up to 22% of the arable land, ranging from none in Lebanon to 55 to 60% in Kuwait and Bahrain. Agriculture consumes 60 to 90% of the accessible water, but contributes significantly less than 25% of GDP across the countries of the Middle East and West Asia. Generally, water is used inefficiently in flood and furrow irrigation systems, and for crops with high water demand. Salinity is increasing through both excessive irrigation and seawater intrusion into depleted coastal aquifers. In some areas, withdrawals are far greater than rates of recharge, and aquifers have become rapidly depleted. Measures adopted to reduce the problem have been largely limited to the introduction of costly sprinkler and drip irrigation systems in areas of capital-intensive agriculture.

Nutrient cycles

Nutrient depletion is a decline in the levels of plant nutrients, such as nitrogen, phosphorous and potassium, and in soil organic matter, which results in declining soil fertility. It is commonly accompanied by soil acidification. The causes and consequences of nutrient depletion are well established: in a wet climate, soluble nutrients are leached from the soil (leaching) at the same time as crops take up nutrients. Unless the nutrients are replenished by manure or inorganic fertilisers, soil fertility declines. Deficiency of plant nutrients in the soil is the most significant physical factor limiting crop production across very large areas in the tropics, where natural soils may well be poor in the first place.

Nutrient pollution has led to eutrophication of waters, with negative environmental effects such as anoxia (a decrease in the level of oxygen) and severe reductions in water quality, fish and other animal populations. Such pollution has led to the creation of coastal dead zones; regions of water that lack the oxygen necessary to support animal life. In the case of the Louisiana coast of the USA, in 2007 the 'dead zone' was the largest it had been in the 22 years since mapping began, with an estimated area of 8,543 square miles. To some extent, oxygen depletion occurs naturally off the coast of all of the major river basins as nutrients are washed out to sea. However, fertilisers and pollution greatly add to the natural nutrients, causing algae to bloom. The algae dies and oxygen is consumed by micro-organisms as part of the decay process. Shrimp, fish and other animals move out of the oxygen-depleted region or die. The dead zone starts forming in the spring and recedes in autumn. In the case of the Louisiana dead zone, the area sometimes shrinks from one year to the next, though it is considerably bigger now than when the mapping began.

Desertification

See ch 3, Climate change (p74).

Desertification [🔗] is defined as the degradation of productive land in arid and semi-arid regions, as a result of a range of factors, including climatic variations and human activities. Climate variability is central to an understanding of desertification, as with the Sahelian and African droughts of the 1970s and 1980s. More recent droughts include the Sahel in 2005 and the Horn of Africa and northern Kenya in 2006. Drought is a persistent feature of tropical Africa. Yet drought may simply mean a dry period that lies within the range of an ecosystem's responses. That is to say, ecosystems are affected by droughts, but survive and are able to return to their former state after a drought. On the other hand, longer droughts (dessication) will kill seed-bearing plants, thereby preventing regeneration of the ecosystem. However, desertification is not always an irreversible process. Some areas thought to have been permanently degraded during droughts have subsequently recovered. For instance, in the Sahel, significant greening took place during the 1990s, following the droughts in the early 1980s. This can be explained largely by increased rainfall, but reduced population pressures as a result of urban migration, along with improved land management, have also played a part.

The UN Convention to Combat Desertification (*www.unccd.int*) has been established in an attempt to tackle issues relating to desertification on a global scale. As a process, desertification is at its most damaging in poor countries, where both socio-economic and biophysical processes adversely affect land resources and human wellbeing. Drylands cover about 40% of the Earth's land surface (see figure 7.4 on p165) and support 2 billion people. Some 90% of these people are found in developing countries, although population levels are rising rapidly in areas such as the south-western USA and the Mediterranean coasts of southern Europe. Desertification is a global development issue, resulting in enforced population movements from affected areas. Desertification endangers the livelihoods of rural people in drylands, particularly the poor, who depend on livestock, crops and fuelwood.

Rangelands are the environment most vulnerable to desertification. Rangelands may be defined as expansive, mostly unimproved lands where a significant proportion of the natural vegetation is native grasses and shrubs. Overgrazing of animals may remove

**Figure 7.4:
Drylands**

Drylands.ppt

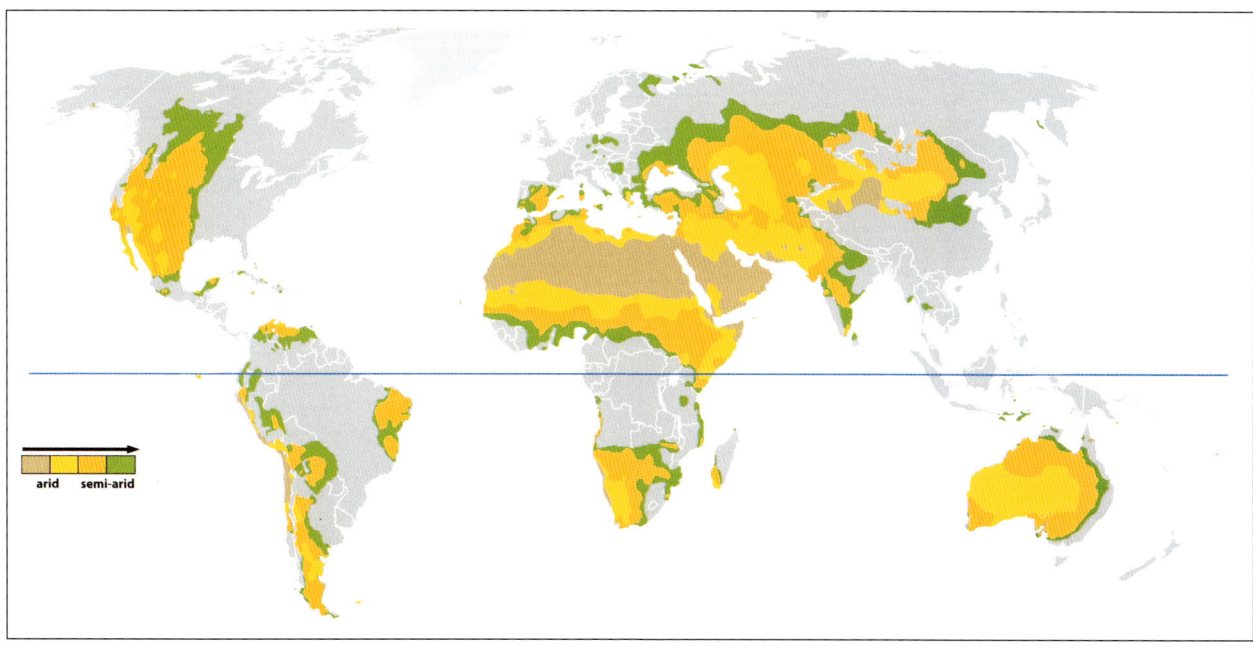

Source: adapted from UNEP, 2007: 107.

both trees and grass cover, while agricultural practices have resulted in the conversion of rangelands to croplands. Without significant new inputs, a loss of productivity and biodiversity, accompanied by erosion, nutrient depletion, salinity and water scarcity, may well be the result (figure 7.5). These lands are already on the margins in terms of suitability for human life. In 2000, the average availability of freshwater for each person in drylands was 1,300 cubic metres per year, significantly below the estimated minimum of 2,000 cubic metres per year needed for human wellbeing. On measures of human wellbeing and development, dryland developing countries lag far behind the rest of the world. For instance, the average infant mortality rate (54 per thousand) is 23% higher than in non-dryland developing countries and ten times that of industrialised countries.

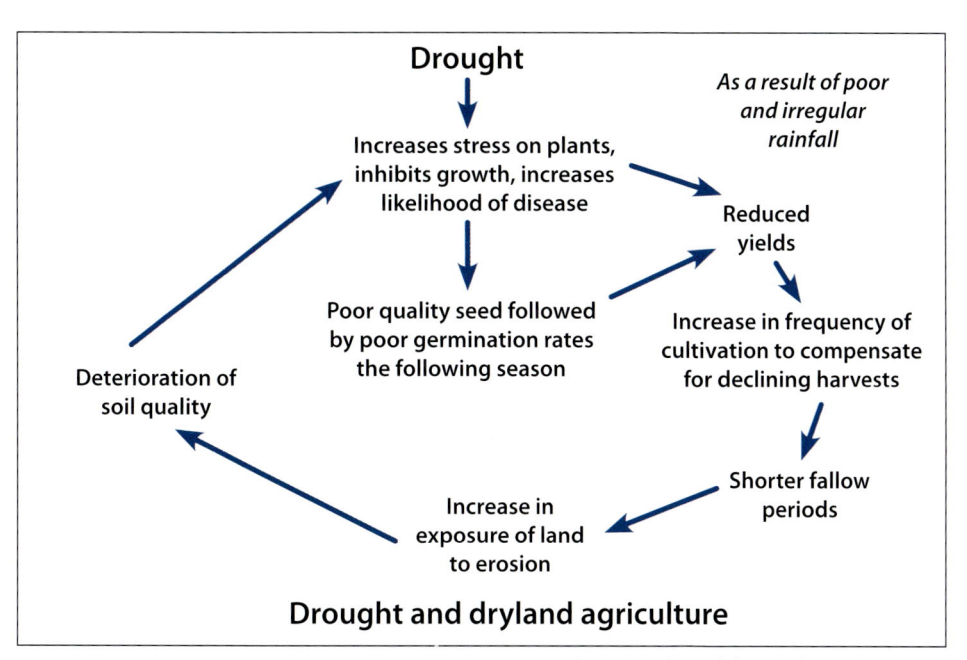

**Figure 7.5:
Drought and dryland agriculture**

Drought and dryland agriculture.ppt

Drought and dryland agriculture

Drought → Increases stress on plants, inhibits growth, increases likelihood of disease

As a result of poor and irregular rainfall → Reduced yields

Poor quality seed followed by poor germination rates the following season

Increase in frequency of cultivation to compensate for declining harvests

Shorter fallow periods

Increase in exposure of land to erosion

Deterioration of soil quality

Source: adapted from Adams, 2009: 203.

Responses to desertification have tended to be focused on short-term issues such as drought, shortfalls of food and the death of livestock. These are issues that reflect the variability of the climate in many of these regions. However, longer-term responses are more important for the overall sustainability of an area. In this context, policies such as effective early warning, assessment and monitoring based on integrating science, technology and local knowledge, and incorporating environmental assessments into all decision making, are more likely to be successful. It is also essential to communicate this information to all involved. Incorporating ecosystem management at the level of local catchments and river basins is also required to produce an integrated approach. Alongside environmental management, it is also essential to promote economic development and alternative livelihoods that are less dependent on crops and livestock. Examples of this might include taking advantage of the abundant sunlight and space in drylands, by introducing solar energy, aquaculture and tourism. Prevention is a better and more cost-effective approach than responding to crises.

Tackling desertification in China

An example of the effective role of government action in reversing desertification processes can be cited from China.[2] The Loess Plateau in China's north-west is home to more than 50 million people. It takes its name from the dry, powdery, wind-blown soil which, as a result of centuries of overuse and overgrazing, has experienced one of the highest erosion rates in the world. The World Bank-funded project encouraged natural regeneration of grasslands, tree and shrub cover on previously cultivated slopes. Replanting of vegetation and bans on grazing allowed the perennial vegetation cover to increase dramatically. Alongside the benefits for agriculture and vegetation, sedimentation of waterways was also dramatically reduced. The flow of sediment into the Yellow River has fallen by more than 100 million tons each year. In turn, this has reduced the risks of flooding, with a network of small dams helping store water for towns and for agriculture when rainfall is low. Before the project, frequent droughts caused crops cultivated on slopes to fail. Terracing of these slopes has both increased average yields and significantly lowered the annual variability of yields, thereby securing food supplies.

In this case, policies to restore areas of the severely degraded Loess Plateau in China have resulted in real environmental improvements and a 20-year trend of increasing biomass, even though rainfall levels have fallen over the same period. In China in the 1990s, about 3,440 square kilometres of land was affected annually by sand encroachment. Since 1999, 1,200 square kilometres have been reclaimed each year. More than 2.5 million people, in four of China's poorest provinces, have been lifted out of poverty. As a result of the introduction of sustainable farming practices, farmers' incomes have doubled and the degraded environment has been revitalised. Even in the lifetime of the project, the ecological balance has been restored in a vast area that was considered by many to be damaged beyond repair.

Forest environments

See ch 1, Ecosystems (p22) and ch 5, Food supply (p127).

The effective management of forest environments on a global scale is a contentious issue. The failure to agree a binding set of 'forest principles' at the Rio Conference in 1992 has been seen as a consequence of contrasting global perspectives between northern environmental organisations and the governments of tropical nations. The environmental organisations of the developed world have become increasingly concerned at the rate of clearance of tropical rainforests, while governments of poor countries have favoured initiatives designed to increase economic wealth. At the same time, these governments have been able to point out that the wealthier nations cleared their extensive forests long ago. A further sticking point concerning the preservation of the rainforests for the benefit of the whole world is related to the difficult question of who would bear the costs of this preservation.

Forests are managed for various functions. In 2005, one-third of global forests were managed primarily for production, one-fifth for conservation and protection, and the remaining forests for social and other purposes. The proportion allocated primarily for production is largest in Europe (73%), and least in North America (7%) and West Asia (3%). Of the total wood production, 60% was industrial wood and 40% was fuel; 70% of industrial wood is produced in North America and Europe, while 82% of fuelwood is produced in the developing world (UNEP, 2007). Non-wood forest products include food, fodder, medicine, rubber and handicrafts. In some countries, these products are more valuable than timber production. Particularly in the wealthier countries of the world, more and more forest areas are being designated for conservation and protection, as governments begin to realise their importance in providing ecosystem services [☞], such as soil and water protection, absorption of pollution, and climate regulation through carbon fixation. At the same time, these forests are being developed as recreational and tourism assets. However, this trend has yet to counteract an overall decline in total forest area across the globe.

See ch 1, Ecosystems (p15).

The development of commercial forestry has proved to be an effective way of generating income in many less developed countries. However, such development has not been without problems. For instance, in recent years, Chile has experienced rapid growth in the production and export of forest products. This production has been based on the expansion and management of exotic species in newly planted forests. Traditional land-use practices relating to the small-scale logging of native forests, the raising of livestock and agricultural cultivation have been replaced by large-scale timber production. Many endangered tree and shrub species have been affected by this growth of planted forest, which has also led to a dramatic reduction of landscape diversity, as well as goods and services from the forests.

Since 1998, Brazilian farmers have had to maintain 80% of their land as forest (50% in some special areas) as a legal forest reserve. There is a range of examples of environmentally enlightened forestry practices that can be cited here. For instance, since 1995, a group of smallholders in the state of Acre, supported by Embrapa (the Brazilian Agricultural Research Corporation), has developed sustainable forest management systems based on traditional forest practices as a new source of income. Forest structure and biodiversity are maintained by low-impact disturbance at short intervals. Small management areas, combined with appropriate management techniques such as short cutting cycles, low intensity harvesting and animal traction, have proved sustainable in an area with limited labour availability and investment. The forest holdings average 40 hectares each, while cooperative agreements among neighbours facilitate the acquisition of oxen, small tractors and solo-operated sawmills, resulting in higher prices in local markets and lower transportation costs. As a result, farmers' incomes have risen 30%. In 2001, the smallholders created the Association of Rural Producers in Forest Management and Agriculture to market their products nationwide and, in 2003, they won Forest Stewardship Council certification from SmartWood (see *www.rainforest-alliance.org/forestry*). Surveys have been conducted to monitor biodiversity. IBAMA (the Brazilian Institute of Environment and Renewable Natural Resource) and BASA (the Bank of the Amazon) use the sustainable forest management system as a benchmark for development and financial policies for similar natural resource management schemes (UNEP, 2007).

However, Brazilian government action has not always been effective in preventing illegal logging. For instance, government clampdowns in 2008 resulted in saw mills being closed and logging activities ceasing. However, the subsequent economic chaos in what were effectively logging towns, such as Tailândia in the state of Pará, resulted in mass protests and after government troops had withdrawn the illegal activities resumed. The difficulties of enforcing legislation can be highlighted by the fact that there are only 300 environmental agents to look after the entire Amazon region in Brazil (*The Observer*, 15 February 2009).

Figure 7.6 illustrates issues relating to deforestation within the Amazon. In the Brazilian state of Mato Grosso, the green of the Amazon rainforest is broken up by broad tracks of pale green and tan deforested land. In 2005, the government of Brazil said that 48% of the deforestation in the Amazon that took place in 2003 and 2004 occurred in Mato Grosso. The transformation from forest to farm is clear in the NASA image. Although some deforestation is part of the country's plans to develop its agriculture and timber industries, other deforestation is the result of illegal logging and squatters. Because the forest is so large and is difficult to access or patrol, satellite images such as this one are being used to tell officials where to look for illegal logging.

Figure 7.6: Deforestation

See accompanying CD-Rom

Deforestation.ppt

Deforestation in Mato Grosso

Source: NASA Visible Earth: *http://visibleearth.nasa.gov/view_rec.php?id=20945*

Coastal, marine and freshwater environments

For centuries, coastal reclamation practice has been to reclaim as much land from the sea as possible. Such practices can be clearly seen in the progressive reclamation of significant tracts of the Fens and the Lincolnshire coast of eastern England. Reclamation of these areas began in Roman times and continued until very recently. The impacts of such policies on coastal ecosystems have been dramatic and, at times, catastrophic. However, a major shift in management practice recently has seen the introduction of managed retreat for many of the marshy coastlines of Western Europe and the United States.

In the UK, 100 hectares of saltmarsh are being lost annually. Land claim for agriculture has been a significant cause, and coastal squeeze resulting from sea level rise will make the situation worse. A number of restoration projects around the British coast have aimed to reverse this loss. Hesketh Outer Marsh in the Ribble Estuary (figure 7.7) was initially claimed in 1980 by the building of a new sea wall. Restoration started in 2008 when the sea wall was breached and 170 hectares of agricultural land were flooded. Excavation of the original creek and lagoon system allowed for the existing sea defences to be reinforced and the restored saltmarsh further reduced flooding risk by expanding the available flood plain of the Ribble. Hesketh Outer Marsh is now managed by the RSPB. Saltmarshes are important breeding and wintering habitats for a range of birds, including declining species such as lapwing, redshank and skylark.

The ecology of the oceans has been transformed by human activity. For instance, it is estimated that the population of large predatory fish is now less than 10% of pre-industrial levels (Adams, 2009: 17). Over the past 50 years, many coastal and marine ecosystems and most freshwater ecosystems have become heavily degraded, with many completely lost, some irreversibly. Since 1980, about 35% of all mangroves have been lost, while about 20% of corals have been lost with a further 20% degraded. Nearly two-thirds of Caribbean coral reefs are reported to be threatened by human activities. The principal cause in the region is overfishing, which affects approximately

Figure 7.7:
Hesketh Outer Marsh

See accompanying CD-Rom

Hesketh Outer Marsh.ppt

60% of Caribbean reefs. Other pressures include large quantities of dust originating from deserts in Africa, which are blown across the Atlantic Ocean and settle on the reefs in the Caribbean, leading to significant coral mortality. Coral degradation has negative impacts on coastal communities, including the loss of fishing livelihoods, protein deficiencies, loss of tourism revenue and increased coastal erosion. It has been projected that many coral reefs will disappear by 2040 because of rising seawater temperatures.

Many freshwater wetlands are relatively species-rich, supporting a disproportionately large number of species of certain faunal groups. This can be illustrated by the case of Wicken Fen in Cambridgeshire, which is believed to have the richest biodiversity in the country, with 15% of all British species having lived there now or in the past (figure 7.8). Nevertheless, the current nature reserve represents a tiny fragment of the original Fenland that existed prior to huge drainage projects in the 17th century (Adams, 2009).

Figure 7.8: Species diversity on Wicken Fen, Cambridgeshire

See accompanying CD-Rom

Environmental management.ppt

No of species	Type of species
30	Mammals
231	Birds
7	Reptiles and amphibians
867	Plants
399	Fungi
74	Lichens
5,781	Insects

Note: for more information on the Wicken Fen data see www.nbn.org.uk

Source: *The Observer*, 5 April 2009.

However, globally, populations of freshwater vertebrate species suffered an average decline of almost 50% between 1987 and 2003, significantly more dramatic than for terrestrial or marine species over the same timescale. Many of these habitats are very much under threat. For instance, the often accidental introduction of invasive alien species, via ship ballast water, aquaculture or other sources, has disrupted biological communities in many coastal and marine aquatic ecosystems. Many inland marine ecosystems have also suffered from invasive plants and animals. Declines in global marine and freshwater fisheries are dramatic examples of large-scale ecosystem degradation that have been caused by persistent overfishing, pollution and habitat disturbance and losses.

Freshwater and marine species are declining more rapidly than those of other ecosystems. Wetlands, as defined by the Ramsar Convention on Wetlands of International Importance (*www.ramsar.org*), cover 9 to 13 million square kilometres globally. However, more than 50% of inland waters, excluding lakes and rivers, have been lost in parts of North America, Europe and Australia. More recently, conversion to alternative land usage or mismanagement of water resources have had significant impacts in other areas of the world. For instance, the surface area of the Mesopotamian marshes had decreased from between 15,000 and 20,000 square kilometres in the 1950s, to less than 400 square kilometres by the year 2000, because of excessive water withdrawals, damming and industrial development. Changes in policy have meant that the marsh area is now recovering. In Bangladesh, more than 50% of mangroves and coastal mudflats outside the protected Sunderbans (tidal mangrove forest) have been converted or degraded. The reclamation of inland and coastal water systems has caused the loss of many coastal and floodplain ecosystems and their services. Wetland losses have resulted in changes in flow regimes, increased flooding in some places, and reduced wildlife habitats.

Marine and freshwater environments: examples from the United States

The impact of Hurricane Katrina [☞] on the Gulf Coast of the United States in 2005 highlighted the consequences of previous developments in the mouth of the Mississippi River and along the Gulf Coast. Natural sea defences had been substantially reduced by human interference with coastal ecosystems, resulting in the coast being particularly vulnerable to extreme wave and surge events. The retention of coastal wetlands around the delta, lost as a consequence of human activities, could have considerably lessened the impacts of the storm surges triggered by the hurricane. These wetlands were deprived of new sediment by river embankment construction, which was designed to increase river flow and ease navigation. As a result, the Mississippi delta has been reduced in extent. The effects of storm surges and high waves generally can be reduced, though not entirely prevented, by healthy coastal ecosystems, such as salt marshes, mangrove forests and coral reefs. Additionally, in the case of Katrina, it became clear in the aftermath that there were conflicting interests within the region and that issues of flood control, fisheries, and oil and gas production required very different responses.

See ch 2, Weather and climate (p48).

Alongside human activity in coastal environments, more than half the major North American rivers have been dammed, diverted or otherwise controlled. These structures provide hydroelectric power and protection from floods, and they supply irrigation water and improve navigation. However, these actions have also changed the hydrological regime and damaged aquatic life. In recent times, the impact of dams has been reassessed in the light of their ecological and economic costs in relation to perceived benefits. As a result, at least 465 dams have been decommissioned in the United States, with about 100 more planned for removal. There has also been a recent trend towards river restoration in the United States, with projects aimed at improving water quality and fluvial environments.

> **Teaching idea 7.2**
>
> Ask students to investigate environmental policies with regards to their local river. What policies are being pursued? What are the purposes of these policies? Have their local rivers suffered as a result of unsustainable environmental practices?

Fisheries

Fisheries are a vital source of income and food in many parts of the world. Fish provides more than 2.6 billion people with at least 20% of their average per capita animal protein intake. However, overfishing has had significant consequences in several areas. It is estimated that over a quarter of all fish stocks are overharvested. The collapse of the Canadian east coast cod fishery, in the late 1980s, had devastating impacts on local fishing communities, and illustrates that developed countries are not immune to the economic implications of mismanaging natural resources. The collapse of the fishery resulted in unemployment for 25,000 fishers and 10,000 other workers. The area, off southern Labrador and to the east of Newfoundland, had yielded an overall annual catch of about 250,000 tons for more than a century, prior to the mid-1950s. Overfishing during the 1970s and 1980s, however, had a catastrophic effect. Although preventative measures were introduced at the beginning of the 1990s, the Canadian fisheries department issued a warning in 1995 that the entire northern cod population had declined to just 1,700 tonnes, down from a 1990 biomass survey showing 400,000 tonnes (figure 7.9). As yet there is no sign of recovery of cod stocks.

Figure 7.9: Fish catch landings, Newfoundland and Labrador

See accompanying CD-Rom

Fish catch landings.ppt

Source: adapted from UNEP, 2007: 327.

Sustainable fisheries are essential for a healthy and diverse marine ecosystem. They are also important for a vibrant and long-term fishing industry. In the case of the UK, during the 1990s, the percentage of fish stocks considered to be harvested sustainably and at full reproductive capacity was no more than 10% (figure 7.10). By 2007, this figure had increased to 25%, which still suggests that up to 75% of UK fish stocks still have either reduced reproductive capacity or have been harvested unsustainably in recent times (Defra, 2009).

Figure 7.10: Sustainability of UK fish stocks, 1990-2007

See accompanying CD-Rom

Fish stocks.ppt

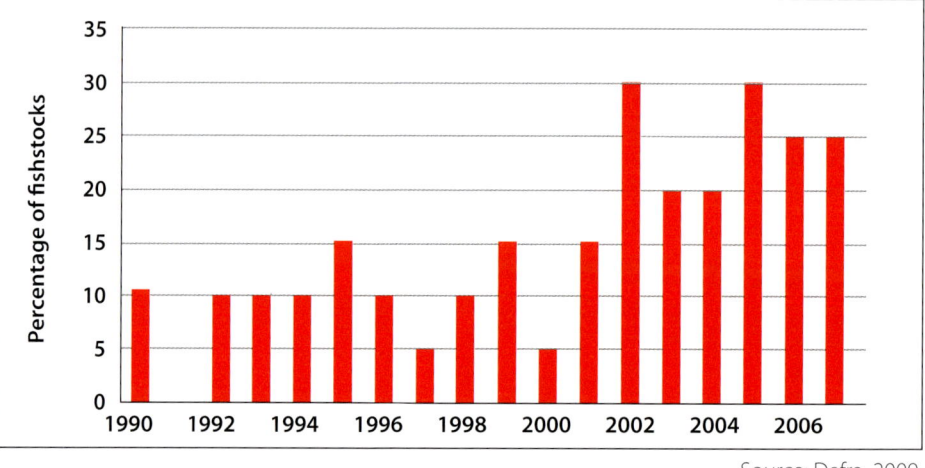

Source: Defra, 2009.

The overfishing of species, such as cod, is also causing major changes in marine ecosystems, as reductions in the numbers of predators result in spectacular growth of other species. While this offers alternative options for some fisheries, it also has serious implications for other human activities, as with the growth in jellyfish and algae along tourist coasts.

Restoring biodiversity

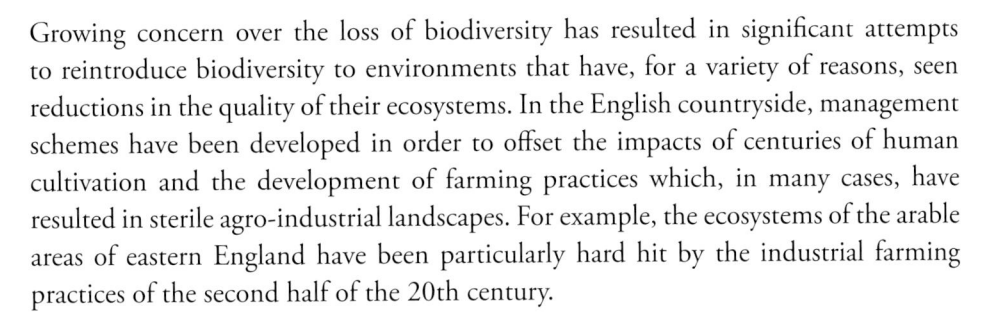

Reducing the rate of biodiversity [☞] loss across the globe will require a package of policies implemented effectively at all levels from the local to the global. Some such policies are already in place, but their full implementation is far from assured. As we have already seen, current patterns of farming [☞] are based on high resource inputs (such as water and fertilisers) and agricultural intensification. As such, they are placing great strains on ecosystems, contributing to nutritional imbalances and reduced access to wild foods. Reducing the rate of loss of biodiversity, and ensuring that decisions made incorporate the full values of goods and services provided by biodiversity, will contribute substantially towards achieving sustainable development [☞].

See ch 1, Ecosystems (p15).
See ch 1, Ecosystems (p18).
See ch 6, Sustainable development (p150).

Growing concern over the loss of biodiversity has resulted in significant attempts to reintroduce biodiversity to environments that have, for a variety of reasons, seen reductions in the quality of their ecosystems. In the English countryside, management schemes have been developed in order to offset the impacts of centuries of human cultivation and the development of farming practices which, in many cases, have resulted in sterile agro-industrial landscapes. For example, the ecosystems of the arable areas of eastern England have been particularly hard hit by the industrial farming practices of the second half of the 20th century.

To place these policies in context, nearly 500 species are known to have been lost from England in the recent past: 12% of land mammals, 22% of amphibians and 24% of our native butterflies. On a regional and local scale, the loss of species has been even more significant. Red squirrels have been lost from most counties in England, while the purple emperor butterfly has been lost from the West Midlands and East of England regions. An assessment of loss of flowering plants from 23 English counties concluded that, on average, one species of plant has been lost every two years since 1900. Rates of loss in southern and eastern counties have generally been highest (*http://naturalengland.etraderstores.com/NaturalEnglandShop/NE233*).

Biodiversity on the Lincolnshire Wolds

The Lincolnshire Wolds (see figure 7.11 on p174) is an Area of Outstanding Natural Beauty. The Wolds form a region of predominantly chalk upland which has been farmed intensively since the beginning of the 19th century. As a result, plant-rich chalk grassland had become increasingly scarce. However, the high biodiversity and relative scarcity of such environments in Britain make calcareous grassland a habitat of significant conservation value. In the case of the Lincolnshire Wolds, the Lincolnshire Biodiversity Action Plan sets targets for maintaining, safeguarding and improving existing areas. Seven grassland sites have been designated as Sites of Special Scientific Interest (SSSI), with four of them being designated nature reserves that are managed by the Lincolnshire Wildlife Trust. In several cases, former arable land has

Chapter 7: Environmental management

**Figure 7.11:
The Lincolnshire Wolds**

See accompanying CD-Rom

Lincolnshire Wolds.ppt

been restored to sheep-grazed grassland. As a result, a range of wildflowers has been returned to the area, along with a variety of butterflies and birds such as skylarks and common buzzards, the latter after an absence of nearly 150 years. Interestingly, the wide roadside verges associated with the landscapes of parliamentary enclosure, which characterise much of the Wolds landscape, have enabled linear nature reserves to be developed in locations such as Fulletby. In this case, an agreement between the Lincolnshire Wildlife Trust and the county council (which normally has responsibility for roadside verges) has resulted in some 16 of the most important verges on the Wolds being managed by the Trust (Smith, 2009).

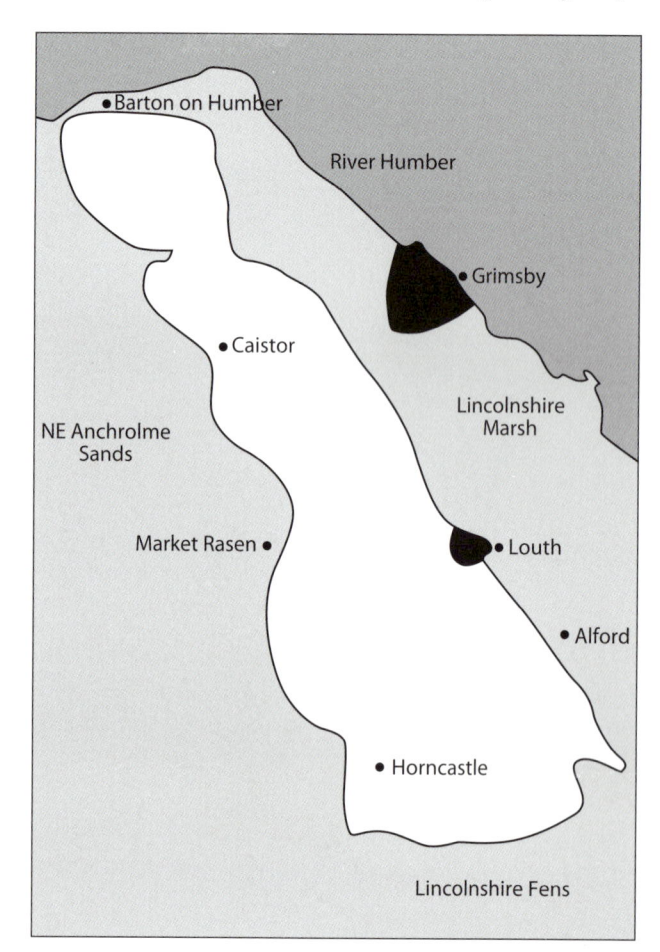

Teaching idea 7.3

Ask students to investigate their local biodiversity action plan. How is their local council attempting to improve the local environment? Which locations have been targeted for specific actions, and why? Alternatively, ask students to investigate a local SSSI. How is it managed for biodiversity? What makes the location sufficiently important to have been granted SSSI status?

Metals, oil and the environment

The impact of the extraction and processing of mineral resources in terms of environmental degradation and social effects has long been a concern to environmentalists. For instance, the production of alumina creates caustic alkaline slurry, while a common way to extract gold involves the use of cyanide. Many mines create huge quantities of overburden, often dumped in streams and rivers. Such practices are common even in industrialised countries, as in the Appalachian region of the eastern USA, where large-scale opencast coal mining has resulted, quite literally, in the removal of forested mountains in West Virginia and Kentucky (456 mountains across 6,000 square kilometres (figure 7.12). Because mines are often in remote locations, effects on people can be both unrecognised and uncompensated.

In the mid-1980s, an Australian corporation, Broken Hill Proprietary (BHP), developed an opencast gold- and copper-mining operation in the western mountains of Papua New Guinea. The government of Papua New Guinea owned 30% of the shares in the company. The mine employed 1,700 people and supplied over 16% of national export earnings. However, it also released daily about 80,000 tonnes of mine tailings, containing a suite of heavy metals, into the Ok Tedi River, which drains into the Fly River system. Over the life of the mine some 250 billion tonnes of waste will have been dumped. According to the company itself, mine waste could seriously damage up to 1,350 square kilometres of forest along the rivers. Independent reviewers, however, fear an even wider impact. The company concedes that, given the sheer volume of tailings already in the river, and continued erosion from the waste rock dumps adjacent to the mine in the mountains, the environmental problems will continue to worsen over the next 40 years (FPP, 2000).

Figure 7.12: Mining and the environment

See accompanying CD-Rom

Mining and the environment.ppt

Penmanmaer Quarry, Anglesey, North Wales

Penrhyn slate quarry, North Wales

Mountain top removal, Kentucky

Parys Mount copper mine, Anglesey, North Wales

> **Teaching idea 7.4**
>
> Ask students to investigate a large-scale mining landscape, using Google Earth to provide an effective aerial view of the extent of the workings. For instance, the extensive china clay workings close to the town of St Austell in Cornwall can be clearly seen. Equally, extensive areas of slate waste can be identified close to the town of Blaenau Ffestiniog in North Wales. Images such as these can then be matched with OS maps to enable students to carry out a detailed consideration of the area.

Substantial numbers of people lived downstream of the mine. Between 1994 and 1996 lawyers successfully sued the company in the Australian courts on behalf of 30,000 people living downstream. The mine, however, continued to operate and is due to close when the ore body is exhausted. In this case, pollution control facilities cost money and their construction cuts profits, and may not be technically feasible. A major attraction of mining in less developed countries is that capital and operating costs can be kept low. Limited statutory protection for workers and weak requirements for the control of pollution often mean that costs are lower than the equivalent mine in a wealthy country, and profits are correspondingly higher (Adams, 2009: 348-350).

The restoration of damaged environments

Over the past 40 years, damaged and degraded industrial landscapes in the UK have been extensively restored and improved. The trigger for this work was undoubtedly the Aberfan disaster of 1966, where a colliery spoil heap in South Wales collapsed, engulfing the village primary school and resulting in the deaths of 144 people, 116 of them children. In the period following this, major work was undertaken to avoid a repetition of the disaster elsewhere, while more recently 'nature' has been restored on many former industrial sites. For instance, on the former Lancashire coalfield, the infamous 'Wigan Alps' have been reduced to the Three Sisters, much lower mounds that are now grassed and planted with woodland, while the Flashes, lakes created by mining subsidence, have become an extensive wetland nature reserve with the remaining colliery spoil and ash providing suitable conditions for a wide variety of wild flowers.

Oakwell Hall Country Park in Kirklees, Yorkshire (*www.kirklees.gov.uk*) (see figure 7.13 on p177) is a good example of how an industrial landscape has been redeveloped over recent years. The area was previously used for mining and gas production as well as agriculture. The park has been developed partly on the site of Gomersal Colliery, which was closed in 1973, leaving behind a large spoil heap and derelict industrial and railway land. The reclamation that followed brought the country park into existence. The present Countryside Centre is on the site of the former pit head and a sculpture and information board commemorates the mine and the men who worked in it. The area of colliery waste has been reseeded to form a wildflower-rich meadow.

In restoring damaged local environments, local authorities have also taken the opportunity to proclaim their industrial heritage with elements of public art, as with the decision of St Helens council, along with former miners, to commission the 20 metre-high 'Dream' statue (see figure 7.14 on p177), portraying the image of a girl with her eyes closed. It is located on the top of a spoil heap overlooking the M62 motorway,

**Figure 7.13:
Oakwell Hall Country Park, Kirklees**

See accompanying CD-Rom

Oakwell.ppt

on the site of the former Sutton Manor Colliery. In this instance, the last coal was mined in 1991. In 2001, the 230-acre site was leased to the Forestry Commission by St Helens council. The Commission developed the Wasteland to Woodland project. Initially, 50,000 young trees, including alder, willow and ash, were planted. A mix of slow and fast-growing trees were chosen. During the planting phase, eight miles of special fencing was used in order to protect the young trees from rabbit damage.

On the other hand, the legacy of previous industrial development can also be taken as an opportunity for new development on brownfield sites. A recent example has been the conversion of the largest opencast coal mine [☞] in Europe, near Llanelli in South Wales, into Britain's newest racecourse, Ffos Las (*www.ffoslasracecourse.com*).

See ch 4, Energy (p86).

**Figure 7.14:
Sutton Manor Country Park and 'Dream'**

See accompanying CD-Rom

Sutton Manor.ppt

Chris Kington Publishing   Contemporary Approaches to Geography Volume 3: Environmental Geography   177

Chapter 7: Environmental management

> **Point for consideration**
>
> To what extent are environmental problems social constructs? Would well-paid miners have considered the spoil heaps to be an environmental issue? [⚙] (the poem on slide 6 of Sutton Manor.ppt might be an interesting starting point for discussions with pupils).

> **Teaching idea 7.5**
>
> Ask students to investigate the industrial history of their area (OS maps from the 1930s may prove to be a good starting point for this activity). Can they identify areas that were previously occupied by heavy industry? What has happened to those areas subsequently?

See accompanying CD-Rom
Sutton Manor.ppt

See Volume 1: Human Geography, ch 5, Rural geographies (p105).

Industrial development can also lead to unexpected ecological consequences. Jones (2008) discusses the example of Sheffield's fig trees. In this instance, the banks of the River Don have been colonised by wild fig trees. It appears that the trees grew from seeds carried downstream in human sewage or waste from food factories. That they germinated in the rather cool climes of South Yorkshire can be attributed to the effect of the steel industry on the waters of the River Don. The waters were used for cooling purposes, thereby raising the ambient temperature in the river, and maintaining a steady temperature of 20°C, warm enough for Mediterranean species to germinate. A combination of stricter controls on industrial usage of the river and the decline of the steel industry has meant that no new trees have grown as river temperatures have cooled. However, a successful campaign by locals to protect the trees, now regarded as an integral part of the local landscape, highlights a rather curious local attachment to an 'invasive species'.

> **Point for consideration**
>
> What do we mean by a native species? By what criteria do 'alien' species become accepted as part and parcel of a new environment?

Environmental disasters

Ironically, a major factor in increasing environmental awareness has been the occurrence of environmental disasters that have attracted the attentions of the world media. Accidents at nuclear power plants [⚙], oil spills from supertankers that have come to grief in coastal waters, and accidents that result in the release of toxic chemicals have all had major prominence in newspapers in recent years.

See ch 4, Energy (p85).

Bhopal 1984

In December 1984, an explosion in a pesticide factory on the outskirts of Bhopal in Madhya Pradesh, India, spread a cloud of pollution over the city. The plant was owned by Union Carbide India Limited (in turn 50.9% owned by the Union Carbide Corporation of the USA). About 30 tonnes of methyl isocyanate gas escaped. Within two days, 5,000 people had died from inhaling the gas, and half the population of the city had fled in terror. The eventual death toll was probably about 20,000 people, with another 200,000 poisoned. Twenty years after the devastating accident at Bhopal the site remained contaminated with highly toxic chemicals. Dangerous chemicals have spread throughout the local environment, even reaching the local drinking water supply.

See ch 8, Globalisation (p193).

The explosion might have been averted if the automatic controls standard in Union Carbide plants in the USA [⚙] had been installed, had the Indian government not insisted that manual controls be fitted, or had the Indian subsidiary of Union Carbide followed plans more closely. The human cost of the disaster would have been much less if the plant had not been built so close to the city.

The pesticides being produced at Bhopal were part of the package of technical inputs of the 'Green Revolution' [☞] intended to revolutionise agricultural production in India and push back hunger and poverty.

See ch 5, Food supply (p112).

The Bhopal disaster has come to epitomise the hazards of industrialisation in the poorly regulated urban environments of the developing world. The hazards of dangerous, poorly understood and under-regulated industrial processes have long offered a threat to the welfare of workers (Adams, 2009: 331-2).

Waste management

The management of waste is a major environmental issue. Households and industry in England and Wales produce more than 100 million tonnes of solid waste each year. The decreasing availability of landfill sites and a raft of environmental measures designed to encourage recycling have resulted in significant shifts in policy and practice in recent years. Indeed, local councils can point towards clear signs of success in their strategies for reduction of waste, although there remains a long way to go. In 2007, across the UK, around 73 million tonnes of waste were disposed of in landfill sites. This includes waste produced by households, commerce and industry and construction and demolition. This represents a decrease of 19.5% since 2002, when 91 million tonnes of waste were disposed of in landfill sites (figure 7.15). Between 2003/4 and 2007/8, household waste per person decreased by 0.9%. Each person currently generates about half a tonne of waste per year on average. Over the same four-year period, the amount of waste recycled or composted has increased. There has also been a year-on-year decrease in the amount of non-recycled waste per person, such that amounts are now at their lowest levels since estimates were first made in 1983/4 (Defra, 2009).

Figure 7.15: Waste in the UK

UK waste.ppt

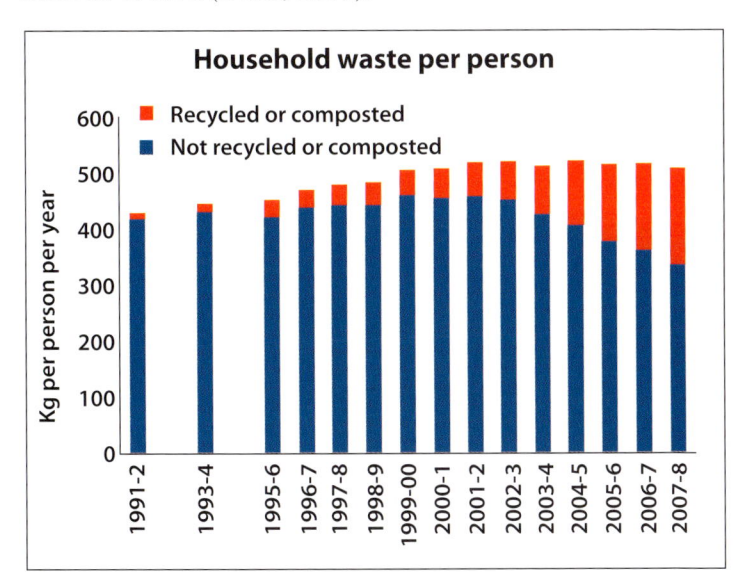

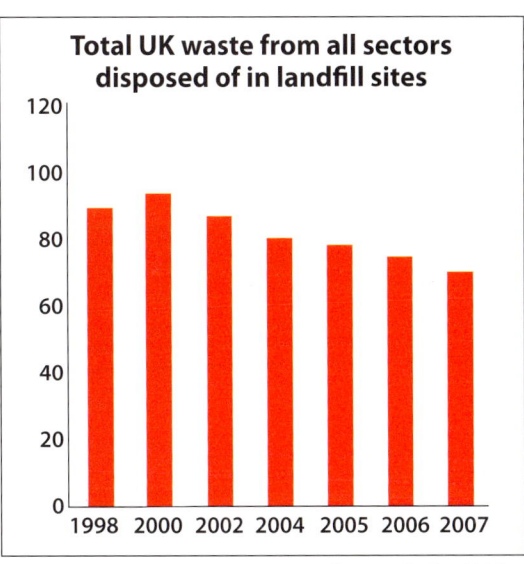

Source: Defra, 2009.

As a consequence of the Waste and Emissions Trading Act 2003, all local authorities are required to produce a municipal waste management strategy, designed to reduce levels of waste in line with government and European Union targets (see figure 7.16 on p180). Figure 7.17 on p180 shows the preferred options for dealing with waste within the waste hierarchy.

Figure 7.16: Summary of key European, national and regional targets for waste reduction

See accompanying CD-Rom

Environmental management.doc

Legislation	Target
European Landfill Directive	Reduce the amount of biodegradable municipal waste (BMW) going to landfill by: • 25% of 1995 levels by 2010 • 50% of 1995 levels by 2013 • 65% of 1995 levels by 2020
Waste Strategy for England 2007	Reduce residual waste (household waste not re-used, recycled or composted) by 29% in 2010 compared with 2000. Aspire to reduce levels by 45% by 2020. Recycle or compost at least 40% of household waste by 2010. Recycle or compost at least 50% of household waste by 2020.
Regional Waste Strategy for the North West	Reduce growth in municipal solid waste (MSW) across the region to 2% by end 2006; 1% by 2010; 0% before 2014. Increase recycling or composting of household waste by 35% by 2010; 45% by 2015; 55% by 2020. Increase recovery of value from MSW by 45% by 2010; 67% by 2015.

Source: JMWMS for Merseyside, 2008: 9.

Figure 7.17: The waste hierarchy

See accompanying CD-Rom

UK waste.ppt

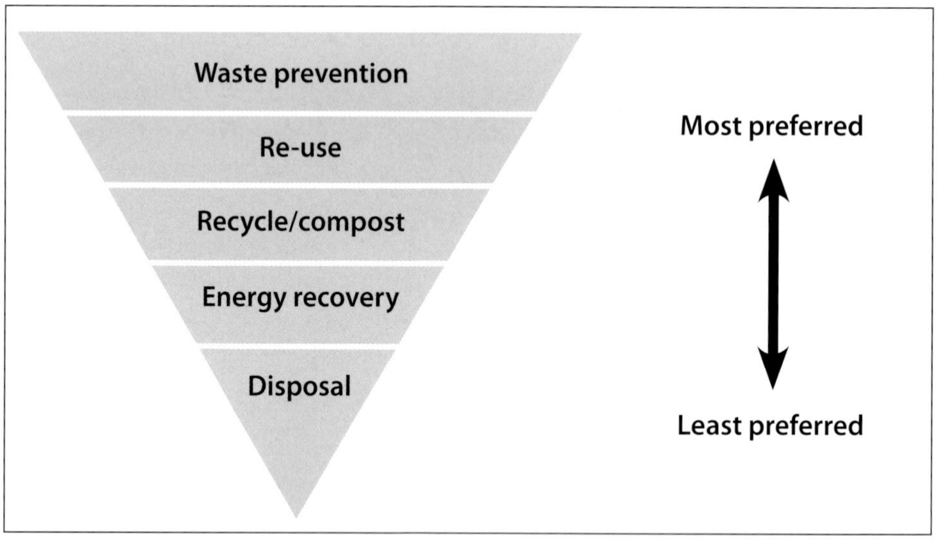
Waste prevention
Re-use
Recycle/compost
Energy recovery
Disposal
Most preferred
Least preferred

Source: JMWMS for Merseyside, 2008: 10.

Teaching idea 7.6

Ask students to investigate their local municipal waste management strategy (usually available as a pdf file via the local authority website). What strategies have been put in place? What are the priorities of their local authority? Why do they think the authority has prioritised these areas? Have they seen any evidence of changing strategies in their own lives?

It should be stressed that, while there is clear evidence of progress on effective waste management strategies, new challenges are also emerging. The most obvious area where levels of waste are increasing is the electronics industry, where rapid product obsolescence is resulting in huge amounts of 'e-waste'.

Summary

Management of the environment is becoming an increasingly important element of government policies at all levels. The growth of policies can be directly attributed to an increasing awareness of the growing nature of environmental problems and the increasing impact of humanity on the environments of the planet. A failure to manage environmental problems effectively may well have wide-reaching consequences for the entire human race.

Endnotes

1. This chapter draws heavily on three major reports on the global environment that are available on the internet:

    Millennium Ecosystem Assessment, available at: *www.millenniumassessment.org*

    United Nations Environment Programme (2007) *Global environment outlook 4*, available at: *www.unep.org/geo/geo4/media/*

    WWF (2008) *Living planet report*, available at: *www.panda.org*

2. For more details of this World Bank-funded project see: *http://web.worldbank.org*

Useful websites

On UK biodiversity see the National Biodiversity Network: *www.nbn.org.uk*

On the collapse of the Canadian cod fishery see: *http://archive.greenpeace.org/comms/cbio/cancod.html*

On UK biodiversity, Natural England (2010) has produced *Lost life: England's lost and threatened species*, available at: *http://naturalengland.etraderstores.com/NaturalEnglandShop/NE233*

On the OK Tedi mines see Forest People's Programme (FPP) (2000) *Undermining the forest: the need to control transnational mining companies*, available at: *www.wrm.org.uy/publications/undermining.pdf*

Defra (2009) *Sustainable development indicators in your pocket* available at: *www.defra.gov.uk/sustainable/government/progress/data-resources/sdiyp.htm*

On waste management see, for instance, (JMWMS) *Joint Municipal Waste Management Strategy for Merseyside 2008: Headline Strategy*, available at: *www.merseysidewda.gov.uk/documents/Main%20Joint%20MWMS%202008.pdf*

Chapter 7: Environmental management

Globalisation

Charles Rawding

Introduction

It is now routine to discuss issues such as air pollution, acid rain, deforestation, climate change and the depletion of the ozone layer in global terms, but this has not always been the case. The consideration of environmental problems in a global context is a relatively recent development. Arguably, the first time that such issues were raised was in Rachel Carson's *Silent Spring*, first published in 1962 (Carson, 1965), which discussed the damage to ecosystems caused by indiscriminate use of pesticides. The book was a big success, selling half a million copies in hardback in the USA alone and triggering legislation that resulted in a ban on the use of DDT and other toxic substances during the early 1970s (Lechner, 2009), while the first major global meeting devoted to the environment was the UN-convened Conference on the Human Environment (UNCHE) in Stockholm in 1972.

However, it should be stressed that this does not necessarily imply that environmental issues are more serious than they have been in the past, merely that perspectives on the environment have changed and with these changes a more overtly global approach has developed. These changing perceptions of environmental issues are extremely important, as they determine society's reaction to them. Where environmental issues become features of the news agenda, contemporary attitudes may shift quite dramatically within a short period of time. To illustrate this point, air pollution was a much more serious issue in industrial cities during the 19th century than it was by the time global environmentalism became a major social movement in the 1960s. Yet, for much of the 19th century, industrial pollution was seen as a sign of progress and prosperity rather than as any sort of a problem. However, the continuing integration of world society and the increasing web of international organisations and social movements, combined with instantaneous access to news from around the world, means that major issues today are more likely to be cast as global problems and be addressed on global agendas. This chapter aims to draw together the strands discussed in earlier chapters within a more explicitly global consideration of environmental issues.

Global environmental trends

Before the 1987 World Commission on Environment and Development (the Brundtland Commission [☞]), 'development' [☞] was associated with industrialisation, and tended to be measured solely in terms of economic activity and increases in wealth. Environmental protection and legislation were perceived by many as obstacles to development. However, it is important that current global environmental issues are not thought of as being fixed entities. The contrasting histories of two global issues, climate change [☞] and ozone depletion, which were prominent during the 1990s, illustrate this point well. Both issues are heavily dependent on scientific evidence and

See ch 6, Sustainability (p135).

See Volume 1: Human Geography, ch 7, Development geographies (p138).

See ch 3, Climate change.

**Figure 8.1:
Global environmental trends**

See accompanying CD-Rom

Global environmental trends.doc

> There are... environmental trends that threaten to radically alter the planet, that threaten the lives of many species upon it, including the human species. Each year another 6 million hectares of productive dryland turns into worthless desert. Over three decades, this would amount to an area roughly as large as Saudi Arabia. More than 11 million hectares of forests are destroyed yearly, and this, over three decades, would equal an area about the size of India. Much of this forest is converted into low-grade farmland unable to support the farmers who settle it. In Europe, acid precipitation kills forests and lakes and damages the artistic and architectural heritage of nations; it may have acidified vast tracts of soil beyond reasonable hope of repair; the burning of fossil fuels puts into the atmosphere carbon dioxide, which is causing gradual global warming. This 'greenhouse effect' may, by early next century, have increased average global temperatures enough to shift agricultural production areas, raise sea levels to flood coastal cities, and disrupt national economies. Other industrial gases threaten to deplete the planet's protective ozone shield to such an extent that the number of human and animal cancers would rise sharply and the ocean's food chain would be disrupted. Industry and agriculture put toxic substances into the human food chain and into underground water tables beyond reach of cleansing.

Source: *The World Commission on Environment and Development: our common future* (1987) cited in Lechner and Boli, 2008: 405.

Teaching idea 8.1

Ask students to study the extract (figure 8.1) from the 1987 World Commission on Environment and Development. Which issues can they identify as being global in context? How do these issues relate to them directly? Which of the issues cited are highest on current environmental agendas? Why do they think that is the case?

the claims of scientists, and both are difficult to conceptualise in a meaningful way at an individual level (unusual weather events may or may not be symptomatic of climate change; similarly, increased levels of skin cancer may or may not be a consequence of the depletion of the ozone layer). The 'hole' in the ozone layer (actually a thinning of the layer) was discovered in 1984. The ozone layer is essential because of its role in absorbing ultra-violet radiation from the Sun. The negative effects of any further diminution became quickly apparent. There were few disagreements about the science, and the ability of the large chemical companies to find alternatives to ozone-depleting chlorofluorocarbons (CFCs) resulted in the issue dropping down global agendas in a relatively short period of time, even though the 'hole' over the Antarctic in the stratospheric ozone is now the largest ever. However, because emissions of ozone-depleting substances (ODS) have decreased over the past 20 years, the challenge has been presented as a global success story. Nevertheless, it is still estimated that the ozone layer over the Antarctic will not fully recover until between 2060 and 2075, assuming world governments continue to act on the production of ODS.

By contrast, as research into climate change has developed, the simplicity of early ideas about 'global warming' has been replaced by a somewhat bewildering complexity of potential outcomes. Although the concept of climate change is now largely taken as fact – it is generally accepted that it is happening to some degree – the mechanisms of it, the consequences of it and the implications for human societies are still hugely debated. Largely as a result of the unpredictability and complexity around the topic, climate change remains a highly contentious issue both at a scientific level and in the political arena (see chapter 3).

Economic development and environmental issues

In the past few decades, there has been a growing realisation that it is impossible to separate economic development from environmental consequences. The products that we consume have to come from somewhere. The inputs of materials and energy and the waste products at the end of the process or the end of the life of the product are ultimately linked to the physical environment. Many forms of development have adverse environmental effects, which may cross national boundaries and may have ramifications for future generations. Three main aspects can be identified:

- overuse of non-renewable and renewable resources (including fossil fuels, depletion of water resources and deforestation)
- overburdening of the natural environment (for instance the increasing concentrations of greenhouse gases in the atmosphere and heavy metals in the soils)
- the destruction of ecosystems to create space for urban and industrial development (Dicken, 2007: 25).

Population growth [☞] in the past 50 years has been dramatic, more than doubling from about 3 billion people in 1960 to just under 7 billion today. At the same time, economic activity has grown more than 50-fold over the past century, with most of this growth occurring during the past 50 years. Worldwide, GDP per capita (purchasing power parity) has increased from US$5,927 in 1987 to US$8,162 in 2004 (UNEP, 2007). These dramatic changes in population, economic activity and income levels have had a massive impact on the biosphere. Much of this economic and population growth has relied on the exploitation of natural resources.

See Volume 1: Human Geography, ch 3, Population geographies (p55).

As we saw in chapter 1 (p15), environmental degradation threatens human wellbeing, it has been linked to human health problems, including some types of cancers, vector-borne diseases, emerging animal-to-human disease transfer, nutritional deficits and respiratory illnesses. The environment provides both resources and an economic base for human activity. Non-sustainable use of natural resources therefore threatens individual livelihoods as well as local, national and international economies. Environmental degradation can also increase human vulnerability, causing forced population movement and insecurity, as in the case of storms, droughts or environmental mismanagement.

At another level, poverty is a major cause of environmental degradation, and attempting to tackle environmental issues produced as a result of poverty without tackling the root causes of poverty may be seen as a pointless exercise, or worse, as a series of policies designed to further marginalise the poor. Solutions to such issues are usually discussed in terms of sustainable development [☞].

See ch 6, Sustainability and Volume 1: Human Geography, ch 7, Development geographies (p147).

Depleting and damaging a local resource base can have major implications elsewhere. Deforestation in upland regions can lead to flooding lower down in the drainage basin, industrial pollution may lead to diminished fish stocks in waters distant from the original polluter, while dryland degradation leads to environmental refugees crossing national borders. The effects of aircraft fuel combustion are clearly transnational in their implications, while on a larger scale, acid precipitation and nuclear fallout have international implications; at the same time, greenhouse gas emissions threaten climate change for the entire planet.

As we have already seen in chapter 3, if current trends in global warming continue, they will generate enormous social and economic damage in many parts of the world. It is expected these will include: the dislocation of climate zones, altering agricultural economies, the flooding of many coastal and low-lying areas, changing patterns of disease and increasing volatility of atmospheric systems (producing more frequent storms).

Global intergovernmental actions

If the UNCHE Stockholm meeting in 1972 had marked the beginning, in many ways the 1987 World Commission on Environment and Development set the tone for subsequent evaluations of the relationship between economy, society and environment, with the result that the UN Conference on Environment and Development (the Rio Declaration) in 1992 proclaimed a range of environmentally related principles (figure 8.2).

**Figure 8.2:
The Rio Declaration on Environment and Development – extracts from the environmental principles**

See accompanying CD-Rom

Rio Declaration.doc

Principle 2	States have... the responsibility to ensure that activities within their jurisdiction or control do not cause damage to the environment of other States or of areas beyond their national jurisdiction.
Principle 3	The right to development must... meet the environmental needs of present and future generations.
Principle 4	Environmental protection shall constitute an integral part of the development process and cannot be considered in isolation from it.
Principle 7	States shall cooperate in a spirit of global partnership to conserve, protect and restore the health and integrity of the Earth's ecosystem.
Principle 10	Environmental issues are best handled with the participation of all concerned citizens at the relevant level.
Principle 11	States shall enact effective environmental legislation. Environmental standards, management objectives and priorities should reflect the environmental and developmental context to which they apply.
Principle 17	Environmental impact assessment shall be undertaken for proposed activities that are likely to have a significant adverse impact on the environment.
Principle 18	States shall immediately notify other States of any natural disasters or other emergencies that are likely to produce sudden harmful effects on the environment of those States.
Principle 22	Indigenous people and... local communities have a vital role in environmental management and development because of their knowledge and traditional practices.
Principle 25	Peace, development and environmental protection are interdependent and indivisible.

Source: adapted from Lechner and Boli, 2008: 411-4.

> **Teaching idea 8.2**
>
> Ask students to look at the principles of the Rio Declaration (figure 8.2) and offer examples of where the principles have been applied in practice, or examples of where the principles are being ignored. How realistic do they think the principles are?

Following on from the Rio Declaration, a number of major environmental agreements were concluded during the 1990s:

- Montreal Protocol on substances that deplete the ozone layer (1989-92)
- convention on biological diversity (1992)
- framework convention on climate change (1992)
- Kyoto Protocol on climate change (1997) (Dicken, 2007: 543).

However, the proliferation of global treaties did not mean that there was a common agreed agenda. For instance, as we have already seen in the case of Rio, delegates from the North called for the protection of forests, while many of those from the South stressed their right to use resources such as timber for urgent development needs. Again the wealthy demanded environmental protection, while the less wealthy required financial support.

Trade, industry and the environment

Prior to the 20th century, most of the impacts of industrial development were relatively localised. However, the dramatic growth in industrial output in the developed world during the 20th century has resulted in much more widespread environmental impacts. Industrial production has been resource intensive, resulting in ever larger mines and quarries and ever growing levels of emissions from factories. While much of the consequent pollution and environmental degradation has had a local impact, other aspects have been transferred around the globe, as we saw in chapter 4 (p95), with the impact of the Chernobyl disaster on the upland farmers of the UK. Transborder pollution and risks such as nuclear power and acid rain, along with activities such as the transport of toxic wastes around the globe, illustrate the global nature of many issues that have arisen as a result of the development of industrial society.

The growth of consumer society in the past half century has resulted in a huge increase in levels of international trade, involving high energy costs with both short-term and long-term environmental consequences. Environmentalists have criticised many aspects of this trade:

> 'More than half of all international trade involves the simultaneous import and export of essentially the same goods. For example, Americans import Danish sugar cookies, and Danes import American sugar cookies. Exchanging recipes would surely be more efficient.'
>
> (Daly cited in Dicken, 2007: 544)

The progressive globalisation of trade and industry [☞] during the past century has been built, to a significant extent, on the basis of the comparative advantage of different locations, in terms of access to raw materials, labour, energy sources and so on. The growth of industry in less economically developed countries (LEDCs) in the past 50 years has been based on the twin 'advantages' of lower labour costs and less strict (and therefore less costly) environmental regulation. Perhaps the most extreme juxtaposition of the poor and wealthy economies and their environmental interconnectedness can be seen on the Mexico-United States border, where the unregulated pollution of the

See Volume 1: Human Geography, ch 10, Geographies of globalisation (p208).

factories set up on the Mexican side to benefit from significantly lower costs than in the United States has led to very high levels of toxicity in water supplies and air pollution, both of which have also impacted on the wealthier side of the border. Such a situation, of course, raises the question of whether variations in environmental standards should be incorporated into international trade regulations and also poses the rather more awkward moral question of whether LEDCs should be required to do things that the more economically developed countries (MEDCs) did not have to do when they were undergoing industrialisation. If they are required to do these things, who should be paying the bill?

In some contexts, environmental problems may be regarded as global where they occur in similar contexts in different countries. Environmental problems are often at their most pronounced in the largest cities of the developing world, where extremely high levels of air pollution can be found as a consequence of very rapid, under-regulated industrialisation combining with increasing levels of car ownership and transport usage generally. Other forms of pollution, such as water pollution and an inability to cope adequately with waste water and sewage, can also be cited in many of these cities. The combination of these problems then results in low life expectancy and high levels of premature deaths. Figure 8.3 shows changes in the relative levels of emissions of nitrogen oxide and sulphur dioxide at a global level. Emissions in the various regions show different trends for SO_2 and NOx. There have been decreases in

Figure 8.3:
Air pollution
(above) sulphur dioxide
(below) nitrogen oxide

See accompanying CD-Rom

Air pollution.ppt

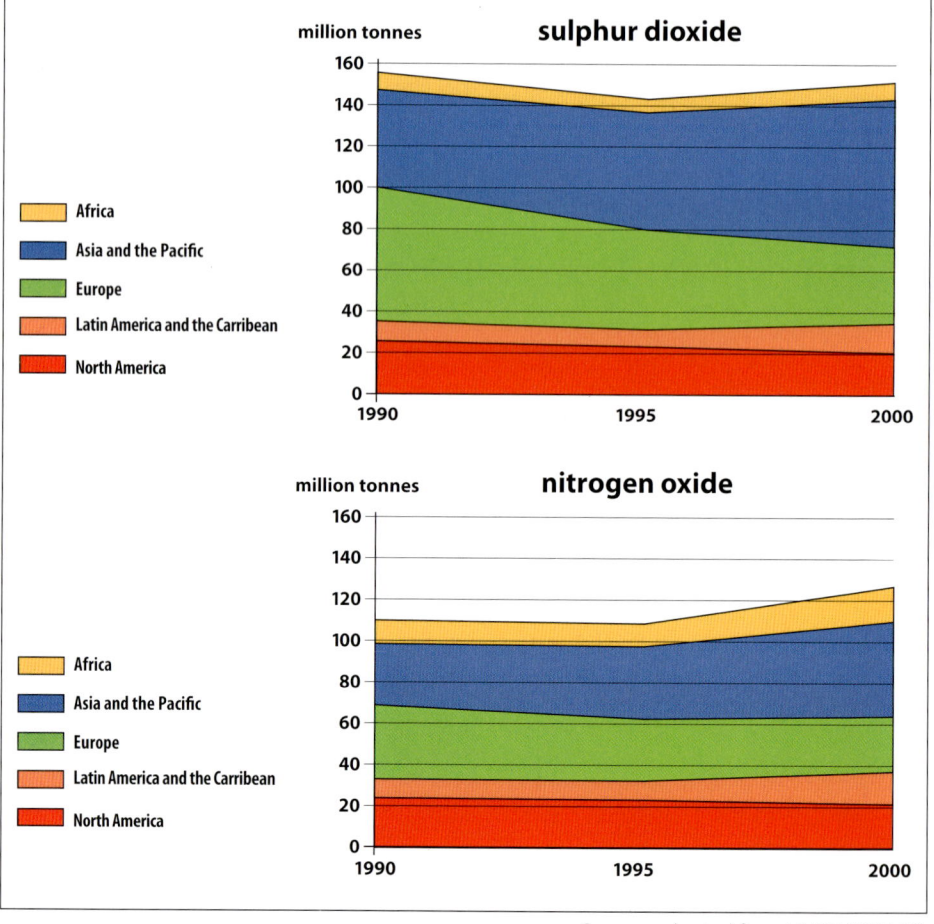

Source: adapted from UNEP, 2007: 52.

the national emissions in the more affluent countries of Europe and North America since 1987. More recently, Europe is as concerned with unregulated sulphur emissions from international shipping as it is with the regulated land-based sources. For the industrialising nations of Asia, emissions have increased, sometimes dramatically, over the past two decades.

Between 2000 and 2005, Chinese SO_2 emissions increased by approximately 28%, while satellite data suggest that NOx emissions in China have grown by 50% between 1996 and 2003. The main result is that global emissions of SO_2 and NOx are increasing compared to 1990 levels. In Africa, and in Latin America and the Caribbean, small increases have been reported (UNEP, 2007).

> **Teaching idea 8.3**
>
> Ask students to study the graphs of air pollution (figure 8.3 on p188). What trends do they notice, both in terms of absolute levels of air pollution and the changes in proportions attributable to the various continents? How do they explain these changes?

Climate change: the ultimate globalisation?

As we have already seen in chapter 3, climate change is probably the single most pressing global issue of the contemporary world. The impacts of climate change will vary across the planet, and their consequences will be different according to the wealth and adaptability of the societies concerned. For those less developed countries of the world where people are heavily dependent on ecological systems for their livelihoods, what might appear to be relatively minor changes in climate may have significant impacts on the environment, and subsequently human societies. A one degree increase in temperature threatens to produce both droughts in Africa and sea-level rise and greater flooding in South Asia. In both locations, it will be the most vulnerable communities that will have the greater difficulty in adapting successfully to new circumstances (Collins, 2009). Because of the present-day patterns in global manufacture and trade, climate change connects household purchases in the UK with industrial pollution in China and deforestation in Brazil. It is an issue that forces us to think geographically [☞] and globally.

See Introduction (p1).

The Earth's average temperature has increased by approximately 0.74°C over the past century. The impacts of this warming include sea-level rise and increasing frequency and intensity of heatwaves, storms, floods and droughts, leading to potentially massive consequences, especially for the most vulnerable, poor and disadvantaged people on the planet. In developing countries, the poor, often relying on rain-fed subsistence agriculture and gathered natural resources, are deeply dependent on climate patterns, such as the monsoons, and are most vulnerable to the devastation of extreme weather events, such as hurricanes. The likelihood of changes in rainfall patterns and water availability also threaten food security, with major changes projected for regions such as Africa, which are the least able to cope. Sea-level rise threatens millions of people and major economic centres in coastal areas, such as the Ganges-Brahmaputra delta in Bangladesh, and the very existence of small island states – for example, the Maldives. It is the poor or vulnerable who suffer most from weather extremes, even within relatively

See ch 7, Environmental management (p171).

See ch 5, Food supply, figure 5.24.

affluent societies, as was demonstrated by the effects of Hurricane Katrina [🔖] in 2005, and by the European heatwave [🔖] of 2003 (UNEP, 2007).

On the other hand, taking action on climate change is likely to prove extremely expensive, which raises issues concerning whether the money might be better spent on alternatives. For instance, Lomborg compares estimates by UNICEF of the costs of providing basic health, education, water and sanitation for all the developing countries with the costs of tackling climate change, and opts for the former:

> *'We should not spend vast amounts of money to cut a tiny slice of the global temperature increase when this constitutes a poor use of resources and when we could probably use these funds far more effectively in the developing world... global warming is not anywhere near the most important problem facing the world. What matters is making the developing countries rich and giving the citizens of developed countries even greater opportunities... the same resources could do much more good, saving many more people from dying...'*

(Lomborg, cited in Held and McGrew, 2007: 71)

See accompanying CD-Rom

Climate change or development. doc

Teaching idea 8.4

Provide students with Lomborg's statement, above, and ask them to consider what they feel to be the most important problems facing the world. Ask them to rank these problems in terms of their perceptions of the relative importance of the problems identified and then justify the ranking [🔖].

Initiatives focusing on global interdependence

Following the initiatives of the 1980s and 1990s discussed above, in 2005 the UN conference in Montreal began to address the issue from the point of view of the interdependence of nations, agreeing three important measures:

- encouraging developed countries to invest in sustainable development projects in developing countries, enabling them to earn emission allowances that could be offset against their own emissions

- allowing developed countries to invest in other developed countries (particularly the transition economies of Eastern Europe), enabling them to earn carbon allowances to meet their own emission reduction targets

- implementing the Kyoto 'compliance' regime; ensuring that countries are accountable for their emission reduction targets (Dicken, 2007: 544).

While criticisms have been made about the relative weakness of the framework and the undemanding nature of some targets relative to the perceived threat to the global environment, there can be no doubt that these changes mark a significant globalisation of the perception of environmental issues.

Global governance?

Global governance of the environment is usually associated with the functions of the United Nations and a range of intergovernmental groupings such as the G8 and G20 groups of nations and the interactions between bodies such as the European Union and the African Union, while bodies such as Greenpeace and Friends of the Earth also operate at a global scale. Figure 8.4 shows the range of organisations associated with environmental governance from the perspective of the United Nations.

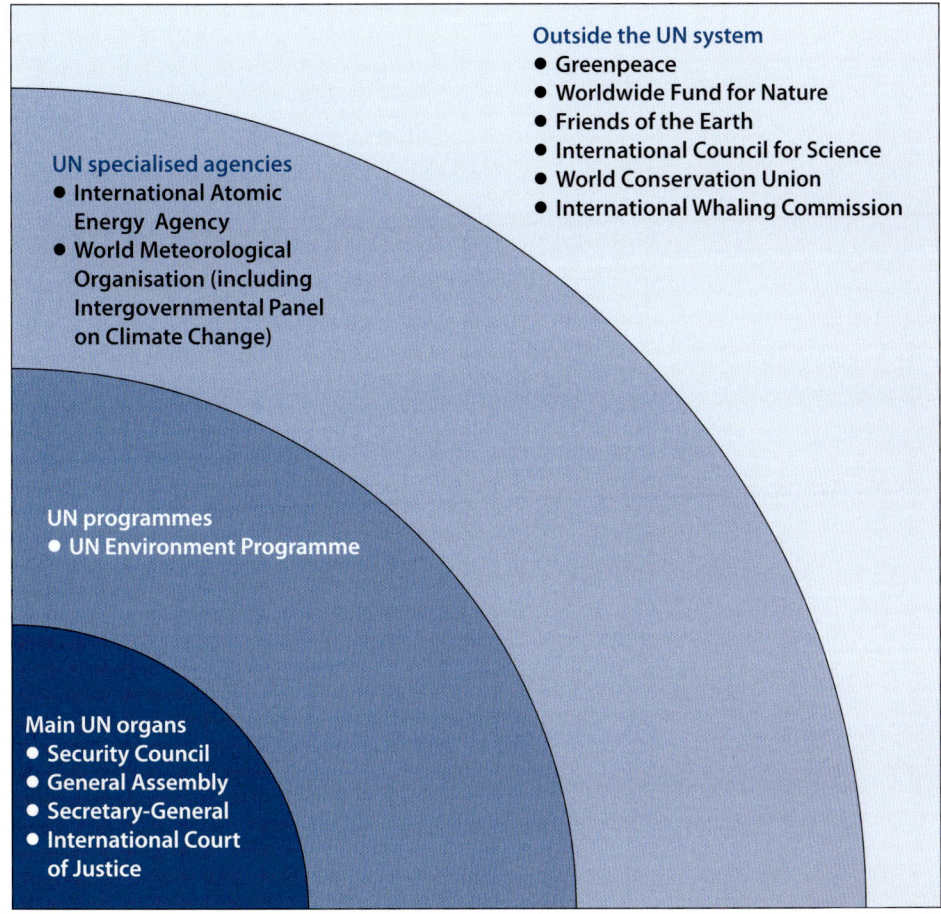

Figure 8.4:
Global governance and the environment – a UN-centred viewpoint

Global governance.ppt

Outside the UN system
- Greenpeace
- Worldwide Fund for Nature
- Friends of the Earth
- International Council for Science
- World Conservation Union
- International Whaling Commission

UN specialised agencies
- International Atomic Energy Agency
- World Meteorological Organisation (including Intergovernmental Panel on Climate Change)

UN programmes
- UN Environment Programme

Main UN organs
- Security Council
- General Assembly
- Secretary-General
- International Court of Justice

Source: adapted from Held and McGrew, 2007: 140-141.

Global governance is clearly a far from neutral concept, and reflects the economic and political realities of power, as reflected in weighted voting systems and institutionalised vetoes at institutions such as the United Nations Security Council. The United Nations is clearly susceptible to the influence of the most powerful states, while many of its operations are relatively weak and underfunded, and many of its environmental policies may be policed inadequately. The United Nations Environment Programme, for instance, relies on member nations' voluntary donations, which have led on occasion to financial issues making it difficult for it to live up to its task of monitoring and coordinating and promoting new environmental activity. On the other hand, it has become an effective clearing house for environmental data with its regular Global Environmental Outlooks and Global Resource Information Database (*www.unep.org*) (Lechner, 2009).

The past 20 years have seen a growth in the number of scientific assessments carried out on a global scale: the Global Environmental Outlook; the Intergovernmental Panel on Climate Change (IPCC); and the Millennium Ecosystem Assessment. The IPCC was established in 1988 to assess the scientific, technical and socio-economic information relevant to climate change (*www.ipcc.ch*). In 2007, the IPCC released its *Fourth Assessment Report*. The Millennium Ecosystem Assessment was launched in 2001 to highlight issues facing the ecosystems of the planet (*www.millenniumassessment.org*). These scientific assessments reflect the work of thousands of experts worldwide, and have led to greater understanding of environmental problems.

While such reports represent a balanced outcome from the world's scientific community, the present world order is very much dominated by the United States (although the rise of China looks set to challenge this position in the coming years). This dominance has had significant implications in terms of approaches to the environment. For instance, the resistance of the Bush administration to ideas relating to climate change clearly hindered efforts to achieve progress on emissions reduction, while the extent to which there will be policy changes during the Obama presidency has yet to become clear. At the same time as there are clear imbalances within global power structures, there are also significant variations in the abilities/willingness of nation states to implement not only their own agendas, but also those of supranational bodies such as the UN. Figure 8.5 shows the variation in levels of effectiveness of governments around the world.

The dominance of the free-market, liberal position can also be seen in the activities of bodies such as the World Trade Organization (*www.wto.org*), which can be contrasted with campaigns such as the Jubilee Debt Campaign (*www.jubileedebtcampaign.org.uk*) and organisations such as Trade Justice (*www.tjm.org.uk*). While it is clear that politics and political power remain centred on the nation state, there has undoubtedly been a shift towards interstate and global perspectives. To a significant extent, this shift

**Figure 8.5:
Government effectiveness**

See accompanying CD-Rom

Government effectiveness.ppt

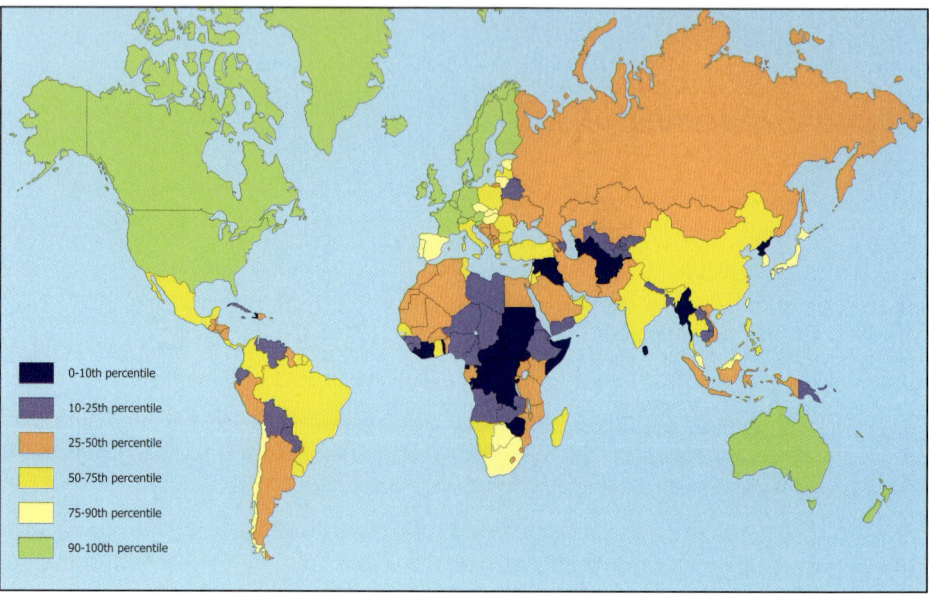

- 0-10th percentile
- 10-25th percentile
- 25-50th percentile
- 50-75th percentile
- 75-90th percentile
- 90-100th percentile

Note: the rankings are based on factors including quality of public services and policy implementation, degree of political independence and levels of government commitment.

Source: adapted from UNEP, 2007: 309.

has been promoted and encouraged by the growth of transnational environmental movements to which we shall now turn our attention.

Transnational environmental movements

As well as describing corporations as transnational [☞], it is also possible to discuss notions of transnational activism where activist networks around the globe interact to tackle global issues. Today we take for granted the existence of global environmental movements such as Greenpeace, Friends of the Earth and the World Wildlife Fund, yet Friends of the Earth was only founded in 1969, while Greenpeace came into existence in 1971 in Vancouver, Canada, as a response to US nuclear tests. Today, Greenpeace is an international organisation based in Amsterdam, the Netherlands, with 2.8 million supporters worldwide, and national as well as regional offices in 41 countries.

See Volume 1: Human Geography, ch 10, Globalisation, figure 10.4.

> We 'bear witness' to environmental destruction in a peaceful, non-violent manner;
>
> We use non-violent confrontation to raise the level and quality of public debate;
>
> In exposing threats to the environment and finding solutions we have no permanent allies or adversaries;
>
> We ensure our financial independence from political or commercial interests;
>
> We seek solutions for, and promote open, informed debate about society's environmental choices.

Source: www.greenpeace.org/international/about/our-core-values

Figure 8.6: Greenpeace 'cornerstone principles'

See accompanying CD-Rom

Greenpeace.doc

Teaching idea 8.5

Ask students to consider the 'cornerstone principles' of Greenpeace (figure 8.6) in the light of one of the campaigns discussed on their website (www.greenpeace.org). How does the organisation set about achieving its aims? Do the students agree with the methods or do they have reservations?

The management structure of Greenpeace reflects its transnational operations. It comprises the Greenpeace Council, with representatives from all the countries where Greenpeace has offices, and meets once a year to decide on organisational policy. Council members come from around the world, with the result that decisions reflect sensitivity to differing regional and local aspects of environmental problems. In addition to the Council, there are regional trustees who are expected to advance a global rather than a national or regional orientation.

Technological changes have aided the effectiveness of organisations such as Greenpeace (see figure 8.7 on p194). In the 1970s, Greenpeace ships used Morse code, which was sent to their offices on land before the information was communicated to the media by telephone. Photographic evidence was only available once the ship had returned to port. Greenpeace ships now use telephones, fax machines and satellite links to communicate with home offices, enabling instantaneous information to be communicated and verified. Video cameras are used to capture action – images which can then be beamed directly into people's homes, enabling issues to be highlighted as they are occurring. Greenpeace has been able to use these techniques to expose incidents such as the illegal activities of a Russian whaling fleet and to highlight the levels of pollution from a manufacturing plant in New Jersey, USA.

Figure 8.7: Improvements in communications technology

See accompanying CD-Rom

Improvements in communications technology.doc

'A number of years ago it was difficult to use direct, non-violent action to change political conditions around the globe. While direct action has always been a tool for those seeking change, the technology did not exist to publicise specific actions to a global audience. Recent innovations in communications technologies have allowed information to whip around the globe within seconds, linking distant corners of the world. Greenpeace plugs into this planet-wide communication system to advertise its direct actions.'

Source: Wapner in Lechner and Boli, 2008: 420.

Teaching idea 8.6

Provide students with the quote in figure 8.7. Ask them to investigate an environmental issue being pursued by bodies such as Greenpeace or Friends of the Earth. How are the organisations using modern media to publicise the issue?

Pollution and transnational activism: an example from South Africa

The south Durban industrial basin is the country's second-largest concentration of industrial activity.[1] It also suffers some of the worst industrial pollution in the country. Local residents, predominantly poor black people, live in close proximity to a range of dirty industries and suffer very high levels of air, ground and water pollution, largely as a result of living close to two oil refineries, a paper and pulp factory and a number of petrochemical plants. The two oil refineries are among the worst polluters. One is jointly owned by Shell and BP (Anglo-Dutch and British transnational corporations respectively), while the other is owned by Petronas, Malaysia's state-owned oil and gas company.

The South African constitution recognises the rights of its citizens to a clean and healthy environment, and ultimately has responsibility for implementing legislation relevant to industrial pollution. Local activists have been successful in attracting a great deal of news coverage of the issues in the south Durban area in both local and national news. As a result, the government has responded by implementing a programme of environmental monitoring and scientific research into the health problems of the region. However, the activists have not limited their activities to the national scale. They have also engaged in transnational activities. For example, they have mobilised foreign scientific expertise by sending local air samples for testing at US universities, enabling them to confront both government and business with their findings. They have also established a collaborative relationship with the largest environmental organisation in Denmark, Danmarks Naturfredningsforening. This collaboration has included a scientific comparison between the levels of air pollution produced by the South African refineries and levels produced by refineries in Denmark. The research showed that the emission of sulphur dioxide from the two South African refineries was far higher than levels from Danish refineries. Emissions of particulate matter were also higher in South Africa. The comparison emphasised the different pollution standards applied in the two countries, and strengthened arguments that TNCs shift their environmentally noxious and more hazardous operations to less developed countries with less stringent environmental and safety standards.

The activists have also turned their attention to the transnational corporations directly, by joining a campaign coordinated by Friends of the Earth that aims to force Shell to be more accountable to the local communities where it has factories. Some of the activists own single shares in Shell, enabling them to attend shareholders' meetings and raise embarrassing questions about the company's operations around the world.

Such strategies demonstrate how global communication technologies have enabled the globalisation of a range of environmental issues, raising awareness and increasing the pressure on relevant actors to instigate change in the face of adverse publicity and evidence of avoidable environmental damage.

Shipbreaking: a green industry?

The industry of shipbreaking highlights a number of environmental issues. At one level it should be applauded, as it effectively recycles very high proportions of technologically obsolete vessels, yet at the same time it is widely regarded as one of the most environmentally polluting of all industries.

India has one of the largest shipbreaking industries in the world. It is a £270 million industry which provides steel for the rapidly growing economy, and much needed jobs for the workforce. Much of the industry is focused on Alang in the state of Gujarat. Alang produces 2.5 million tonnes of steel a year for India's rolling mills, and everything that can be sold from the ship is available. However, for critics, it is an industry with appalling working conditions paying low wages to people living in inhumane conditions. Most of the workers are migrants who live close to the yards in slum conditions, having arrived from the poorest states of India in search of work.

Alang has developed from a small village to the world's biggest shipbreaking yard for several reasons. The area experiences high tides and has steeply sloping beaches which meant there was no need to build dry docks and piers. It also offers a location not subject to environmental and safety regulations, along with a plentiful supply of very cheap labour.

Figure 8.8: Shipbreaking

Shipbreaking.ppt

Along the coast the environmental consequences of shipbreaking are being felt by local fishermen, who have noticed coastal pollution and dwindling fish stocks. However, the industry claims that increasing environmental and safety awareness in India is persuading shipowners to find alternative destinations for their vessels, including Pakistan, Bangladesh and China, which has taken over from India as the country with the largest shipbreaking industry.

The nature of the shipping industry also makes effective regulation more difficult, since many of the world's ships are owned by offshore companies, and fly flags of convenience, with crews recruited from locations where wages are very low. As such, the shipping and shipbreaking industries, both global in outlook and operation, present formidable environmental challenges at a global scale (Ramesh, 2008: 285-7).

The globalisation of fauna and flora

For much of human history, the main way in which environmental impacts were spread around the world was through the unintentional transport of flora and fauna and microbes. The 'discovery' of the Americas, the growth of trade with Asia and the development of colonial empires by European nations, all resulted in increasing levels of transfer of environmental resources around the globe. Such transfers have had both positive and negative consequences. On the negative side, diseases of European origin caused havoc in the Americas, where natives had little immunity, while diseases of African origin were imported to the Americas via the slave trade; equally 'invasive species' have had a range of unpredicted consequences for ecosystems [✱]. On the positive side, in terms of human health and lifestyle, the spread of food and cash crops from their source regions to other areas of the world has generally had positive benefits for recipient societies and economies (figure 8.9). The potato is an early example of the globalisation of fauna and flora, introduced to Europe from its native Americas in 1536. The potato is now the fourth-largest food crop in the world. Large numbers of plants and animals have been transferred around the globe. While modern policies

See ch 1, Ecosystems (p21-22).

Figure 8.9:
World plants – origins and distribution

See accompanying CD-Rom

World plants.doc

Plant	Source region	Newer areas of cultivation
Cocoa	North-east South America	West Africa/Indonesia
Maize	Western South America/Central America	Eastern USA/all of South America/Europe/West and South Africa/India/South-east Asia/eastern Australia
Rubber	Amazonia	West Africa/South-east Asia
Sugar cane	Eastern India	Caribbean/eastern South America/South-east Asia/East Africa/north-east Australia
Coffee	Horn of Africa/Central Africa	Central America/north-east Brazil/India/wider areas of Africa
Wheat	Middle East	Europe/Central Asia/eastern USA/south-east South America/South Africa/southern Australia
Potato	Western South America	All the Americas (except the cold north)/Europe/South and East Asia/East Africa/southern Australia

Source: adapted from Bingham, 2008: 114-5.

on bio-protection have much reduced this trade, during the Victorian period the collection of exotic species was a common hobby of the wealthy. The Royal Botanic Gardens at Kew (*www.kew.org*) were effectively established as a botanical home for the empire under the patronage of Queen Victoria.

On the other hand, concerns over the extinction of species have resulted in attempts to encourage biodiversity [☞], itself a relatively recent concept. Moves towards recognising biodiversity at a global level began with the Brundtland Report of 1987, which was followed by the United Nations Convention on Biological Diversity (*www.cbd.int*) in 1992. 2010 is the International Year of Biodiversity. The potentially fragile nature of biodiversity is highlighted by the fact that just 12 countries contain 70% of the world's plant biodiversity (figure 8.10).

See ch 1, Ecosystems (p15).

USA	Ecuador	Democratic Republic of Congo	China
Mexico	Peru	Madagascar	Indonesia
Colombia	Brazil	India	Australia

Source: Bingham, 2008: 122.

Figure 8.10: Countries containing 70% of the world's plant biodiversity

See accompanying CD-Rom

World plants.doc

Teaching idea 8.7

Ask students to map the 12 countries listed in figure 8.10 and then suggest reasons why these countries contain significant elements of the world's biodiversity. Which areas of the world are not represented on the map? Why do they think this is the case?

Undoubtedly, part of the drive to sustain and promote biodiversity came from altruistic environmental campaigners alarmed by the accelerating rates of extinctions being identified across the planet. However, a second, and in some ways more powerful, group of proponents was to be found within the pharmaceutical industry (figure 8.11). Significant changes took place in the approaches of pharmaceutical companies from the 1980s; where previous research had focused on synthetic chemistry, there was now a switch to screening and modifying existing compounds (see figure 8.12 on p198).

Figure 8.11: GlaxoSmithKline, Brentford, UK

See accompanying CD-Rom

Pharmaceutical.ppt

**Figure 8.12:
The use of plants in medicine**

See accompanying CD-Rom

World plants.doc

Plant-based traditional medicine systems continue to play an essential role in health care, with about 80% of the world's inhabitants relying mainly on traditional medicines for their primary health care. Plant products also play an important role in the health care of the remaining 20% who reside in developed countries. About 25% of prescription drugs dispensed from community pharmacies in the United States from 1959 to 1980 contained plant extracts or active principles derived from higher plants. At least 119 chemical substances derived from 90 plant species are important drugs currently in use. Of these 199 drugs, 74% were discovered as a result of research directed at the isolation of active compounds from plants used in traditional medicine. Based on 1991 sales, half of the leading pharmaceuticals were either derived from natural products or contained a pharmacophore* that was based on natural products. In 1993, 57% of the top 150 brand-name products prescribed contained at least one major active compound, or were derived or patterned after compounds, reflecting biological diversity.

Note: a pharmacophore is the molecular framework that carries the essential features responsible for a drug's biological activity.

Source: Lewis, 2004, cited in Bingham, 2008: 122-3.

At an international level, the Convention on Biological Diversity provided in Article 16 an explicit requirement of reciprocity between countries, as a way of attempting to generate a greater level of equality between MEDCs and LEDCs and to ensure that poorer countries are able to benefit from bio-prospecting. At the same time, the Convention also requires resources to be made available to outside parties, to enable the whole planet to benefit from the bio-resources of a particular area.

An interesting example, which illustrates the global nature of biodiversity and the potential far-reaching consequences of human action, relates to research into the disappearance of songbirds in the US Midwest. It was found that conversion of forests in Central America to coffee plantations substantially reduced the winter habitats for many migratory birds, reducing their breeding success and their numbers. Researchers at the Smithsonian Institution worked with coffee producers to test methods of 'bird friendly' planting, using intact or minimally thinned forests for coffee tree planting. This method of planting produces coffee beans, but they are of higher quality, and require fewer pesticides and fertilisers. Additionally, the coffee can be marketed as coming from environmentally friendly sources, potentially bringing in higher prices (UNEP, 2007).

The globalisation of food

We have already discussed the issue of 'food miles' in chapter 6. However, it is worth reiterating some of the issues here in order to stress the increasingly globalised nature of food production and consumption in wealthy societies. For example, a basket of 20 fresh foods bought from major UK retailers was found to have clocked up a total of 100,943 miles. For such products to be purchasable requires an effective global cool chain to ensure the freshness of the product when it arrives at its destination. The situation today is in marked contrast to that of 40 years ago. Before the 1970s, as much as 90% of world food production was consumed in the country in which it was produced (Dicken, 2007: 360-4). During this period, food regulation was very much the preserve of national governments. However, the dramatic increases in world trade since then have resulted in a range of international regulations, principally overseen by the Food and Agriculture Organization (FAO) and the World Health Organization (WHO). There are now 'over 200 standards, 40 codes and guidelines for food production and processing, maximum levels for about 500 food additives, and 2,700 maximum-residue limits for pesticide residues in foods and food crops' (cited in Dicken, 2007: 264).

However, there are also variations in regulation between nations, even within trading units such as the EU, where national interests appear to come to the fore during times of food crisis, as with the French approach to British beef during and subsequent to the outbreak of bovine spongiform encephalopathy (BSE). There are also clear differences in emphasis between the US and the EU over issues such as genetically modified crops. A further area of international conflict relates to levels of subsidy and protection for agro-food industries – issues which frequently preoccupy the regulators at the World Trade Organization negotiations.

The most obvious manifestations of the globalisation of food relate, on the one hand, to the increasing dominance of TNCs such as McDonald's on our high streets, and, on the other, to the growth of global movements such as Fairtrade, which now incorporates more than 5 million farmers and workers in LEDCs. These somewhat contradictory strands lead to divergent approaches to significant issues relating to food production and consumption. The economic success of McDonald's clearly indicates a demand for the products in its restaurants, yet at the same time there has been widespread opposition to the alleged quality of its products and the ethics of its marketing strategies with films such as *Super Size Me* highlighting popular concerns. Parallel concerns here might be the opposition to genetically modified products and the power of the agro-chemical TNCs [☞]. In many cases, there are accompanying demands for the relocalisation of food. In this context, it is interesting to note that McDonald's now advertises that it only uses British beef in its UK products.

See ch 5, Food supply (p114).

An interesting consequence of what might be termed the globalisation of diet has been the cultivation of 'exotic' species to cater for changing tastes. For instance, bean sprouts and pak choi are now grown in the Vale of Evesham to cater for the growing demand for Chinese-style cuisine. Indeed, such developments might appear to be a somewhat perverse form of the 'alien species' discussed in chapter 1.

The converse, and at times contradictory, approach to globalisation, which is reflected in demands for a diverse diet and the desire to support the economic development of rural societies in LEDCs, is a reflection of the choices of wealthy consumers in richer societies. Choosing to buy fair trade food from farmers' cooperatives in Africa is not an option for many of the less wealthy members of society, for whom low-price, mass-produced commodities are an essential element in their economic survival.

Point for consideration

To what extent are our moral/ethical positions on issues such as fair trade and transnational corporations governed by our own financial situation?

Beyond these more high-profile approaches to the globalisation of food, there has been a steady concentration of power in the hands of an ever smaller group of very large transnational corporations in areas such as the provision of seeds (for instance, DuPont and Monsanto), pesticides (Bayer and Syngenta), food and drinks (Nestlé and Unilever) and retailing (Walmart and Tesco).[2] The February 2010 takeover of Cadbury, a UK-based TNC, by Kraft, a US-based TNC, is merely the latest in a sequence of acquisitions and mergers within the food sector, which have resulted in ever larger corporations with greater market share and dominance.

A more recent development in terms of the globalisation of food has been the acquisition of large agricultural areas in Africa by wealthier nations, to guarantee food supplies for their own markets (figure 8.13). Ethiopia is one of more than 20 African countries where land has been acquired for large-scale intensive agriculture destined for export to wealthier markets. These developments have been attributed to worldwide food shortages following sharp rises in the price of oil in 2008, which have resulted in increasing acreages of biofuels, along with growing water shortages in some regions. For instance, China has signed a contract with the Democratic Republic of Congo to grow 2.8 million hectares of palm oil for biofuels; while in 2008, Saudi Arabia announced a reduction in domestic arable production in order to conserve water supplies.

See ch 4, Energy (p99).

See ch 7, Environmental management (p161).

Figure 8.13: Ethiopia's largest greenhouse

See accompanying CD-Rom

Ethiopia's largest greenhouse.doc

Nestling below an escarpment of the Rift Valley, the development is far from finished, but the plastic and steel structure already stretches over 20 hectares – the size of 20 football pitches.

The farm manager shows us millions of tomatoes, peppers and other vegetables being grown in 500-metre rows in computer controlled conditions. Spanish engineers are building the steel structure, Dutch technology minimises water use from two bore-holes and 1,000 women pick and pack 50 tonnes of food a day. Within 24 hours it has been driven 200 miles to Addis Ababa and flown 1,000 miles to the shops and restaurants of Dubai, Jeddah and elsewhere in the Middle East.

Ethiopia is one of the hungriest countries in the world with more than 13 million people needing food aid, but paradoxically the government is offering at least 3 million hectares of its most fertile land to rich countries and some of the world's most wealthy individuals to export food for their own populations.

The 1,000 hectares of land that contain the Awassa greenhouses are leased for 99 years to Saudi billionaire businessman, Ethiopian-born Sheikh Mohammed al-Amoudi, one of the 50 richest men in the world. His Saudi Star company plans to spend up to US$2 billion acquiring and developing 500,000 hectares of land in Ethiopia in the next few years. So far, it has bought four farms and is already growing wheat, rice, vegetables and flowers for the Saudi market. It expects eventually to employ more than 10,000 people.

The al-Amoudi farm uses as much water a year as 100,000 Ethiopians.

Source: *The Observer*, 7 March 2010.

Teaching idea 8.8

Ask students to study figure 8.13. Why has the Ethiopian government decided to lease farming land to foreign corporations? Why have foreign companies decided to invest in Ethiopia? What are the moral issues raised by such developments? What insights does this article offer into current trends in globalisation?

Clearly such development provides both employment and investment opportunities, but also risks creating political and social tensions, particularly if indigenous populations are ignored and developments are imposed against the wishes of local peoples. In many cases, lands that governments and investors regard as 'empty' are used by farmers, herders and gatherers, local people who may have no written proof of ownership of land, and only weak legal rights to the resources that they regard as their own.

There are significant disagreements between experts about the merits of large-scale intensive farming in such regions. They may well provide employment and income to regions that would otherwise not receive such economic benefits, but intensive farming also requires pesticides and fertilisers as well as intensive water use and large-scale transport, storage and distribution capacity.

It is important when considering such discourses that the inequalities between wealthier and poorer countries in terms of ecological impacts are kept in mind. Figure 8.14 demonstrates the relative impacts of different countries on the global environment.

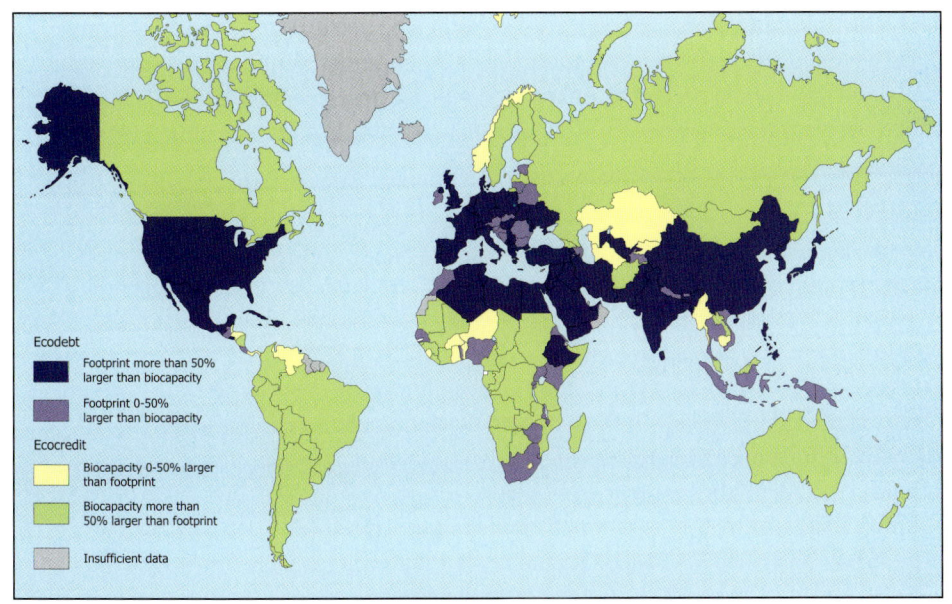

Figure 8.14: Ecological creditors and debtors

Ecological creditors.ppt

Source: adapted from UNEP, 2007: 289.

Regional perspectives on global issues

While the issues discussed in this chapter are of a global nature, it is clear that there are different priorities for many of these issues in different parts of the world. A summary of the United Nations Environment Programmes overview of how these issues relate to specific regions can be seen in figure 8.15 on p202. It should be stressed that there are obvious overlaps between regions, as with the case of Africa, Europe and West Asia, where the Mediterranean forms a common border (see figure 8.16 on p202), and that of Latin America and the Caribbean and the North American regions, with their shared boundaries.

**Figure 8.15:
Regional environmental priority issues**

See accompanying CD-Rom

Regional environmental priority issues.doc

Region	Issues
Africa	Land degradation and its impacts on forests, freshwater, marine and coastal resources. Pressures such as drought, climate variability and change, and urbanisation.
Asia and Pacific	Transport and urban air quality, freshwater stress, valuable ecosystems, agricultural land use, and waste management.
Europe	Climate change and energy, unsustainable production and consumption, air quality and transport, biodiversity loss and land-use change, and freshwater stress.
Latin America and the Caribbean	Growing cities, biodiversity and ecosystems, degrading coasts and polluted seas, and regional vulnerability to climate change.
North America	Energy and climate change, urban sprawl and freshwater stress.
West Asia	Freshwater stress, land degradation, degrading coasts and marine ecosystems, urban management, and peace and security.
Polar regions	Climate change, persistent pollutants, the ozone layer, development and commercial activity.

Source: UNEP, 2007: 203.

**Figure 8.16:
The Mediterranean Sea – taking a holistic approach**

See accompanying CD-Rom

The Mediterranean Sea.doc

The Mediterranean Sea is bordered by 21 countries. More than 130 million people live permanently along its coastline, a figure that doubles during the summer tourist season. The sea and its shores are the biggest tourist destination on Earth. Because of its geographical and historical characteristics, and its distinctive natural and cultural heritage, the Mediterranean is a unique ecoregion.

Local, regional and national authorities, international organisations and financing institutions have devoted a great deal of effort to protecting the Mediterranean region's environment, but many environmental problems continue to plague it. In recent decades, environmental degradation has accelerated. Valuable agricultural land is being lost to urbanisation and salinisation (80% of arid and semi-arid areas in the southern Mediterranean countries are affected by desertification, as well as 63% of the semi-arid land in the northern bordering countries). Scarce, overused water resources are threatened with depletion or degradation. Traffic congestion, noise, poor air quality and the rapid growth of waste generation are compromising urban standards of living and health. Coastal areas and the sea are affected by pollution, and coastlines are being built up and/or eroded, while fish resources are being depleted. In short, overexploitation is disrupting the Mediterranean's unique landscapes and biodiversity.

There are two major current initiatives to improve the state of the environment in the Mediterranean region. The Mediterranean Strategy for Sustainable Development, developed by UNEP's Mediterranean Action Plan and adopted in 2005, focuses on seven priority fields of action: water resources management, energy, transport, tourism, agriculture, urban development, and the marine and coastal environments. Complementary to this is the Horizon 2020 initiative under the Euro-Mediterranean Partnership. The aim of this initiative is to 'de-pollute the Mediterranean by 2020' through tackling all the major sources, including industrial emissions, and municipal waste, particularly urban wastewater.

Source: UNEP, 2007: 288.

> **Teaching idea 8.9**
>
> Ask students to investigate either the Mediterranean Strategy for Sustainable Development (*www.planbleu.org*) or the Horizon 2020 initiative (*http://ec.europa.eu/environment/enlarg/med/horizon_2020_en.htm*). What policies are being introduced to improve the environment of the Mediterranean basin?

Linking the local to the global

The relatively abstract nature of many global environmental issues may result in an inability to conceptualise problems in a meaningful and relevant manner. One way in which global issues have been rendered more accessible has been through notions such as Agenda 21 [☞], where global problems have been translated into local issues requiring local responses, which are aimed at having local impacts as well as contributing towards more effective global solutions. Agenda 21 was a major output of the United Nations Conference on Environment and Development (the 'Rio Conference') in 1992. Agenda 21 is structured around a huge document outlining the ideals of sustainable development, and covers how the social, environmental and economic aspects of sustainability should be realised. One of the significant areas for action included in the Agenda was the 'Strengthening of Major Groups', which in the UK included local authorities. There is therefore now a regularly adopted acronym of LA21 – Local Agenda 21. These are the guidelines for local authority councils to set out their plans for promoting, encouraging, and implementing the sustainable development within their area of influence, and for promoting and communicating those plans to the public and all stakeholders.

See ch 6, Sustainability (p153).

Summary

The world is continually changing as a result of processes that range from the very local to the global in scale. Issues such as climate change clearly have a global dimension which requires a global response as well as specific local responses to the impacts of change. If we are to understand notions of a globalised world, then it is important to consider the territories that make up that world and also the flows that occur between them. At the same time, we have to consider notions of borderlessness, where flows occur across territories irrespective of their territoriality. In many ways, the environment can be viewed as borderless, and while ecosystems clearly have specific locations, the boundaries between ecosystems are more usually blurred rather than being readily identifiable. In a world where trade flows are increasingly global, and the social, economic and environmental consequences of global interactions are becoming increasingly apparent, it is essential that a global perspective is incorporated if we are to achieve an effective understanding of environmental geographies.

When we analyse the issues and problems of the contemporary world, there are clear interlinkages between climate change, ozone depletion, air pollution, biodiversity loss, land degradation, water degradation and chemical pollution. Figure 8.15 on p202 shows some of these linkages between climate change, desertification and biodiversity. Human activities and pressures create multiple environmental changes. Environmental changes are linked across scales and between geographical regions through both biophysical and social processes.

**Figure 8.17:
Linkages between climate change, desertification and biodiversity**

See accompanying CD-Rom

Linkages.ppt

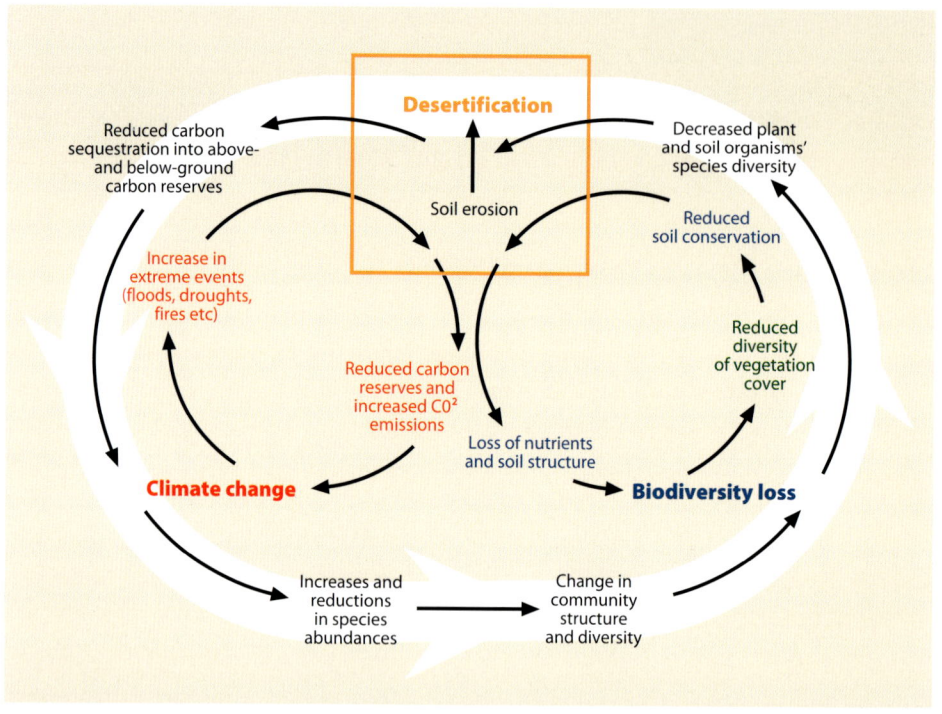

Diagram labels: Desertification; Reduced carbon sequestration into above- and below-ground carbon reserves; Decreased plant and soil organisms' species diversity; Soil erosion; Reduced soil conservation; Increase in extreme events (floods, droughts, fires etc); Reduced carbon reserves and increased CO_2 emissions; Reduced diversity of vegetation cover; Loss of nutrients and soil structure; Climate change; Biodiversity loss; Increases and reductions in species abundances; Change in community structure and diversity.

Source: based on UNEP, 2007: 372.

For our students, their world is an increasingly global one, where the mass media and the World Wide Web continuously bring distant places, events and people into their lives, which represents both a huge opportunity and a real challenge for the geography teacher. It provides the opportunity to assert the relevance of the subject by stressing the topicality of the issues. It also provides an opportunity to stress the unity of the subject through developing an understanding of the clear links between humanity and global environments.

At the same time, there is a very real danger that the subject comes to be seen through a negative lens with an excessive focus on the global problems and issues that are always highlighted (and often exaggerated) by the media, while equally important perspectives on the diversity and wonder of our planet are marginalised or even ignored. For a range of indicators, the rate of global environmental change slows or even reverses towards the middle of the present century.[3] This slowing down is important because it gives us hope that society and nature can more successfully cope with the pace of change and adjust to it before experiencing too many negative consequences (UNEP, 2007). It is essential that we strike an appropriate balance between attempting to solve the problems of the world and inspiring our students with the awe and wonder that also represents the planet we live on.

Endnotes

1. For a more detailed discussion see Barnett in Barnett et al (2008) pp130-141.

2. For a more detailed discussion see Dicken (2007) pp367-375.

3. For a range of futures scenarios relating to the global environment see UNEP (2007) chapter 9.

Useful websites

www.foe.co.uk for information about Friends of the Earth.

www.greenpeace.org for information about Greenpeace.

United Nations Environment Programme (2007) *Global environment outlook 4*, available at: *www.unep.org/geo/geo4/media/*

References

Adams, WM (2009) *Green development* (3rd Ed). London, Routledge.

Adams, WM (2009) 'Sustainability' in Cloke, P, Crang, P and Goodwin, M (Eds) *Introducing Human Geographies (2nd Ed)*. London, Hodder Arnold.

Barnett, C, Robinson, J and Rose, G (Eds) (2008)*Geographies of globalisation: a demanding world*. London, Sage.

Bingham, N, 'Bioprospecting and the global entanglement of people, plant and pills' in Clark, N, Massey, D and Sarre, P (Eds) (2008) *Material geographies: a world in the making*, pp105-160. London, Sage.

Binns, AJ, 'Making development work in Africa (part 2): enhancing sustainability' in *Geography*, 94, 2, Summer 2009, pp100-107.

Browmilow, J, 'Zero carbon futures' in *Geography*, 94, 3, Autumn 2009, pp219-222.

Butlin, RA (2009) *Geographies of empire: European empires and colonies c.1880-1960*. Cambridge, Cambridge University Press.

Cabinet Office (2008a) *Food: an analysis of the issues*. www.cabinetoffice.gov.uk/media/cabinetoffice/strategy/assets/food/food_analysis.pdf

Cabinet Office (2008b) *Food Matters: Towards a strategy for the 21st Century*. www.cabinetoffice.gov.uk/media/cabinetoffice/strategy/assets/food/food_matters_es.pdf

Carson, R (1965) *Silent Spring*. Harmondsworth, Penguin.

Christopherson, RW (2005) *Geosystems* (5th Ed). New Jersey, Pearson Prentice Hall.

Clark, N, Massey, D and Sarre, P (Eds) (2008) *Material geographies: a world in the making*. London, Sage.

Colinvaux, P (1990) *Why Big, Fierce Animals are Rare* (3rd Ed). Harmondsworth, Penguin.

Collins, A (2009) *Disaster and development*. Abingdon, Routledge.

Convention on Biological Diversity (2000) *Sustaining Life on Earth*. Secretariat of the Convention on Biological Diversity/UNEP/Government of the United Kingdom. www.cbd.int/iyb/doc/prints/cbd-sustain-en.pdf

Daniels, P, Bradshaw, M, Shaw, D and Sidaway, J (Eds) (2005) *An introduction to Human Geography: issues for the 21st century* (2nd Ed). Harlow, Pearson.

Department for Business, Innovation and Skills and Department of Energy and Climate Change (2009) *Low Carbon Industry Strategy: A Vision*. HM Government. www.berr.gov.uk/files/file50373.pdf

Department for Communities and Local Government (2007) *Homes for the future: more affordable, more sustainable*. www.communities.gov.uk/documents/housing/pdf/439986.pdf

Department for Communities and Local Government (2008) *The Code for Sustainable Homes*. www.communities.gov.uk/documents/planningandbuilding/pdf/codesustainhomesstandard.pdf

Department for Environment, Food and Rural Affairs (2006) *Food security and the UK*. www.defra.gov.uk/evidence/economics/foodfarm/reports/documents/foodsecurity.pdf

Department for Environment, Food and Rural Affairs (2005) *One Future – Different Paths*. London, Defra. www.defra.gov.uk/sustainable/government/documents/SDFramework.pdf

Dicken, P (2007) *Global shift: mapping the changing contours of the world economy (5th Ed)*. London, Sage.

Elliott, JA (2006) *An introduction to sustainable development*. London, Routledge.

Environment Agency (2008) *Managing Water Abstraction*. http://publications.environment-agency.gov.uk/pdf/GEH00508BOAH-E-E.pdf

Eyre, SR (1963) *Vegetation and soils*. London, Edward Arnold.

Financial Times, 'The future of energy' in Supplement, 2 November 2009.

Forest Peoples Programme (FPP) (2000) *Undermining the forest: the need to control transnational mining companies*. www.wrm.org.uy/publications/undermining.pdf

Garcier, R, 'The nuclear "renaissance" and the geography of the uranium fuel cycle' in *Geography*, 94, 3, Autumn 2009, pp198-206.

Held, D and McGrew, A (2007) *Globalization/Anti-globalisation*. Cambridge, Polity.

HM Government (2005) *Securing the future. The UK Government Sustainable Development Strategy*. HMSO. www.defra.gov.uk/sustainable/government/publications/uk-strategy/documents/SecFut_complete.pdf

Intergovernmental Panel on Climate Change (IPCC) (2007) *Climate Change 2007: Synthesis Report*. Summary document. www.ipcc.ch/pdf/assessment-report/ar4/syr/ar4_syr_spm.pdf

International Plant Genetic Resources Institute (IPGRI) (2002) *Neglected and Underutilized Plant Species: Strategic Action Plan of the International Plant Genetic Resources Institute*. Rome, IPGRI.

International Transport Forum (2008) *Transport and Energy: The Challenge of Climate Change*. OECD.

JMWMS (2008) *Joint Municipal Waste Management Strategy for Merseyside 2008: Headline Strategy*. www.merseysidewda.gov.uk/documents/Main%20Joint%20MWMS%202008.pdf

References

Jones, O, 'Of Trees and Trails: place in a globalised world' in Clark, N, Massey, D and Sarre, P (Eds) (2008) *Material geographies: a world in the making*. London, Sage.

Lambert, D and Morgan, J (2010) *Teaching geography 11-18: a conceptual approach*. Maidenhead, Open University Press.

Laszlo, E (1972) *Introduction to Systems Philosophy: Toward a new paradigm of contemporary thought*. New York, Gordon and Breach.

Lovelock, J (1989) *The Ages of Gaia. A Biography of Our Living Earth*. Oxford, Oxford University Press.

Lovelock, J (2009) *The Revenge of Gaia*. Oxford, Oxford University Press, Oxford.

Lechner, FJ (2009) *Globalisation: the making of world society*. Chichester, Wiley-Blackwell.

Lechner, FJ and Boli, J (Eds) (2008) *The globalization reader*. Oxford, Blackwell.

Massey, D, Allen, J and Sarre, P (Eds) (1999) *Human geography today*. Cambridge, Polity.

Met Office Hadley Centre (2005) *Climate Change and the Greenhouse Effect*. www.metoffice.gov.uk/publications/brochures/2005/climate_greenhouse.pdf

Met Office (2007) Fact Sheet No.10 – Air Masses and Weather Fronts. National Meteorological Library and Archive. www.metoffice.gov.uk/corporate/library/factsheets/factsheet10.pdf

Met Office (2008) *Avoiding Dangerous Climate Change*. www.metoffice.gov.uk/publications/brochures/cop14.pdf

Met Office (2009) *Warming: Climate change – the facts*. www.metoffice.gov.uk/climatechange/guide/downloads/quick_guide.pdf

Mitchell, D (Ed) (2009) *Living geography*. London, Chris Kington.

Murry, M, 'The Value of Biodiversity' in Kirkby, J, O'Keefe, P and Timberlake, L (Eds) (1999) *Sustainable Development*, pp17-29. London, Earthscan Publications Ltd.

Oldfield, F, Worsley, AT and Appleby, PG, 'Evidence from lake sediments from recent erosion rates in the Highlands of Papua New Guinea' in Douglas, I and Spencer, T (Eds) (1985) *Environmental Change and Tropical Geomorphology*, pp185-196. Allen & Unwin.

Potter, RB, Binns, T, Elliott JA and Smith, D (2008) *Geographies of development*. Harlow, Pearson.

Pretor-Pinney, G (2006) *The Cloudspotter's Guide*. London, Sceptre.

Proctor, MCF, 'Malham Tarn Moss: The Surface-Water Chemistry of an Ombrotrophic Bog' in *Field Studies*, 10 (2003) 553-578.

Pugh, D (2004) *Changing Sea Levels: Effects of Tides, Weather and Climate*. Cambridge, Cambridge University Press.

Ramesh, R, 'Toiling in India's ship graveyard for £1 a day' in Barnett, C, Robinson, J and Rose, G (Eds) (2008) *Geographies of globalisation: a demanding world*, pp285-7. London, Sage.

Royal Society (2008) *Climate Change Controversies. A Simple Guide*. London, The Royal Society. http://royalsociety.org/uploadedFiles/Royal_Society_Content/News_and_Issues/Science_Issues/Climate_change/Climate_booklet_RS1420_reprint_Dec08.pdf

Ruddiman, WF (2005) *Plows, Plagues and Petroleum: How Humans Took Control of Climate*. Princeton University Press.

Smith, J, 'Interdependence day' in *The Geographical Association Magazine*, Spring 2009.

Smith, T, 'Restoring biodiversity' in Robinson, DN (Ed) (2009) *The Lincolnshire Wolds*, pp103-113. Oxford, Windgather Press.

Tansley, AG (1939) *The British Isles and their Vegetation*. Cambridge, Cambridge University Press.

UK Biodiversity Partnership (2007) *Conserving Biodiversity – The UK Approach*. London, Department for Environment, Food and Rural Affairs. www.ukbap.org.uk/library/UKSC/DEF-PB12772-ConBio-UK.pdf

UK Climate Impacts Programme (UKCIP) (2009) *A local climate impacts profile: how to do an LCLIP*. Oxford, UKCIP. www.ukcip.org.uk/images/stories/LCLIP/LCLIP_guidance.pdf

United Nations Environment Programme (2007) *Global environment outlook 4*. www.unep.org/geo/geo4/media/

United Nations World Commission on Environment and Development (WCED) (1987) *Our Common Future*. Oxford, Oxford University Press.

Valiela, I (2006) *Global Coastal Change*. Oxford, Blackwell Publishing.

Wapner, P, 'Greenpeace and political globalism' in Lechner, FJ and Boli, J (Eds) (2008) *The globalization reader,* pp415-422. Oxford, Blackwell.

Whatmore, S and Clark, N, 'Good Food: ethical consumption and global change' in Clark, N, Massey, D and Sarre, P (Eds) (2008) *Material geographies: a world in the making*. London, Sage.

Wildlife & Countryside Link (2007) *Bioenergy in the UK: turning green promises into environmental reality*. http://wcl.org.uk/Bioenergy%20in%20the%20UK.htm

Winchester, A (2006) *England's landscape : The North West*. London, Collins.

WWF (2008) *Living Planet Report 2008*. Available at www.panda.org/

Woodworth, PL, 'High waters at Liverpool since 1768: the UK's longest sea level record' in *Geophysical Research Letters*, 26 (1999) 1589-1592.

World Health Organization (WHO) *Obesity and overweight*. www.who.int/dietphysicalactivity/publications/facts/obesity/en/

Young, EW and Lowry, JH (1979) *A Course in World Geography* (5th Ed). London, Arnold.

Examination specification references

	AS/A2 Specifications			GCSE Specifications				
	AQA	Edexcel	OCR	AQA A	AQA B	Edexcel A	Edexcel B	OCR A	OCR B
1. Ecosystems									
Populations, communities and ecosystems	✓	✓	✓	✓			✓		
Biomes and geographical regions	✓	✓	✓	✓			✓		
Understanding ecosystems	✓	✓	✓	✓			✓		
Ecosystem services	✓	✓	✓	✓			✓		
Biodiversity	✓	✓	✓	✓			✓		
Ecosystems under pressure	✓	✓	✓	✓	✓	✓	✓		
Forest ecosystems and change	✓	✓	✓		✓	✓	✓		
The impact of energy usage on biodiversity	✓	✓	✓				✓		
The effects of ecosystem change on human health	✓	✓	✓				✓		✓
Ecosystem thresholds	✓	✓	✓	✓			✓		
2. Climate and weather									
The role of the Sun	✓		✓						
Dynamics between land masses and oceans	✓		✓						
The importance of topographical features	✓		✓						
Atmospheric air pressure and winds	✓		✓					✓	
Atmospheric moisture and the hydrological cycle	✓	✓	✓			✓	✓		
Biomes	✓								
Extreme global weather		✓	✓	✓	✓			✓	✓
Local climatic variations	✓			✓					
UK climate	✓			✓					
3. Climate change									
How climate works: the greenhouse effect	✓	✓		✓		✓	✓	✓	
Evidence of short term changes	✓	✓		✓	✓	✓	✓	✓	
Evidence of long term changes	✓	✓		✓	✓	✓	✓		
What's wrong with climate change?	✓	✓		✓		✓	✓		
Biodiversity and ecosystems		✓		✓		✓	✓	✓	
Agriculture and food supply		✓		✓		✓	✓	✓	
Rising sea levels	✓	✓		✓		✓	✓	✓	
Marine ecosystems	✓	✓		✓		✓	✓		
Human health	✓			✓		✓	✓	✓	
Water availability		✓		✓		✓	✓		
How can human-induced changes be stabilised?		✓		✓		✓	✓	✓	
The UK		✓		✓		✓	✓	✓	

Examination specification references *Continued*

	AS/A2 Specifications					GCSE Specifications				
	AQA	Edexcel	OCR	AQA A	AQA B	Edexcel A	Edexcel B	OCR A	OCR B
4. Energy								
Historical geographies of energy	✓								
Fossil fuels	✓	✓	✓	✓		✓			
Coal	✓	✓	✓	✓		✓			
Oil production	✓	✓	✓	✓		✓	✓		
Energy from wood and deforestation	✓	✓	✓	✓	✓	✓			
Carbon capture	✓	✓	✓	✓		✓			
Carbon neutral	✓	✓	✓	✓		✓			
Carbon footprint	✓	✓	✓	✓		✓	✓		
Nuclear power	✓	✓	✓	✓		✓			
Renewable energy	✓	✓	✓	✓		✓			
Biofuels	✓	✓	✓	✓		✓			
The localisation of energy	✓	✓	✓	✓					
Energy and development	✓	✓	✓	✓					
Energy futures	✓	✓	✓	✓		✓	✓		
5. Food supply								
Food supply chain	✓	✓				✓			
The involvement of government	✓	✓				✓			
Population and food supply	✓	✓		✓		✓	✓		
Globalisation and food	✓	✓		✓		✓		✓	
Food miles	✓	✓				✓		✓	
Environmental impacts	✓	✓		✓		✓		✓	
Alternative food networks	✓	✓				✓		✓	✓
Organic farming	✓	✓				✓		✓	
The ethics of food supply	✓	✓		✓		✓		✓	
Food supply and carbon footprints	✓	✓				✓		✓	
Forestry	✓	✓			✓	✓	✓		
Food security and food shortages	✓	✓		✓		✓	✓		

Examination specification references *Continued*

	AS/ A2 Specifications			GCSE Specifications			
	AQA	Edexcel	OCR	AQA A	AQA B	Edexcel A	Edexcel B	OCR A	OCR B
6. Sustainability								
What is sustainability?		✓	✓	✓		✓	✓	✓	✓
Social development and sustainability		✓	✓	✓		✓	✓		✓
Social development in LEDCs		✓	✓	✓		✓	✓		✓
Social development in MEDCs		✓	✓	✓		✓	✓		✓
Economic growth and sustainability		✓	✓	✓		✓	✓		✓
Transport and sustainability				✓		✓			
Natural ecosystems and sustainability		✓	✓	✓		✓	✓		
Sustainability and biodiversity		✓		✓		✓	✓		
Human use of natural resources		✓	✓	✓		✓	✓		✓
Sustainability and political process: the role of Agenda 21		✓		✓		✓	✓	✓	
7. Environmental management								
Land degradation	✓	✓	✓		✓		✓		
Agricultural practices: soil erosion		✓	✓				✓		
Chemical contamination		✓	✓				✓		
Water scarcity	✓	✓	✓			✓	✓		
Salinity		✓	✓				✓		
Nutrient cycles		✓	✓				✓		
Desertification	✓	✓	✓				✓		
Forest environments	✓	✓	✓		✓	✓	✓		
Coastal, marine and freshwater environments	✓	✓	✓	✓	✓		✓		
Fisheries	✓	✓	✓	✓	✓				
Restoring biodiversity		✓	✓	✓					
Restoration of damaged environments		✓						✓	
Environmental disasters		✓							
Waste management		✓	✓			✓		✓	

Examination specification references *Continued*

8. Globalisation

	AS/A2 Specifications					GCSE Specifications			
	AQA	Edexcel	OCR	AQA A	AQA B	Edexcel A	Edexcel B	OCR A	OCR B
Global environmental trends	✓	✓	✓	✓	✓			✓	
Economic development and environmental issues	✓	✓	✓	✓	✓		✓	✓	
Global inter-governmental actions	✓	✓		✓		✓		✓	
Trade, industry and the environment	✓	✓	✓	✓	✓		✓	✓	
Climate change: the ultimate globalisation?	✓	✓		✓	✓	✓	✓	✓	
Global governance?	✓	✓		✓		✓			
Transnational environmental movements		✓				✓			
Pollution and transnational activism		✓							
The globalisation of fauna and flora		✓		✓					
The globalisation of food	✓	✓							
Regional perspectives of global issues		✓		✓	✓				
Linking the local to the global	✓	✓						✓	

Index

Afforestation	23-24
Agenda 21	153-154, 203
Agriculture and food supply	74-76
Air pollution	188-189
Alternative food networks	120
Amazon rainforest	143
Atmospheric moisture and the hydrological cycle	44-45
Atmospheric pressure and winds	38-41
Bhopal	178-179
Biodiversity	15-17, 74, 150-152, 173-174, 197
energy usage	24-25
Biofuels	99-102
Biomes	7-13, 47
Brazil	99-100, 139, 167-168, 189
Brundtland Report	135-136
Canada	90
Canadian cod fishery	172
Carbon capture	92-93
Carbon footprints	93-94, 124-126
Carbon Trust	124
Carbon-neutral	93
Chemical contamination	160-161
Chernobyl	85, 95, 187
China	1-2, 95, 97, 166, 189
Climate and weather	31-62
Climate change	63-82, 189-190
UK	80-81
stability?	79-81
Climate	
air masses	57-59
local variations	55-56
long-term changes	71-74
short-term changes	67-71
the British Isles	56
the Sun	33-34
topographical features	37-38
weather fronts	59-60
Clouds	45-46
Clough Bottom Farm	122-123
Coal	86-88
Coastal, marine and freshwater environments	169-173
Common Agricultural Policy	110
Coriolis effect	38
Daw Mill	87
DDT	161
Desertification	164-166
Dust Bowl, USA	159-160
Dynamics between land masses and oceans	34-35
Ecology	14
Economic development	185-186
Ecosystem services	15-17
Ecosystem thresholds	29-30
Ecosystems	3-29
habitats and niches	12
marine	78
population, communities	6-7
sustainability	148-150
under pressure	18-22
valuing	17-18
Ecuador	143
Edge Hill University	104-105
El Niño	36
Energy	83-105
Energy and development	107
Energy	
current situation	86
futures	107
global production	85
historical geographies	85
localisation	103-106
wood	92
sustainability	153
Environmental disasters	178-179
Environmental geographies, social construction	3-4
Environmental management	157-181
Ethiopia	200
Extreme weather	48
Fairtrade	120-121, 199
Fishing and fisheries	149, 171-173
Flora and fauna	196-198
Food miles	116-118
Food security	128-130
Food shortages	130-132
Food supply	109-132
diet	111-112
ethics	123-124
government involvement	110-111
population	112-114
Forest ecosystems	22-23, 166-168
Forestry	127
Fort McMurray	90
Fossil fuels	86-94
Galapagos Islands	142, 144
Geothermal	102-103
Global environmental trends	183-184
Global governance	191-193
Global interdependence	190
Globalisation	183-204

Index

Globalisation and food	114-116, 198-200
Greenhouse effect	66-67
Greenpeace	193-194
Harworth	87
Health	26-29, 78-79, 150
Heatwaves	131
Hesketh Outer Marsh	169
Hoover Dam	96-97
Hurricane Katrina	49-52, 171
Hurricanes	48-52
Hydroelectric power	95-97
India	195-196
Inter Tropical Convergence Zone	39
Intergovernmental Panel on Climate Change	79-81
Intergovernmental actions	186-187
Jet streams	40
Kellingley	87
Kenya	119-120, 144
Lake District	23-24, 43
Lake sediments	71-73
Land degradation	158
LEDCs	
economic growth	141-144
local cropping practices	126-127
social development	138-139
Lincolnshire Wolds	173-174
Living Planet Index	19-20
Malthus	112
McDonald's	199
MEDCs	
economic growth	144-146
social development	140-141
Mediterranean biome	8-9
Mediterranean Sea	202
Metals and oils	175-176
Mexico-US border	187-188
Mid-latitude depressions	41
Millennium Development Goals	18, 107
Millenium Ecosystem Assessment	18
Monsoon	34-35, 37
Natural resources	152-153
North Wales	175
North-west England	97-98
Nuclear power	94-95
Nutrient cycles	163-164
Oakwell Hall Country Park	176-177
Oil	88-90
Organic farming	121-123
Papua New Guinea	148, 175-176
Peak oil	91
Peat bogs	73-74
Pendle Vale campus	106
Population growth	185
Psammosere	11-12
Ramsar Convention on Wetlands of International Importance	170
Red bush tea	115
Regional distribution centres	117
Restoration of damaged environments	176-178
Ribble Estuary	77
Rio Declaration on Environment and Development	186-187
Salinity	163
Satellite measurements	68
Sea-level change	68-70, 76-78
Sefton	77
Sheffield's fig trees	178
Shipbreaking	195-196
Snow and ice stores	70-71
Soil erosion	159-160
Solar power	99
South Africa	194-195
Southern Asia	34-35, 37
Sustainability	135-156
definitions	135
economic growth	141-146
social development	137-138
transport	146-147
Sutton Manor Country Park	177
Synoptic charts	60-62
Tesco	124-125, 200
The National Forest	24
Thoresby	87
Thunderstorms	54-55
Tidal and wave power	102
Tornadoes	52-54
Trade, industry and the environment	187-189
Transnational environmental movements	193-195
Tropical biome	9-11
UK ports	119
UK, water supply	162
UN Convention to Combat Desertification	164
Walkers crisps	124-125
Waste management	179-180
Water availability	79
Water scarcity	161-162
Weather forecasting	60-62
Weather stations	67-68
Welbeck	87
Wetlands	13
Wicken Fen	170
Wildlife tourism	144
Wind measurement	42-43
Wind power	97-98